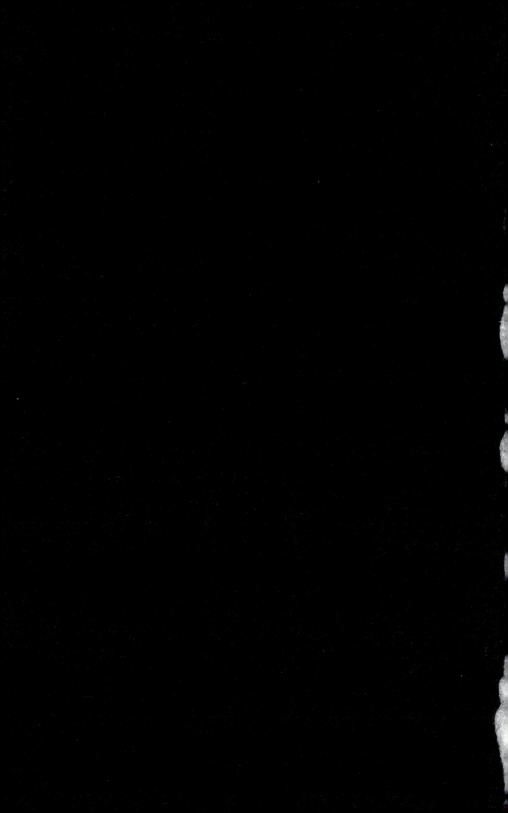

# TOO HOT TO HANDLE

# TOO HOT
# TO HANDLE

## A GLOBAL HISTORY OF
## SEX EDUCATION

## JONATHAN ZIMMERMAN

PRINCETON UNIVERSITY PRESS
PRINCETON AND OXFORD

Copyright © 2015 by Princeton University Press
Requests for permission to reproduce material from this work should be sent to
Permissions, Princeton University Press
Published by Princeton University Press, 41 William Street, Princeton, New Jersey 08540
In the United Kingdom: Princeton University Press, 6 Oxford Street, Woodstock,
Oxfordshire OX20 1TW
press.princeton.edu

Jacket art © Volodymyr Krasyuk/Shutterstock

Library of Congress Cataloging-in-Publication Data

Zimmerman, Jonathan, 1961–
Too hot to handle : a global history of sex education / Jonathan Zimmerman.
pages cm
Includes bibliographical references and index.
ISBN 978-0-691-14310-1 (hardback)
1. Sex instruction—History. 2. Sex instruction for teenagers—History. I. Title.
HQ57.3.Z56 2015
613.9071'2—dc23        2014043559

British Library Cataloging-in-Publication Data is available
This book has been composed in Janson Text LT Std
Printed on acid-free paper. ∞
Printed in the United States of America
1 3 5 7 9 10 8 6 4 2

FOR
# MARGOT LURIE ZIMMERMAN,
FAMILY PLANNER EXTRAORDINAIRE

# CONTENTS

# ACKNOWLEDGMENTS

I wrote this book while serving as chair of the Department of Humanities and Social Sciences in the Professions at New York University's Steinhardt School of Culture, Education, and Human Development. There's simply no way I could have completed it without the help and support of my terrific colleagues and staff. Special thanks to Lucy Frazier, Jessica Cole, Letizia Larosa, and Erinn Bernstein, who kept the department running when I flew off to an archive or speaking engagement. Thanks, too, to the intrepid graduate students who have served as my teaching assistants during these years: Janet Bordelon, Christian Bracho, Ben Davidson, Cody Ewert, Noah Kippley-Ogman, Dominique Jean-Louis, Lauren Lefty, Maia Merin, Naomi Moland, Amy Scallon, Rachel Wahl, and Ashley White. I'm also grateful to the leaders of the Steinhardt School, especially Dean Mary Brabeck. Mary made Steinhardt the best place to think, teach, and write about education in the United States. I wish her all the best in her post-dean endeavors.

Clara Platter first suggested this book to me, and Brigitta van Rheinberg brought it to Princeton University Press. I owe the title to my sister-in-law, Sharon Weinberg, who reads more—and more carefully—than anyone I know. Thanks, too, to friends and colleagues who read parts of the book or invited me to share them with audiences: Mary Ann Dzuback, Dagmar Herzog, Richard Hull, Peter Kallaway, Dan Segal, and David Spandorfer. I'm grateful to the Arthur and Elizabeth Schlesinger Library for a grant to conduct research in its superb collections. Finally, *medase* (thanks) to my incomparably kind hosts at NYU's campus in Accra, Ghana, which has provided a home-away-from-home for several summers as well as a terrific place to try out the ideas in this book.

For the past eighteen years, I have been commuting between New York and my home in suburban Philadelphia. This placed extraordinary burdens on Susan Coffin in caring for our two beautiful daughters, Sarah and Rebecca. They're grown up now, and building their own lives, so we're embarking on a new chapter. I feel incredibly fortunate that I get to write it with Susan, who remains the anchor of my world.

This book is dedicated to my mother, Margot Lurie Zimmerman, who spent her career in family planning and sex education. As I grew up, she imbued me with the standard liberal assumption that the United States was somehow "behind" more "progressive" countries—particularly those in Western Europe—when it comes to sex education. But the United States actually pioneered the subject, as the ensuing pages will show. Then Europeans created a different *type* of sex education; one focused less on public consequences and dangers than on individual rights and pleasures. This challenges another liberal storyline from my youth, in which Americans emphasize individual freedoms while Europeans attend to the collective good. In sex education, it was precisely the opposite. Nobody was "ahead" or "behind" in this game; instead, different countries came to it with contrasting goals, expectations, and ideas.

I hope my mother won't mind that some of the ideas in this book depart from her own. The most important thing she taught me was that our beliefs about sex, love, and family matter. Obviously, that's one lesson I've never forgotten. Enjoy the book, Mom. It's yours.

# TOO HOT TO HANDLE

# Introduction
## THE CENTURY OF SCHOOL, AND THE CENTURY OF SEX

In 1900, the Swedish schoolteacher and author Ellen Key published a best-selling book with an auspicious title: *The Century of the Child*. Translated into several languages, Key's book, and its title, would become rallying cries for reform-minded critics, scholars, and educators around the world. Children were the hope of the future, Key wrote, but everywhere they were enchained by adults' rigid rules and stern rebukes. Here she took special aim at the West's signature child-rearing institution, the public school, which prescribed irrelevant "doses of knowledge" and pretended to measure the same with terrifying tests and examinations. But children learned best on their own and with their own parents, who had surrendered too much influence and authority to schools. Whereas gymnastics and art were formerly taught at home, for example, children increasingly learned them in the classroom. In the twentieth century, Key hoped, children would be "emancipated" from the sterile curricula and harsh pedagogy of the school. And parents would regain rightful control over the child, who could best develop "individuality"—including conscience, judgment, and free will—at home.[1]

In many ways, however, the world was moving in the opposite direction. The ensuing century witnessed a dramatic explosion of state-run schools, which became ubiquitous across the West and—eventually—around the globe. Between 1950 and 1970, the percentage of children who attended primary school rose from 58 to 83 percent; by 1985, 90 percent of the world's children had spent at least some part of their lives at school. Secondary schools increased at an even faster rate, roughly tripling in number and size over the same span.[2] Official policies and curricula proclaimed that these institutions would cultivate the freedom and agency of each individual, much as Ellen Key had wished. In practice, though, they frequently diverged from her ideal. In the developed world, child-centered classrooms were often distributed by social class: wealthier children received personalized attention and instruction, while poorer ones were more likely to experience the lockstep lessons and dry drills that Key detested. So did the vast majority of students in the so-called Third World, where skyrocketing class sizes and dwindling resources made "individuated instruction" impossible. How could a teacher with fifty or a hundred students—and without much formal preparation herself—do anything *other* than force-feed selected facts, which the children would dutifully regurgitate on their end-of-year exams? The twentieth century would not be the Century of the Child, at least not in the manner that Ellen Key had hoped. It was, instead, the Century of the School.

It was also the Century of Sex, which Key more presciently forecasted. "People have commenced already to experiment with unions outside marriage," she wrote. "The whole problem is being made the subject of debate." An avowed enemy of Christianity, particularly in its denigration of bodily pleasures, Key looked forward to the day when more and more individuals could determine their own sexual destinies. And so they did. Especially in the second half of the century—and especially in the West—human beings would attain a level of sexual freedom beyond anything Ellen Key could envision. A new model of companionate marriage promised sexual pleasure for men and women alike, aided by birth control technologies that separated lovemaking from reproduction; homosexuals gained increased visibility and rights, including—most recently—the right to get married; and formerly tabooed sexual themes became commonplace in literature and mass media, as censorship laws and regulations fell away. Many of these trends occurred earlier—and more forcefully—in the developed than in the developing world, where older traditions and restrictions held sway. Nor was it clear that the "liberalization" of sexual mores was always liberating; for women, especially, the heightened public discourse around sex could feel more like a new set of expectations than a new license for freedom. Surely, though, a greater number of people experienced a greater degree of sexual autonomy than ever before.[3]

But how would they learn to exercise that freedom? The modern answer was sex education, where the Century of the School met the Century of Sex. Starting in Europe and the United States, and then spreading around the globe, nation-states looked to their burgeoning educational systems to describe, explain, and especially control sex. But the marriage between school and sex proved to be both stormy and delicate, spawning heated controversy outside of the schools and surprisingly little instruction inside of them. Part of the reason lay in deep popular unease and disagreement about childhood sexuality; whereas advocates saw sex education as a check upon youth sexual activity, critics worried that it would corrupt otherwise innocent minds. Another factor was the organizational structure of the schools, which were never the bloodlessly efficient behemoths that Ellen Key imagined; even in highly oppressive and totalitarian societies, nervous principals or shy teachers could evade national sex education directives if they wished. Most of all, many people around the world continued to insist that the family—not the classroom— was the proper locus of sexual instruction. Even Ellen Key, an early tribune of sexual liberation, balked at the first attempts to teach about sex in schools. "I objected at that time to this plan, showing that the school was not the place for such knowledge," she wrote in 1900. "It should be slowly and carefully communicated by the mother herself."[4] Across the globe, just as Key feared, the state-sponsored school would come to dominate nearly every aspect of children's lives. But it rarely—and then only gingerly—touched on sex, which proved too divisive and unstable for schools to accommodate. In the Century of the School, and the Century of Sex, the school struggled to master sex. And, for the most part, the school failed.

To be sure, sex education varied across space and time. In the early twentieth century, when strong taboos on public sexual discussion remained in place, sex education mostly assumed the form of plant and animal analogies; by studying roses or rabbits, the argument went, children could learn about human reproduction without prematurely igniting their interest in practicing the sexual act. After

World War II, as the United States assumed new power and prominence on the global stage, Americans refashioned sex education as "family life education"; emphasizing gender roles and proper child rearing, it made sexual continence a key to world peace as well as to national survival. In Europe, meanwhile, Swedes took the lead in promoting new curricula aimed at liberating individuals to discover and develop their own sexual selves, much as Ellen Key had wanted (but via her bête noire, the state-sponsored school). International aid and educational associations took up that ideal in the 1960s and 1970s, which in turn triggered a right-wing reaction in the United States, Great Britain, and other parts of the West. These conservatives would join hands with like-minded critics in the developing world in the 1980s and 1990s, when the HIV/AIDS crisis lent a renewed global urgency to sex education. But the terms of the battle remained much the same, even as the battlefield changed. Around the world, liberal educators sought to empower individuals to assert their sexual "rights"—including the right to sexual pleasure—while conservatives emphasized abstinence outside marriage. One side stressed "the right of young human beings to have sexual feelings," as a Dutch educator wrote in 2000, while the other urged the young "to say NO to sex."[5]

Yet even countries that officially embraced "liberal" sexual philosophies often struggled to provide much real sexual *instruction* in their schools. Consider Ellen Key's homeland of Sweden, the first nation to require sex education and a symbol of sexual freedom (or, depending on one's perspective, sexual excess) around the world. In 1969, more than a decade after the subject became compulsory, one-third of Swedish students had still not encountered it in school. Moreover, half of Swedish teachers admitted that they avoided or ignored sex education in their classrooms. Many teachers confessed to being "embarrassed" by the subject, while others complained that they lacked sufficient education in it themselves; as late as 2006, more than 90 percent of teachers reported receiving "little or no preparation" for delivering sex education. But the limited instruction in Swedish schools dwarfed most other countries, where the subject resembled the small town of American cliché: blink twice and you might miss it. In Hong Kong, the average high school student received two hours of sex education per year in 2001; students in France averaged exactly the same amount, belying their country's libertine image; in Chile, half of students received sex education no more than twice per year; and so on. In the United States, where local authorities mostly controlled education, the average school provided 6.5 hours per year of sex education in 1989; in the United Kingdom, which was similarly decentralized, half of local districts did not bother to record what—if anything—their schools were teaching about it. Significantly, however, even countries with highly nationalized education systems often ceded *sex* education to local officials and teachers. In most of the world, "every course other than sex education is centrally programmed," a 1976 international survey concluded. "Only in the area of sex education is the initiative and responsibility left to individuals."[6]

Indeed, only in the area of sex education would modern school systems fail so dramatically—and so universally—to impose themselves *upon* individuals. It was not for want of trying. By the 1970s, nearly every country in the Western world had instituted some form of sex education; most nations in the developing world would do the same during the HIV/AIDS crisis of the 1980s and 1990s, which made it impossible to ignore sex entirely in their schools. But from the dawn of the twentieth century into the present, and from one corner of the world to another, the reach of sex education radically exceeded its grasp. "The child growing up in the midst of civilization receives from its parents and teachers something of the accumulated experience of the world on all other subjects save upon that of sex," the prominent American reformer Jane Addams complained in 1912. "On this one subject alone each generation learns little from its predecessors." Similar jeremiads mark the reports and memoirs of sex education advocates from Addams's day into our own, when—as one African educator observed—children "learn complicated mathematics they will never use in their lifetimes" but "nothing about their sexual organs, which they will be using every day of their lives." In the Century of the School, as Ellen Key feared, children's lives came to revolve around formal educational institutions. But in the Century of Sex, Key would be relieved to know, schools were never able to bring sex fully into their orbit. This book tries to explain why.[7]

\* \* \*

The first reason, unsurprisingly, was deep-rooted controversy and disquiet surrounding sex itself. Starting in the early twentieth century, adults around the world worried that youth sexual behavior was spinning out of control. But they disagreed sharply about how it should be brought back *into* control, and by whom. To its advocates, school-based sex education represented a "Prophylactic Coefficient against Sexuality," as an Italian physician titled his 1914 plea for the subject; if young people were armed with proper information about sex, the argument went, they would resist its seductive perils. "The sex appetite is a powerful appetite," a New Zealand advocate explained. "A powerful appetite needs control. It must be intelligent control. There cannot be intelligent control without knowledge." The same theme marked imperial officials' scattered attempts at school-based sex instruction in Africa and Asia, where a leading British educator worried that racy Western films and magazines were "inflicting a grave injury on the moral and ethical standards of the Eastern races." The fears continued into the postcolonial period, as newly independent nations gradually established sex education programs to repel promiscuous winds from overseas. "The influence of western culture is increasingly pervading present-day society," three Indian physicians warned in 1976, bemoaning "new sexual trends towards greater liberty and experimentation" and a corresponding rise of illegitimate births and illegal abortions in their country. School-based sex education would provide a "preventive measure" against these developments, they concluded, restoring the traditional continence of the subcontinent.[8]

From the very start, however, critics condemned sex education for fostering the same promiscuity it purported to control. For the half century before Sweden instituted nationwide sex education, parents blocked or limited the subject by arguing that it might "awaken the sleeping bear"—that is, encourage sexual activity. In Japan, opponents warned that sex education would "wake a sleeping child"; in Thailand, that it would "show nuts to the squirrel"; and in Vietnam, that it risked "showing the way to the deer." Beneath these colorfully metaphoric objections lay fundamental disagreements not just about sexuality but also about rationality, and—most of all—about whether the latter could reasonably affect the former. "Knowledge is the cry. Crude, undigested knowledge, without limit and without reserve," wrote the American essayist Agnes Repplier in 1914, in a typical admonishment against sex education. "If knowledge alone could save us from sin, the salvation of the world would be easy work." Six years later, a German critic noted that the most highly educated members of his society also exhibited the highest degree of "sexual indulgence" outside marriage. "Have we not been guilty of the Socratic fallacy that knowledge of the good is sufficient for the avoiding of evil?" he asked. "Reason, as such, does not suffice to check the sex impulse." By the late twentieth century, when nearly every country had adopted some kind of sex-related instruction in schools, deep-rooted disputes about sex continued to hamper the subject almost everywhere it appeared. "There's an old saying that 'there are only two things for certain in this world; death and taxes,'" an American school board member wrote in 1986. "A third certainly might be added: disagreement about sex education."[9]

Faced with these inevitable objections, educators often tried to disguise sex education with different names—or with no name at all. In the 1920s, Denmark taught about sex under labels such as Mothercraft, Baby Nursing, and Moral Education; Germany included sex in lessons on Marriage and Motherhood, Human Development, or Social Hygiene; and Norway changed the last term to "*slekts* hygiene," borrowing the Norwegian term for "family." "This change in nomenclature has been useful inasmuch as it does away with the reaction common in so many people, especially the less enlightened and the prudish, against the 'vulgar' and sensational feeling associated with the word sex," a local physician explained. The word "family" also featured heavily in postwar formulations, starting in the United States; although "a rose by any other name" was nevertheless a rose, as one American advocate quipped, a course called Family Life Education drew far less public attention and controversy than "Sex Education" did. The international drive for family planning in the 1960s and 1970s birthed Population Education, while the HIV epidemic of the 1980s and 1990s led many countries to reframe sex education as AIDS Education. But even the term "AIDS" was too controversial for some countries, which adopted more anodyne titles like Life Skills or Adolescence Education. "So far, no clear consensus exists regarding a universally acceptable term," a 2007 global study of sex education noted. "In some settings, use of the terms 'sex' or 'sexuality' in the title of a programme is simply too explicit for the comfort of parents, teachers, or politicians. And yet, terms such as 'family life education,' 'life skills education' or 'population education' may provide an opportunity to ignore discussion of sex altogether."[10]

So did efforts to "integrate" sex into regular school subjects, as educators repeatedly discovered. According to a 1975 survey of seventeen European countries, only two taught sex education as a "separate" subject in the curriculum; the rest folded it into biology, civics, social studies, or religious instruction. Like the different names that educators devised for sex instruction, "integrating" the subject into others was a strategy to minimize public controversy; if sex education received "special and dramatic emphasis" in the school timetable, one American warned, it would be more likely to draw special—and derogatory—attention. In practice, however, curricular integration often allowed schools to neglect or ignore the topic. Countries that purportedly integrated it into the major subjects rarely included questions about sex in their national examinations of these subjects, so there was little incentive for schools or students to take sexual knowledge seriously. Most of all, spreading sex education across the curriculum also defused responsibility for it. Only ten of eighty Swedish schools in a 2001 survey had designated a staff member to oversee sex education, which still lacked any official space in the national timetable of subjects. "I wish the Government would have the balls to make it statutory and say, 'Right, this has to be timetabled' or get rid of it completely," a British educator groused in 2007. "It just doesn't work, this half-way house."[11]

In the doorway of the house stood classroom teachers, the "foot soldiers on the sex education firing line," as an American visitor to Sweden wrote in 1971. Yet even in that famously "sex-positive" country, many of these instructors found themselves trapped between *competing* lines of fire. "If you want your children to have sex education, I think this is very good. But other parents don't. What should I do?" one Swedish teacher asked the following year. "They come to me and say: why did you tell them—I don't want that—I told you you mustn't do it." Around the world, teachers had to tread a delicate path; more tightrope walkers than foot soldiers, they sought most of all to avoid controversy—and to keep their jobs. "In an ideal world parents would give their children sex education but it falls back on the poor old teachers who are caught between a rock and a hard place," one sympathetic English observer wrote in 2000. "Be fair and totally objective and the moralisers attack them, push a traditionalist 'family and marriage' line and the progressives pan them." Nor were teachers helped by the large amount of discretion that most school systems granted them on sex education; to the contrary, that very "freedom" exposed them to even more potential discord. "In the absence of clarity," an Irish educator explained, "teachers ... adopted a conservative approach and said, 'Well, I'm not sticking my neck out here in case, you know, I say something wrong.'"[12]

The dangers were greatest of all in the developing world, where sex education threatened to erode teachers' tenuous authority inside of classrooms as well as outside of them. As school attendance escalated in the second half of the century, young nations were often forced to hire teachers with little more schooling or preparation than the students in their charge. Some of these students were almost as old the teachers, which added another obvious challenge. Finally, these same years witnessed the mass arrival of female students into schools around the world. So classrooms were also transformed into "amorous" spaces that spawned "early sexual contacts" outside of parental control, as one observer in Ghana wrote in 1976. Some of these new relationships were between students; others paired students and teachers, who sometimes traded sex for school fees, grades, or cash. In such a highly sexualized space, any mention of the subject risked putting teachers' already fragile control on even weaker ground. Male students hissed, giggled, or grunted through sex education lessons; girls stayed quiet or even stayed at home, to avoid embarrassment; and teachers often received intrusive questions about their own sexuality, especially if they were female. To be sure, teachers around the world—and across the twentieth century—faced awkward insinuations whenever they broached the subject; women instructors, especially, were seen as young hussies who were too interested in sex or as "old maids" who were not interested (or experienced) *enough*. But the problem was particularly acute for teachers in the Third World, who had to govern crowded classrooms even as they negotiated the perilous terrain of sex in a rapidly globalizing world.[13]

Indeed, the set of circumstances that scholars have called "globalization"—the compression of the world, and the intensification of our consciousness of it—have mostly served to curtail rather than to expand school-based sexual instruction. From its origins in Europe and the Americas into the present, sex education has remained a strongly international movement. For example, China's first modern sex educator drew heavily on the work of British sexologist Havelock Ellis; in India, meanwhile, a popular American sex education textbook was translated into Marathi and illustrated with local drawings and photographs. But a Norwegian teacher who used the same textbook in his classroom in the early 1950s was fired for spreading "immoral" ideas from the United States; in France, likewise, Catholic critics condemned sex education as an unwelcome American import. Over the next half century, Scandinavia would come to replace the United States as the acknowledged world leader in the subject. No matter where it was taught, however, opponents continued to blast sex education as a "foreign" or alien intrusion upon local or national values. The more the world globalized, in short, the more that sex education came under attack.[14]

Nowhere was that more true than inside the United States, where western Europe—and, especially, Sweden—became a symbol of sex education gone awry. Around AD 1000, one American educator quipped, Scandinavian Leif Erikson discovered America; roughly a thousand years later, Americans "on the prowl for ammunition to use against sex education" discovered Sweden. "Most high school Swedes regard premarital sexual relations as natural and acceptable," a conservative minister told a California school board in 1969. "It is your responsibility to recommend a course of action.... Will it be the plan of God or the failure of Sweden?" Hyperbole aside, the minister's remark spoke to real and important differences between educational approaches in the United States and Sweden; one emphasized the perils of sex and the need for restraint, while the other prized individual discretion and pleasure. But such contrasts were often lost in the developing world and in post-Communist Eastern Europe, where sex education critics denounced the subject with a single, all-encompassing adjective—"Western." In India, the secular left and religious right both blasted sex education as a "Western attack" upon "Indian cultural values"; Chinese critics dismissed it as "just another effort to mimic the Westerners"; and in Russia, opponents charged that a "world sexological-industrial complex" was foisting the subject on the rest of the globe. Some critics said that "Western pharmaceutical companies" and intelligence services were secretly promoting sex education among unwitting Russians; even more darkly, others suggested that a worldwide "Jewish conspiracy" lurked behind it.[15]

Yet these diverse and nationalistic critics united across national borders, posing a new and thoroughly globalized check upon the growth and development of sex education around the globe. After spearheading the movement for sex education in the first half of the twentieth century, the United States would also galvanize the more recent international campaign to remove or restrict it. The key shift occurred in the late 1960s and early 1970s, when the American "New Right" helped organize protests against the subject in several Western countries. "It's up to us to set the standard that we want for our youngsters," a New Zealand activist wrote in 1973, quoting several American and British conservatives. "Do you like the idea of New Zealand being the Sweden of the South Seas?" The effort did not become thoroughly global until the 1980s and 1990s, spurred not just by the spread of HIV/AIDS but also by the enormous transnational migration of human beings. By 2005, 190 million people had moved from one country to another; together they made up 3 percent of the world's population, more than double their proportion three decades earlier. Even a formerly monochrome society like Sweden counted one million immigrants among its nine million people; in Holland, meanwhile, newcomers were so numerous that its largest city, Amsterdam, was expected to become majority-immigrant by 2015. Most of these migrants came from Muslim or Hindu societies in South Asia, the Middle East, or North Africa; not surprisingly, they often objected to the more liberal messages taught about sex in European schools.[16]

By the end of the twentieth century, indeed, the battle over sex education had spawned new armies that cut across races, religions, ethnicities, and—most of all—across nations. In many places, opponents of sex education shared more with conservatives in another part of their country—or in another part of the world—than they did with the people who ran their own schools. One Lebanese journalist described the entire sex education dispute as an example of "Ideological Globalization," pitting traditional and orthodox communities around the world against liberal-minded citizens and educators. In Western Europe, especially, sex education spawned new alliances—or "strange bedfellows," as skeptical journalists quipped—between "the most reactionary believers of different faiths," as a conservative American noted approvingly. "In the case of fundamental norms, we find more common grounds between Islam and Christianity," a British Muslim leader added, in an attack on sex education, "but many Westerners are so distant from their religious roots that it often requires a Muslim to point out the meeting points between these two faiths." As nativist sentiment soared across the continent, sparking electoral gains for right-wing political parties, sex education also provided a rare spot of consensus between Muslim immigrants and conservative whites. On most matters—including civil liberties, foreign policy, and immigration itself—these groups stood in stark opposition. But they joined hands on sex education, creating multiracial coalitions to stalemate or roll back the subject.[17]

To sex educators, across the twentieth century and around the world, the key to improving sexual behavior was spreading knowledge about it; like any other social issue or dilemma, the problem of sex would be solved by more information, discussion, and understanding. "The world has probably never known any such universal consensus as the present belief in education," wrote G. Stanley Hall, perhaps America's best-known psychologist, in 1911. But when it came to sex, Hall added, "it would almost seem as if civilized man was afraid of knowledge, laid a heavy ban upon instruction and deliberately chose darkness rather than life." That same year, but an ocean away, France's most famous sociologist took a very different tack on sex education. Debating a physician who demanded that schools teach the "facts of life" about sex, which religion had made into something frightening and "mysterious," Émile Durkheim rejected the idea that sex could be anything *other* than religious—or mysterious. Even the "crudest and most primitive religions" regarded sex as a "grave, solemn, and deeply religious act," Durkheim observed. Such ideas were not simply "superstitions" or "deceptions," he cautioned; they instead reflected social reality, "some sentiment which men of all times have truly felt." To Durkheim, sex could never be reduced to a matter of health, science, or even knowledge. This book is about the possibility that he was right.[18]

# CHAPTER ONE

# The Birds, the Bees, and the Globe
## THE ORIGINS OF SEX EDUCATION, 1898–1939

In March 1928, a British delegation presented a resolution on behalf of "Biological Education" to the League of Nations' Advisory Committee on Traffic in Women and Protection of Children. Thus far the committee had focused mainly on international treaties and other legal mechanisms to stem prostitution and venereal disease. Yet the "root cause" of these ills lay in the "demand for promiscuity," the British delegation wrote, which could only be lowered via education. "A carefully devised scheme of biological training could not fail to stimulate a sense of individual responsibility in the exercise of the racial function," the British resolution declared. Here it drew upon eugenic theory, which held that sexual impropriety—especially relations outside of marriage—threatened to erode the strength and dominance of white populations. The resolution also announced a gift from the American Social Hygiene Association, which had pledged $5,000 to the committee for "an inquiry into the methods adopted in various countries for the imparting of sex knowledge to young people." In an attached outline of the proposed study, the British delegates noted that "isolated experiments" in sex education were already underway in several nations. A full investigation would allow them to pool their knowledge, which would in turn unleash a worldwide wave of "sexual enlightenment."[1]

But the League of Nations committee rejected the proposal as well as the American money attached to it, highlighting deep ambivalence about sex education around the globe. Even as he denounced the "fairy tales and half-truths" told to children about sex, a Danish representative insisted that "private persons or organisations"—not state-run schools—should counter these falsehoods. In Japan, where sex instruction was part of the school biology curriculum, the subject had come under fire from conservatives; the "burning question" was whether it would continue, a Japanese delegate said, and "much would depend upon the example of other countries." As the ensuing discussion demonstrated, there were few consistent examples to follow. A Belgian delegate said sex should be explained by parents— "particularly by mothers"—rather than by schools; to a Spanish spokesman, meanwhile, the entire subject "raised controversial points of religious morality and pedagogics" that educators would be wise to avoid. Behind the scenes, meanwhile, some British representatives distanced themselves from their own delegation's proposal. "The first step should be to educate parents to do their own job," a British official told his Swiss counterpart. In an exchange with a Belgian delegate, meanwhile, the same official doubted whether sex education lent itself to international rules or principles in the first place. "Adolescence varies in different countries," the British delegate declared, "and the different countries would have to interpret the question in the light of existing facts."[2]

And so they did. During the first few decades of the twentieth century, Western nation-states took delicate first steps to teach about sex in their schools. They also sought to spread the subject to their overseas colonies and territories via missionaries as well as secular instructors. The content and purpose of these courses was remarkably similar across national borders. Using models and metaphors from the animal world, sex education sought to communicate "the facts of life" while simultaneously discouraging human sexual activity outside of marriage. But the popular response to the subject varied considerably. In southern Europe and Latin America, the Catholic Church took the lead in opposing any school-based sex instruction; in Mexico, most notably, sex education became a key issue in the violent struggle between state and religious authorities. In western Europe and North America, meanwhile, new democratic and labor movements spawned unexpected forms of resistance against sex education. As the playwright and social reformer George Bernard Shaw told a group of sex educators in 1929, advocates for such instruction tended to assume that "what makes for liberty in one thing will make for liberty in all things." But the more "the people at large" could influence government, Shaw cautioned, the more they could inhibit sex education. "Do not think your own particular morality can be imposed on the whole nation," Shaw warned, "and do not dream that such liberality is inherent in Democracy; for that is the greatest mistake you can possibly make."[3]

But sex educators were slow to learn Shaw's lesson. Around the world, they assumed that informed parents would accept the virtues and necessity of sex education; when the educators' hopes were dashed, they demanded that schools teach about sex to save innocent children from parental ignorance. The subject took root most readily in America, which European educators would later revile for its conservative or "Puritan" views on sex. But the United States invested in public education earlier—and to a greater degree—than most other countries did. Whenever a social problem arose, Americans were more inclined to view education as a solvent for it; they also sent more adolescents to secondary schools, which were the most common locus of sexual instruction around the world.[4] Finally, the American pattern of local school control required educators to win popular support for sex education; by the same token, the absence of strong national authority in school matters helped sex educators avoid the broadscale controversy that hounded the subject elsewhere. In the latter half of the twentieth century, conservative critics would swarm American school districts and severely constrain sex education. In the early part of the century, however, America took the lead in the subject—both at home and abroad. "Even in Buenos Aries and Rio de Janeiro *mañana* becomes *to-day* when a social-hygiene motion picture is to be exhibited," exulted an official at the American Social Hygiene Association, which sent sex education films around the world. Even when international organizations like the League of Nations rejected its approach, Americans would still find ways to influence how different nations taught about sex.[5]

## DAMAGED GOODS

In 1901, the French dramatist Eugène Brieux published a controversial new play, *Les Avariés* (*Damaged Goods*), about a married couple with venereal disease. When censors in Paris barred the production of the play, it was staged for the first time in Brussels the following year. Exposing ignorance and hypocrisy about sex, the play concluded with a ringing affirmation of education as an antidote to both. A physician declares that sex education must start early, in schools, lest young people engage in dangerous and immoral behavior. When the father of the "damaged" wife suggests that such instruction will awaken adolescent "curiosities," the physician replies that youth are already interested in sex; the only question is what they will do with it. "We must elevate the soul of the young man by taking these facts out of the realm of mystery and slang," the doctor urges, adding a jibe at the "conspiracy of silence" that enshrouded the subject. "We must make him understand that he is a sort of temple in which is prepared the future of the race."[6]

The same year that *Damaged Goods* was produced, Brussels also hosted the Second International Congress for Prophylaxis of Syphilis and Venereal Disease. Attendees included an American dermatologist, Prince Morrow, whose European colleagues charged him with establishing an anti-VD organization in the United States. Upon his return Morrow published a translation of a book by French physician and syphilis expert Alfred Fournier, who had helped found his country's *Société française de prophylaxie sanitaire et morale*. In February 1905, at a medical academy in New York, Morrow started America's own Society for Sanitary and Moral Prophylaxis. Dominated by physicians, the international anti-VD movement emphasized medical interventions and legal controls—not education—as a check on the disease. True, the 1902 Brussels congress resolved that schoolchildren should receive "information" about VD. Yet nobody seemed to comment on this brief and unelaborated plea; nor did the congress suggest any specific measures to implement it. Attention focused instead on the convention's recommendations that hospitals provide free treatment for VD—and that governments slap penalties on people who knowingly infected others with it.[7]

## THE UNITED STATES: SEX EDUCATION, LOCAL AND NATIONAL

By contrast, Morrow's spin-off organization in the United States focused on education about sex—especially in public schools—as well as on efforts to regulate it. So did dozens of other new groups that sprouted simultaneously across the American landscape in the first decade of the twentieth century. By 1910, an umbrella organization called the American Federation for Sex Hygiene counted twenty-seven different societies with six thousand members; three years after that, it would merge with another group to form the American Social Hygiene Association (ASHA). Like its counterparts in Europe, the ASHA was dedicated to eradicating venereal disease and prostitution. But it emphasized education as a route to reform; unless young minds thought differently, the ASHA insisted, their behavior would remain the same. "After a great many years of trying this and that, we finally recognized that the whole situation will never be improved until there is a change in the attitude of the people, about sex," an ASHA official told a teachers' conference in 1922. "We cannot do much with the adults. The hope lies in the development of the next generation."[8] Anti-VD campaigners around the world peppered their reports and speeches with similar statements; indeed, they occasionally borrowed such rhetoric from American sources.[9] But education was a minor key in the global chorus against venereal disease, which remained firmly focused on legal and medical interventions. The exception was America, as a British visitor noted in 1920. In Europe, she wrote, "comparatively little" sex education took place in schools; in the United States, by contrast, "much has been done."[10]

That year, a survey returned by over six thousand American high schools confirmed that 40 percent provided "sex instruction of some sort." Nearly half of those schools reported teaching about sex as part of "courses already in the curriculum"; the most common venue was biology, followed by "physiology and hygiene" and "social sciences." The rest of the schools providing sex education gave what the survey described as "emergency" instruction via lectures, exhibits, and pamphlets. Some school districts hired physicians or other special speakers to address student assemblies, which were almost always segregated by gender. Others simply relied on the leaflets produced by the ASHA and other private organizations, which likewise tailored their wares to the different sexes. (The most popular ASHA pamphlet for boys was called *Keeping Fit*, while its female counterpart was titled *Healthy Happy Womanhood*.) Noting the lack of a central national authority in US education, one observer marveled that "sex instruction has developed here and there without regard to locality." Paradoxically, it seemed, the highly decentralized American school system was generating an informal national curriculum about sex.[11]

But it was hardly a coincidence. As historians of American education have shown, private foundations and university professors joined hands with state authorities to construct a school system that was simultaneously local *and* national. Ceding a wide set of decisions to communities, they generated popular support for policies as well as standardization across them. In the case of sex education, early support from the Rockefeller Foundation—much of it veiled from the general public—fostered a degree of uniformity across districts and schools. Of $177,000 donated to the ASHA in 1918, a whopping $145,000 came from the Rockefellers. A devout believer in sex education, John D. Rockefeller Jr. also made personal—and mostly secret—contributions to local districts to promote it. In 1912, for example, he surreptitiously paid for a well-known lecturer to give eighteen talks about sex to teachers on New York's Lower East Side. As Rockefeller told the district's renowned superintendent, Julia Richman, he hoped the talks would help teachers "break down the barrier of mistaken modesty which has so long prevented the proper discussion of this most important subject." But if Richman was asked who sponsored the lectures, Rockefeller advised, she should dodge the question. "You could say that a small group of persons interested in the subject had asked you to see whether anything could be done," he suggested.[12]

Rockefeller's interest in sex education reflected his concerns about "the frightful ravages of venereal disease," as he told an associate in 1910. That same year he had served as foreman of a special grand jury investigating the so-called white slave trade in New York City. Despite muckraking newspaper exposés of a widespread prostitution ring, the investigation failed to uncover any such syndicate. But it did reinforce Rockefeller's worries about sexually transmitted diseases and—especially—about public panic and misinformation on such subjects; hence, the need for sex education, which would replace lurid media accounts with sober scientific knowledge. Rockefeller helped fund the 1913 Broadway premiere of *Damaged Goods*, which he praised for its matter-of-fact approach to a topic previously shrouded in ignorance and shame. He also sponsored several lengthy surveys of prostitution in the United States and Europe, contrasting their dispassionate, objective style to the tacky tabloids and scandal sheets of the day. Later in the century, the Rockefeller Foundation would join other big American donors—especially the Ford Foundation—in promoting sex education overseas. Yet during the early "experimental stage" of sex education, as one of his lieutenants called it, Rockefeller resolved to establish "a strong, constructive program in our own country" rather than in others. The key was to enlist experts to work quietly with local public school leaders like Richman—and without arousing too much interest or opposition from an easily swayed public.[13]

Meanwhile, the federal government also played an important part in promoting American sex instruction during these years. Because the United States has lacked a department of education for most of its history, other federal agencies have often stepped into the breach to assist schools at moments of stress or crisis. The first such crisis for sex education arrived with America's entry into World War I, when reports of rampant VD among enlistees and soldiers triggered a national panic. Congress responded by establishing the Interdepartmental Social Hygiene Board, composed of the secretaries of the treasury, war, and navy departments along with representatives of the United States Public Health Service and the Army and Navy Medical Corps. Its budget included $100,000 per year for colleges and universities to develop "more effective medical measures" to control VD. But three times that amount was allotted to the universities to design "more effective educational measures" to prevent the spread of the disease. During its three years of operation, the board helped establish new departments of hygiene at thirty-nine colleges, universities, and normal schools; beneficiaries included elite private institutions like Harvard and Reed, large state universities such as the University of North Carolina, and three historically black colleges. The board also funded sex education films, which soon became a staple of urban high school classrooms. In 1925, for example, forty thousand New York City students watched sixty-one separate screenings of *The Science of Life*, which was narrated by a guest lecturer from the US Public Health Service.[14]

## EUROPE: THE UNITED KINGDOM AND BEYOND

The closest parallel to the American situation arose in the United Kingdom, where worries about VD during World War I also spawned a new nationwide drive for sex education. Several prominent physicians and educators met three days before the war started to form the National Council for Combating Venereal Disease (NCCVD), which organized courses for teachers and sent speakers into schools. Unlike the ASHA, the NCCVD—later renamed the British Social Hygiene Council (BSHC)—received funds from the central government. But when the government withdrew this grant in 1929, calling on local authorities to allocate their own funds for sex education, most declined to do so. Part of the reason might have been the government grant itself, which reduced the incentive for local schools to promote the subject. But dejected advocates also pointed to the perennial British squeamishness about the physical body, which inhibited public debate on sex education as well as the instruction itself. "Queen Victoria died in 1901," one BSHC official quipped, "but the Victorian age lingered on." Only a small fraction of British teens attended high school, which did not become free and compulsory until after World War II. But in a large 1949 survey, even people who had been to high school remembered little or no instruction about sex there.[15] The exceptions were found in communities with active voluntary societies, which sponsored lectures for students as well as for their parents.[16]

In Continental Europe, likewise, the rare instances of sex education in schools more often came from volunteers outside the schools than from officials or teachers within them. In 1908, a disciple of Alfred Fournier—and a member of his Sanitary and Moral Prophylaxis Society—proposed nationwide sex instruction in France. "This has to be learned in school," he insisted. "Among young French boys and girls, the sexual instinct must be trained and educated, like other instincts." As elsewhere, the drive for sex education picked up again during World War I; in 1923, a survey of school inspectors, principals, and teachers revealed qualified support for the subject. But many principals balked at interviewing students and their parents, as the survey requested, which in turn made the results "too meager for scientific comment," as one observer noted. Whatever instruction took place fell to the Sanitary Society and to a Feminine Education Committee of the National Council of French Women, which held hundreds of conferences and distributed nearly a million brochures; by 1935, one-third of female schoolteachers had received its materials. But the teachers mostly ignored the subject, lest they alienate an already dubious public. "The English, Americans, Germans, and Swedes have preceded the Latin races in this teaching," one dejected sex education supporter noted. The only question was whether France would follow along.[17]

Yet other countries were hardly as "advanced" as the Frenchman assumed. Repeating a common cliché, the French imagined that Germany, especially, taught about sex in a highly detailed and clinical manner. As a French visitor to the Hygiene Pavilion at the 1927 Dusseldorf Exposition remarked, Germans approached the human body "like a machine" and thereby robbed it of romance and passion. "There is the utmost plainness in sex education," he observed. "Germany is placing before her youth, with a sincerity stripped of all artifice and reticence, every problem of life." Here the visitor gave too much credence to the exhibition, which reflected a long tradition of German social critique rather than actual instruction in the schools. The best-known text in this critical tradition was *Spring Awakening*, an 1891 play by Frank Wedekind. Like *Damaged Goods*, Wedekind's play blasted polite society's mythmaking—and mixed messages—surrounding sex. But *Spring Awakening* concerned the sexuality of adolescents, not of married adults, and also touched on a host of other controversial topics: abortion, homosexuality, rape, and suicide. Censored by German authorities, the play sparked new demands for sex education when it finally premiered in 1906. In one of the play's most quoted scenes, a teen turns to his school's encyclopedia for information about sex—and finds nothing. "What's the good of an encyclopedia that doesn't answer the most pertinent question in the world?" he asks.[18]

The following year, a renowned Viennese psychiatrist posed a similar question. In one of his only published essays about sex education, written at the request of a Hamburg physician, Sigmund Freud rehearsed his theory of child sexuality: children were sexual beings, from birth, so "a child's intellectual interest in the riddles of sex … shows itself accordingly at an unexpectedly early age." But children rarely received solid answers from parents, who confused and harmed their offspring by lying or dissembling about the subject. Hence the need for teachers to tell them the truth at school, Freud argued. "The main facts of reproduction and their significance should be included in lessons about the animal kingdom," he wrote, "and at the same time stress should be laid on the fact that man shares every essential in his organization with the higher animals." So why did so many schools resist this duty? To Freud, the answer lay in a single word: religion. So long as clerical authorities held sway over the school curriculum, as they did across much of Europe, sex education would be suppressed. "A priest will never admit that men and animals have the same nature," Freud concluded.[19]

But his own examples suggested a much more complicated story. Following the principle of *laïcité*, or secularism, Freud noted, France had wisely replaced its school catechism with a primer about ethics and citizenship, but the same book excluded mention of sex, rendering the text "seriously deficient." In Freud's native Austria, meanwhile, the resolutely anticlerical socialist parties offered only lukewarm support for sex education; if such instruction piqued children's interest in sex, the argument went, they would be diverted from the revolutionary struggle. Likewise, avowedly secular Germans remained deeply divided about whether—and how—to teach about sex in their schools. In 1907, as Freud's essay went to press, the German Society for Combating Venereal Disease backed "sex pedagogy" in schools, but the following year, the German Medical Congress declined to take a position on it. Unlike Austria, where the leading women's organization rejected sex education as an attack on maternal authority, Germany's League for Protection of Mothers said instruction about sex should be taken "from the sphere of the home" and transferred to schools. But when the group's leader tried to give a scheduled 1908 lecture in Hamburg, which had barred sex education, police prevented her from speaking. She delivered the talk instead in nearby Altona, which was more supportive of the subject.[20]

Ironically, Hamburg would become one of the German cities to lift its ban on sex education after World War I. But rural states like Oldenburg rejected Hamburg's so-called modern curriculum, which—shockingly for the time—included explanations of human as well as animal reproduction. Even in Hamburg and other "modern" districts, meanwhile, many schools elected to ignore the subject. Two universities did establish chairs in "sexual pedagogics," while some states required teachers to pass an examination in the same. But even these scattered developments came to an abrupt halt in April 1933, when the new Nazi regime barred sex education as the work of "Marxists" and—confusingly—of "bourgeois individualists." As in other parts of the world, sex instruction in German schools was hardly libertine; one popular textbook in the 1920s flatly told students to avoid all sexual activity outside of marriage, including masturbation and homosexuality. But the mere mention of these subjects was too liberal for Nazi censors, who replaced them with passages about racial heredity and "systematic elimination of inferior strains." In Italy, similarly, the rise of Fascism put an end to the handful of sex education experiments in schools. Like coeducational classrooms and birth control, which were also banned, sex education was savaged as a "Communistic" practice that sapped the virility of the Italian fatherland.[21]

## SEEING RED: SEX EDUCATION AND THE SPECTER OF REVOLUTION

The Fascists were right about one thing: in the world's first Communist country, some schools had embraced doctrines of sexual liberation and pleasure. After the Bolshevik Revolution of 1917, elements of the Komsomol (Communist Youth) propagated what became known across the new Soviet Union as the "glass of water" theory. Just as people drank a glass of water to quench their thirst, the theory went, so should they have sex to satisfy a different physical urge; there was no need to complicate the matter with romance or love, which Komsomol ideologues dismissed as a "bourgeois fable." As always, it is hard to know whether—and to what degree—such ideas actually entered school classrooms. Visiting a large Moscow high school in 1925, a local university president found brightly colored wall charts reporting on a poll of students' sexual attitudes. According to the charts, only 2.4 percent of the male students and 1.7 percent of the females believed that the "ideal sexual life" could be found in marriage. The rest preferred "other forms of sexual relations": two-thirds of the females and one-half of the males favored "prolonged love affairs outside of marriage," while the rest sought "brief love relations" or even "chance sexual relations." Another wall chart compared the ages at which male and female students in the class had experienced "sexual feelings," while a third compared their masturbation habits. (Over half of the male students had engaged in the practice, while only 15 percent of women had done so.)[22]

But the same Moscow visitor went on to denounce the school's "highly dubious" and "insufficiently chaste" brand of sex education, marking an important shift away from the brief libertinism of early Bolshevik years. The revolutionary leader V. I. Lenin never liked the glass-of-water theory, which he called "un-Marxist" and "bourgeois" (despite its own antibourgeois pretensions) in a 1920 private interview. Yes, Lenin acknowledged, "thirst must be quenched" in all human beings. "But would a normal person normally lie down in the gutter and drink from a puddle?" he asked. "Or even from a glass whose edge has been greased by many lips?" Most of all, he worried that "sexual excesses" would divert Soviet youth from their revolutionary duties. By 1925, when Lenin's remarks were published, the tide was clearly turning. In an essay on "Sexual Education in the Context of Marxist Pedagogy," which appeared the same year, one educator even suggested that masturbation was "selfish" and hence counterrevolutionary. "All autoerotic processes, moments of self-satisfaction that do not require contact with another, occasion a pathological increase in egocentrism," he asserted, "and produce shy loners imprisoned in themselves and unconcerned with the life of society." Indeed, one could measure students' commitment to the collective by whether they pleasured themselves. "If the adolescent is firmly tied to the communist youth movement," another educator surmised, "then that adolescent will never become an inveterate masturbator."[23]

By the 1930s, Soviet educators had slapped strict restrictions on sex education. The key figure in the field was Anton Makarenko, who published several books on the subject and also hosted a popular radio show. Makarenko received thousands of letters from readers and listeners seeking his counsel about when and what to tell their children about sex. His answer was simple: not too early, and not too much. When children asked where they came from, the best answer was, "You are still too small. When you grow up, you will understand"; alternatively, he wrote, parents "may tactfully dodge the answer, or reply by a joke or a smile." Better to wait until the child was in school, Makarenko added, where teachers could explain the "facts of life" with simple descriptions of animal reproduction. But he also cautioned teachers against giving too many details about the human kind, noting that students "will figure it out when they get married." Lest they run afoul of these restrictions, most teachers probably avoided the subject altogether. In 1935, when Leningrad school officials discovered that a civics teacher was holding question-and-answer sessions about sex—addressing, by one report, which gender "receives satisfaction first" during intercourse—the class was banned. But that was not enough for agents in the state intelligence service, who complained that the school had not fired the offending teacher. "So on the one hand we have the vilest class," one agent wrote, "and on the other, utter political illiteracy." Left-leaning visitors from the West were disappointed to discover that "socialist" sex education was even more prim and straitlaced than the clipped version in their own schools.[24]

In Mexico, by contrast, foreign observers charged that socialist regimes promoted sexual debauchery—not prudery—in the schools. In a 1922 letter to her family at home, an American missionary in the Yucatán region noted that the local socialist government was distributing a pamphlet on birth control to its mostly female—and unmarried—teaching force. "It really is a dreadful thing to get into the hands of young girls," the outraged missionary wrote, alluding to the teachers, "when the high officials say openly that they believe in free love and that a man has a right to take any woman he fancies." But she added that several of the teachers' fathers had barred them from reading the birth-control leaflet, suggesting deep popular discomfort with sex education; the "only good that will come from it," she predicted, "is that the people will revolt." She was right. In 1933, when the socialist-led national government announced plans to provide sex instruction to correct "misperceptions" foisted by "repressive" parents, the country's largest parent organization denounced sex education as "a Communist plot to destroy social stability." The following year, at a crowded Mexico City movie house, three teenaged boys stood up and condemned sex education for corrupting their female classmates. Arrested by police and sentenced to short jail terms, the boys went on a hunger strike; then news of their plight sparked a widespread *school* strike, along with street riots that injured more than twenty parents. Until sex education stopped, parents said, they would keep their children at home.[25]

As best we can tell, though, the government's sex education program never really started. Education officials did release a teachers' manual, which blasted parents' "absolute silence" on the subject—and provided classroom lessons for addressing it. But most teachers seem to have ignored it, too, whether out of fear or conviction. That did not stop local newspapers from publishing scandalous—and almost certainly fictitious—accounts of children stripping for sex education "exhibitions," prostitutes recruited as "instructors," or teachers seducing students as part of their "lessons." Protests also spread north to the United States, where Catholic prelates rallied parishioners against Mexican sex education. At a rally of thirty thousand demonstrators in Philadelphia, one cardinal reviled it as a plot to snuff out religion; in New York, another cleric led a six-day prayer vigil to end "persecution of Catholics"—including "compulsory sex education"—in Mexico. As far away as Ireland, finally, critics noted that a Mexican governor who imposed sex instruction had named his three children "Lenin, Lucifer, and Satan," to underscore his "hatred of Christianity." Back in Mexico, however, officials were already backing off. After charging seven teachers with "subversive activities" for supporting the parent strike, the national minister of education resigned; four days later, parents called off the strike. To one jaundiced American observer, the entire episode showed "how readily the Mexican mind turns to new and untried formulae."[26]

Actually, it showed the opposite. Mexican parents and teachers blocked state-formulated sex education *because* it was "new and untried." Most of all, they rejected sex instruction because of its link to the state. The sex education dispute in Mexico was part of a larger struggle between secular and clerical authority, in Latin America and around the world. Beneath that battle, in turn, lay an even more fundamental one: who owns the child, the parent or the state? Sex educators imagined a world where knowledge—as transmitted through the state—would govern human affairs; indeed, it would penetrate into the most intimate realms of thought and behavior. "Sex is so vital to the individual and community," a Canadian educator wrote in 1922, "that its development and guidance cannot be left to chance." So it could not be left to parents, either. "The home, as in so many other matters, had fallen down in this task, and the burden has been shifted to the school," the Canadian continued. "Our grandmothers would have been horrified to learn that cooking and sewing were taught in schools, nay, that university degrees were given in domestic science, but we view such progress with a dispassionate eye. So it will be with sex education." Across their national differences and idiosyncrasies, sex educators stood united in the conviction that people—especially young people—"need experts to tell them ... the truth about sex," as the American judge and sex education advocate Ben Lindsey wrote in 1927. But the experts confronted a world of faith and family, which frequently rejected state authority—and jealously guarded its own.[27]

## SEX EDUCATION IN THE MODERN WORLD: THE MAIN ARGUMENT

At its root, the argument for sex education was about modernity; old controls had melted away, but nothing solid had arisen in their place. "Times have altered," a British sex educator told a parents' meeting in 1921. "We turn out our children now—we let them loose far more than *you* were let loose—on a far more immoral world today than *you* were let loose upon." In particular, young people were flooded with a constant deluge of sexual imagery and messages from fashion, film, and other forms of popular entertainment. Ironically, much of this material came from the acknowledged world leader in sex education: the United States. At a 1927 YMCA conference in Finland on "Problems of Sex," for example, delegates from fifty countries agreed that "many American-made films were international nuisances." Their discussion yielded some amusing moments: American representatives acknowledged that sex-laden movies encouraged "petting," especially in automobiles, while other delegates confessed that they "did not understand what 'petting' meant." ("Attempts to define it revealed that the word might mean much or little," one account noted.) But everyone seemed to believe that popular culture posed grave risks to young people around the world, along with grave injury to America's global reputation. In 1926, the American Social Hygiene Association reprinted a Chinese report that US films were "debauching" audiences there. "Missionaries in Eastern lands are said to be having a most difficult time explaining to the natives that American men are *not* 'barbaric savages' who gamble for a living," the ASHA editorialized, "and that American women are *not* dance-hall girls, who smoke and drink continuously, and 'sell themselves for a coin and a smile.'"[28]

So sex educators would have to stem the tide, in their own countries and around the world. The issue was especially urgent in the so-called tropics of Asia and Africa, where Western incursions threatened to corrupt the allegedly fragile sexual morals of nonwhite races. "All who read are exposed to birth-control propaganda, the highly sexed novels of the railway bookstall and the loose standards of the cinema," a missionary teacher wrote from India. "Can any school that is really Christian be content until it has tried its utmost to fortify its adolescent pupils with 'self-reverence, self-knowledge, self-control'?" Missionary and government teachers in the British Empire received materials from the British Social Hygiene Council, which boasted nineteen overseas branches by 1930. But after BSHC director Sybil Neville-Rolfe visited India, the organization also decided not to seek compulsory sex education there, or anywhere else in the empire; until there were competent teachers for the subject, Neville-Rolfe argued, it would do more harm than good. So the BSHC sponsored summer courses for missionaries on furlough, who heard lectures from Bronisław Malinowski and other prominent anthropologists about sexual values and practices around the world. In a 1931 lecture to the summer school, Malinowski warned against judging non-Europeans too harshly; upon inspection, he suggested, the teachers might find some "common measure" between "heathen and Christian morality." Indeed, a second lecturer added, one could barely find a place on earth that did not already bear some mark of "the white man's influence."[29]

Ironically, some missionaries maintained, one of the white habits that "natives" acquired was reticence about sex. According to this line of argument, Africans and Asians were "naturally" easygoing and matter-of-fact about the topic. With the advent of colonialism, however, they adopted the same "conspiracy of silence" that prevailed in the West. "The openness and realism of primitive tribalism on this question contrast sharply with the White man's tendency to treat sex as a poor disgraced relation of the human family body, whose very existence is not to be admitted or allowed for in daily life," a missionary conference reported from Southern Rhodesia in 1935. "The result of this attitude upon youthful Native students [is] to develop in both sexes a furtiveness and hypocrisy which is quite unnatural to the raw Native." At the same time, ironically, new work and settlement patterns were isolating young Africans from their families—and promoting even more promiscuity than Western youth exhibited. "The very rhythm and quality of life has changed," one South African educator cautioned. "The ancient norms that once guaranteed stability have broken down." So now schools had to build them back up, teaching a new set of values for the modern era. "The task of restoring our youth ... and of circumventing the perils inherent in their new freedom, devolves upon the State, acting through its Departments of Education," the South African asserted.[30]

Even as they railed against commercial movies, meanwhile, sex educators often found that educational films could be their own best weapon. In France, which lacked any official sex education curriculum, government-sponsored "motor car groups" brought films and projectors to schools across the countryside. They also traveled into colonial Algeria, showing a movie that was specially produced to "impress and instruct the natives of Northern Africa," as one educator wrote. The movie profiled "Mohamed," a "young native" who is "strong as a lion and lithe as a panther." He is also "thoughtless and incautious," however, and he contracts VD. But Mohamed receives treatment and regains his former strength, even winning a camel race in the final scene. As one enthusiast gushed, film was "the universal language"; indeed, another advocate added, it was "absolutely international" in scope and reach. But movies also had to be adapted for different audiences, abroad as well as at home. Although the "Mohamed" film was well received in Algiers and Tunis, for example, viewers in Cairo struggled to understand its North African dialect of Arabic. French films were projected to schoolchildren via "traveling cinemas" in at least a half dozen other countries, from Poland and Romania to Uruguay and Brazil. But the most commonly shown movies came from the United States and especially the ASHA, which produced twelve motion pictures by 1924. That year, educators in Chile borrowed ten ASHA films; in Egypt, the initial screening of the ASHA movie *The Gift of Life* concluded with "three cheers for 'America and Science,'" as one witness reported.[31]

## SCIENCE, RACE, AND SEX

The ASHA film began with florid descriptions of plant and animal reproduction and concluded with veiled, indirect explanations of sex among humans, plus fearsome warnings about its "misuse." So it also followed the standard pattern of sex education lessons around the world, which typically took place as part of biology, physiology, or hygiene classes. If teachers began with plant and lower-animal life and gradually worked up to human beings, one American spokesman explained, the entire subject would be "robbed of its unwholesome mystery"; as a British educator added, plants and animals "excite no wonder in the young mind, and certainly no curiosity." Lest children become too interested in human mating, however, many teachers simply excluded mention of it; echoing their textbooks, others described it in such vague and oblique terms that students were often left shaking their heads. When her students asked whether babies "grow in the same way as the seeds" in plants, a Welsh teacher stammered, "Oh, no, babies grow more like chickens hatch, only it is not nearly such a beautiful process, and I don't want to talk about it now." A 463-page British physiology textbook assigned exactly one paragraph—headlined "Testes and Ovaries"—to human reproductive organs; the passage excluded reference to the uterus or vagina, and to the term "sex." "Older children may for some time content themselves with the information about the pollination of flowers," a Polish observer wrote hopefully in 1931, "and the false conviction that this is how all fertilisation takes place can be enough for them for a long time."[32]

The inimitable American journalist H. L. Mencken satirized this evasive strategy in a 1925 article for a New York newspaper, published the same year that Mencken filed his famous reports from the Scopes Trial about evolution instruction in Dayton, Tennessee. Despite their ritualized paeans to scientific knowledge, Mencken wrote, sex educators were "moralists first and scientists only afterwards." Reviewing over a hundred books that were used to teach the subject, Mencken decried their "thumping non sequitur" between human beings and lower forms of life:

> They start off with attempts to show that the phenomena of sex in the lower organisms—usually dahlias, herring or frogs—are beautiful and instructive, and they close with horrible warnings that the phenomena of sex in man are ugly and not to be maintained.... First they describe romantically the mating of the calla lilies and the June bugs, then they plunge furiously into their revolting treatises [on] kissing games, necking, and the dance.... There is, on the one hand, the chaste, automatic philandering of the rose and the honey bee, and there is, on the other hand, the appalling pathological fate of sinful Homo sapiens.

Whereas Sigmund Freud had hoped that studies of plants and animals would spawn a matter-of-fact acceptance of humans' own sexual nature, then, the actual practice of sex education tended to do the opposite. Privately, sex educators acknowledged the validity of Mencken's critique; if he possessed the same "facile pen" as Mencken, one ASHA veteran told John D. Rockefeller, he "would have written exactly in the same tenor." In their publications and pronouncements, however, they hewed closely to the party line: animal sexuality was natural and positive, while the human version was nefarious and problematic. So schools needed to give students—especially boys—the "mighty resolve" to resist it, as a Canadian educator emphasized. Abstaining from sex until marriage was "the most heroic, the most patriotic, in truth the most God-like work a boy can ever aim at," he added. Keeping his body clean and safe, the boy would also aid "unborn generations of Canadians" that followed him.[33]

The last remark alluded to eugenics, the other key arrow in sex educators' avowedly scientific arsenal. Emphasizing the individual's duty to "the race," eugenics was part and parcel of the social politics embraced by self-described Progressives in Europe and the Americas. If people were sexually promiscuous, the argument went, they did not merely place themselves at risk; they would also injure others, exposing spouses and offspring to disease and—even worse—weakening the overall strength of their nation and race. Just as unregulated food and pharmaceuticals represented a "crime against the common weal," one American wrote, so did unchecked sexual behavior; yet the former problem could be controlled by legislation (namely, the Pure Food and Drug Act of 1906), while the latter could only be solved by teaching young people about their collective obligations. "The ultimate aim of sex education [is] the eugenic or racial responsibility of the individual," a British educator wrote in 1916. "We should seek to ... mould the choice towards that which is best and fittest in every sense of the word." That meant urging boys to foreswear premarital sex and also masturbation, the ultimate selfish act; weakening the individual's social commitments, it was also said to promote a variety of mental and physical ailments that could be passed on to succeeding generations. Girls were warned not to "excite" boys with flirtatious dress or behavior, even as they scrutinized male classmates as potential coparents. "At the moment when the two cells unite, the qualities of the new individual are inherited, so it is important that the stock be sound," an American lecturer told a girls' high school assembly in 1932. "In the choice of a mate, therefore, we must be very careful to have high ideals."[34]

Eugenic thinking cut across countries as well as traditional left-right ideological boundaries, drawing feminists and socialists alongside hardline nationalists and fascists. The stillborn Mexican sex education program of the 1930s was initially designed by the Mexican Eugenics Society, at the behest of the National Block of Revolutionary Women; both groups came under angry fire in the conservative press, which charged that the eugenics society—under the direction of a divorced female, no less—harbored "*inconformes sexuales*" (sexual deviants). Sex education in Uruguay was spearheaded by the country's first female doctor and one of its most vocal feminists, who railed against the double standard that allowed men to patronize prostitutes while requiring women to remain chaste. Schools should teach sexual continence to *both* genders, she said, so they learned to value their racial and eugenic responsibilities over the pursuit of personal pleasure. Although birth control methods were almost never mentioned in schools, meanwhile, sex educators sometimes taught the "social"—that is, eugenic—advantages of family planning. As British birth control pioneer Marie Stopes wrote, all children could tell the difference between a "valuable pedigree dog" and a mongrel. "If dogs should be mated carefully to produce valuable puppies," Stopes continued, "should not human beings be mated as carefully in the interest of their children?" Amid fears of "race suicide" in the Americas and Europe, sex education could encourage whites to protect their racial "stock" by avoiding "intermixing" with others. It might also teach the so-called lesser breeds to limit their own reproduction, lest they drown the white race in a sea of color.[35]

Not surprisingly, sex educators tended to omit explicit claims of racial hierarchy in their entreaties to populations in Asia and Africa. They spoke instead of the dangers posed to "the African race" or "the Eastern race," much as they did with respect to the perils facing white people. Some of these appeals seem to have been well received in Asia and Africa, dovetailing with long-standing local concerns about dissolute sexuality and its threat to national strength. In Japan, for example, worries about masturbation—and its enervating effect on young men—led several experts to visit Germany, which addressed the issue "in a scientific way," as one Japanese physician wrote; upon his return, he confidently announced that almost no German above the age of twenty still masturbated. In India, meanwhile, a high school teacher noted strong parallels between the "new science" of sex education and the Hindu tradition of Brahmacharya, or sexual continence. Ironically, the tradition had been revived in the nineteenth century to strengthen young men for the anticolonial struggle against Great Britain. The most famous practitioner was independence leader Mohandas Gandhi, who had taken a vow of celibacy after his wife bore their last child; to Gandhi, sexual activity for any purpose other than reproduction was a "criminal waste of precious energy" and a danger to long-term health. But Gandhi also opposed sex education—of any kind—in Indian classrooms, declaring it "too special and sacred a subject" for teachers to address. Around the world, indeed, many people who supported the goals of sex education—abstinence outside of marriage, and continence within it—rejected the idea of providing it in schools.[36]

## QUESTIONING SEXUAL KNOWLEDGE

In the early 1900s, Dutch parents rallied against the small but growing movement for sex education in the Netherlands, using a simple slogan: "Don't Do It." They quoted the German educator Friedrich Foerster, who called school-based sex instruction a "rationalist error"; it supposed that children were swayed by reason and knowledge, which rarely affected how they actually behaved. The parents also invoked a well-known Catholic aphorism, *ignoti nulla cupido*, which they translated as "one does not desire what one does not know." Finally, they cited the Dutch social worker Emilie Knappert, who published a short book with a loud title: *Speak by Keeping Silent*. Too much sexual information harmed innocent children, critics said, all in the guise of protecting them. "We can't bear those haughty wise children who look upon their pregnant mother with a knowing glance," one spokesman wrote. "If one were able to consult the children, one would probably find that they are not as eager to learn about these things as the pamphlet-writing lady pedagogues suppose." The last remark was a jab at female reformers, who formed the core of sex education supporters. But other females opposed it as a threat to women, especially to those who taught in schools. "Isn't it bad enough that men speak and write so coarsely?" one woman wrote. "Must women too step forward without blushing and tell the public about things that our mother and grandmothers whispered to their daughters in their boudoirs?"[37]

Together, the Dutch opponents captured the main arguments against sex education in the early twentieth century: it exaggerated the protective value of knowledge, violated children's innocence, and trampled on the rights of parents to raise their young in the manner they saw fit. All three objections were routinely invoked by Catholic laypeople and clergy, who represented the most consistent critics of the subject around the world. "Information, nay even love of learning, cannot keep a man upright before God," an American priest and professor told an international meeting on school hygiene in 1913. "Knowledge is not moral power.... Christ, not hygiene, saved the world. Christ, not hygiene, will clean the world and keep it clean." Chicago school superintendent Ella Flagg Young replied that many public schools in the United States "dare not mention the name of Lord Jesus," thanks to the American separation of church and state, so secular knowledge would have to suffice. But when Young tried to institute a series of sex education lectures by visiting doctors in Chicago schools, Catholics spearheaded a successful campaign to cancel them. "What every one knows is not what every one wills, much less what every one does," one Catholic journal explained, commenting on the Chicago controversy. "The drunkard in presence of temptation is not going to be saved from his indulgence by tables of statistics."[38] Across Europe, Catholic priests and spokesmen echoed this objection.[39] And in 1929, Pope Pius XI devoted one of his encyclicals to it:

There are many people who in their stupidity proclaim and propagate this dangerous educational method known under the disgusting name of sex education. They wrongly think that by purely natural means, excluding the help of religion and piety, they will succeed in preventing young people from seeking sensual pleasure and debauchery.... These people are gravely mistaken. They do not recognize man's inborn imperfection.... Young people frequently fall into the sin of unchastity not so much because of a lack of knowledge as because their weak will is exposed to temptation and deprived of God's help.[40]

But the attack on sexual knowledge was hardly confined to Catholics, or even to religious objectors. The most famous American treatise against sex education was authored by the Harvard psychologist Hugo Münsterberg, a secularized German-Jewish immigrant and self-proclaimed rationalist. Münsterberg had made headlines by exposing frauds among psychics and mediums in America's burgeoning spiritualist community. But sex education was equally fraudulent, he insisted, especially in its claim that knowledge would deter immoral practices; instead, it would more likely promote them. Sex education "is one of the most dangerous causes of that evil which it hopes to destroy," Münsterberg wrote in 1914. "We may instruct with the best intention to suppress, and yet our instruction itself must become a source of stimulation, which necessarily creates the desire for improper conduct." Similar concerns surfaced across the West among educators, particularly those charged most directly with providing sex education: school principals. Testifying before a Parliamentary committee on venereal disease, an Australian headmaster recounted a talk to his male students by a member of the White Cross League, the nation's leading sex education organization. "The whole business was so sickening that it was repulsive, and my soul recoiled from it," he recalled. "To go and warn boys against these things is, in many cases, to give them the first intimation that such things exist." In nearby New Zealand, likewise, a principal warned a government investigatory commission that sex education posed "a grave danger of arousing prurient curiosity and unlikely discussion."[41]

Beneath this objection lay the belief in child sexual innocence, which would be harmed by too much sexual information. To Sigmund Freud and his followers, sexual feelings began at birth, or even in the womb; the real harm lurked in denying these instincts or shrouding them in mystery, which would foist guilt and confusion upon the young. But that notion was anathema to many people— probably, to most people—around the world. "Children ... are to have thrust upon their innocent, childish consciousness subjects much too deep and far reaching for their understanding," complained one mother in Washington, DC; in London, likewise, another critic warned that sex education would "break down the children's natural modesty and reserve." Even some sex education supporters evinced similar concerns, urging schools to teach sexual continence via "the welfare of posterity"—that is, eugenics—rather than through em-barrassing and potentially corrupting details about human anatomy, as a 1906 German conference resolved. Out in the schools, however, many parents opposed *any* form of sex education as a threat to this innocence. In 1913, for example, parents in a rural English commu-nity condemned a teacher for reading her class two sex-related sto-ries; one concerned a married couple and the "little egg" growing in the wife, while the other described a father talking to his son in their family workroom. Showing the boy an electrical dynamo, the father notes that electricity is a "mysterious power":

> No one knows what it is. We only know that if *we treat it in the right way* it will enable us to do wonderful things.... There is another power, very like this in its results. There is the myste-rious feeling that men have for women and women have for men. Treat it right, and it will bless your life and ennoble it. But, treat that feeling wrong, and it will curse you, and blast your life, and *kill your immortal soul*.

Both stories—however elliptical they might seem in retrospect— were too graphic for the village's working-class parents, who con-verged upon the school committee to call for the teacher's dismissal. "It is too disgusting for the children to know," one mother said, weeping. "They have not the same respect for their parents when they know that." When the committee refused to fire the teacher, two-thirds of the girls in her class were withdrawn by their families.[42]

## THE PROBLEM OF PARENTS

Wherever sex education was taught, indeed, parents reviled it as an attack on their own authority. Catholics again took the lead in articulating this objection, which Pope Pius underscored in his encyclical on the subject. Emphasizing that education "belongs to the family," Pius went on to quote the US Supreme Court's 1925 decision in *Pierce v. Society of Sisters*: "a child is not the mere creature of the state." Back in the United States, meanwhile, priests and theologians linked sex education to the world's most drastic examples of unchecked state power: fascism and communism. Sex education echoed "the standardization imposed by the dictatorships of soviet Russia and Nazi Germany," a national Catholic official wrote in 1937, "wherein the state despotically guides each and every life in an arbitrary pattern; and the privacy of home and family is ruthlessly disrespected." (He failed to note that both regimes had severely restricted or eliminated sex education.) Catholic leaders in Europe also mounted a fresh defense of parental prerogative, adding a dose of skepticism about the new "science" of education; mothers and fathers could instruct their children about sex, one Austrian theologian wrote, "even when they have never read a 'teaching guide' and perhaps have never heard the word 'pedagogy.'" In France, a mother founded an organization in 1929 for fellow Catholics who thought sex education should remain inside families. Its name told the whole story: *L'Ecole des parents.*[43]

Again, though, this argument extended far beyond Catholic or religious circles; indeed, many secular critics embraced it. In Switzerland, for example, a leading feminist author decried school-based sex instruction as an incursion of mostly male experts upon maternal authority. "We cannot leave it ... to specialists," she declared. "*We* are the specialists." Even more, a British critic added, mothers wished to teach about the subject in accord with their diverse beliefs; so a "general course of instruction"—provided to all pupils, regardless of background—would inevitably "give offense" to somebody. "Teachers cannot know individual pupils sufficiently well, certainly not as well as the parents," a school board member in New York noted, "and if there is to be an interpretation of ethical standards, such interpretation belongs to the parent." Likewise, a city physical education supervisor in the United States complained that sex education was enhancing the power of school leaders—including himself!—at the expense of average citizens. "If we put sex hygiene instruction in our schools the homes of America will continue to lose ground," he wrote, "and will give up the few privileges they now have to train the children." He added a jab at well-to-do mothers who supported the subject, thereby ceding what was rightfully theirs. "We should have only the strongest condemnation for the wealthy, club-going woman, who has not the time to teach her child the fundamental truths of life, but who would throw the responsibility upon a teacher or a football coach," the supervisor fumed.[44]

But as sex educators pointed out, over and over again, most parents did not teach their children anything—at least not much that was true—about sex. They either ignored the subject or taught absurd myths, which varied from country to country. In America, parents told their children that God or even Santa Claus made babies and dropped them down to earth, where women or doctors caught them; in the United Kingdom, that they were found under a gooseberry bush; in China, that they were fished out of a river; and in Germany, that they were excreted like feces. Across cultures, the most common tale was that babies came out of a mother's navel or from "the stork"; one scholar held that a frog writhing in a stork's bill resembled a tiny human, which in turn accounted for the myth. As Freud documented, most children realized that these explanations were false. But when they asked parents for the truth, they were met with angry stares, whispered rebukes, or a slap to the bottom. So they turned to their peers, where they received even more misinformation. Girls in the United Kingdom learned that they could get pregnant from kissing a boy, or by sitting on a toilet seat after he had done so. Upon getting her first menstrual period in 1930, one young woman thought she was dying; she also spent "many shameful secret hours" trying to cut off her pubic hair, believing she was the only girl who grew it. Clearly, a British sex education advocate declared, "few parents are fitted by education, sentiment, or inclination, to give this knowledge"—at least not to their own children.[45]

So schools would have to give it to them. Once upon a time, sex educators argued, parents could teach children everything they needed to know. But that was impossible in the complex modern world, where more and more parental duties were "relegated to the educator"—and to the state. "The parents ... should be no more expected to teach the subject of sex, than to teach biology, anatomy, or mathematics," one British sex education advocate wrote. It might even be *worse* for parents to teach about sex, she added, because they are "especially liable to sex complexes"—which would in turn be visited on their children. As one American noted, in a plea for mandatory sex education over "elective" instruction, parents who chose to enroll their children in the optional course had usually taught them about sex already. The students who "needed the course most" were the ones whose parents "were too embarrassed or too warped in their own attitudes to discuss sex with their children"—and who forbade them from studying it at school. Indeed, a South African educator added, parents' opposition to sex education was the best evidence for why it was needed. "Being uneducated themselves in regard to sex matters, they oppose sex education for their children, and so produce another generation of bigoted parents who in turn pass on their ignorance to succeeding generations," he wrote. "A vicious circle of bigotry, ignorance and intolerance is produced."[46]

Indeed, many sex educators came to believe that sex education was "impossible" under "democratic conditions," as the prominent British sexologist Havelock Ellis observed in 1913. "A coarse and ill-bred community moves in a vicious circle," Ellis wrote, borrowing the same metaphor as the South African author. "Its members are brought up to believe that sex matters are filthy, and when they become adults they protest violently against their children being taught filthy knowledge." So the only thing to do was to "hasten slowly," as one British educator wrote, adding small bits of sex education while taking care not to arouse a volatile and ignorant public. After Ella Flagg Young's 1913 Chicago experiment was canceled, one New York educator said her mistake was mentioning the matter in public at all. "The temptation always is for the people at the head of school systems to be anxious to have a reputation for doing a new thing first and to announce that sex instruction has been introduced in the schools," he noted, in an undisguised swipe at Young. In New York, by contrast, several high schools were already teaching sex education "and the Board of Education has never been consulted about it," he proudly added. Fifteen years later, the same educator warned once more against "public announcement" of sex education efforts. Newspapers would inevitably distort the matter, taking statements out of context and further hardening "prejudice" against the subject. Better to tiptoe silently ahead, a British educational panel suggested, without asking anyone's permission; most parents would tolerate sex education after the fact, it noted, "but get foolishly hot and bothered if their wishes are consulted beforehand."[47]

## TEACHERS, CAUGHT IN THE MIDDLE

When parents did object to sex education, their first target was typically their local teacher. The British village teacher who told her students about sex—and who was retained by her school board, even when parents demanded her dismissal—was the exception that proved the rule; across the Western world, teachers who breached public opinion on the matter usually lost their jobs. In Denmark, for example, a teacher was fired in 1937 for discussing contraception with his students; upholding his removal, a court told him that he "was not allowed to go any further ... than the general knowledge of the average Danish population." Even though the "sexual standard of values" was changing rapidly, a German observed that same year, teachers "in many different countries" addressed the subject at their peril. Like the publics they served, meanwhile, teachers were divided in their views of sex education. In Germany, for example, a 1912 survey of Berlin head teachers found that twenty-three favored sex instruction in school and thirty opposed it; in the United States, meanwhile, a conservative teachers' union blasted the subject as a "usurpation of parental rights," while a leader of a left-leaning union supported it. But he also noted that most of his members were "afraid to approach the problem," and with good reason. As another

American teacher warned, the Scopes Trial had underscored teachers' tenuous security in the face of public controversy. "The wise teacher whose livelihood depends on his salary from the city fathers does well to keep silent on certain subjects," the teacher added, cautioning against mentioning sex as well as evolution.[48]

To leaders in the sex education movement, however, such teachers were simply cowards, prudes, or ignoramuses; anguished and confused about sex, they lacked both the confidence and the knowledge to teach young people about it. Educators worried especially about single women—or "celibate schoolmistresses," as one British critic called them—teaching the subtleties of sex. "The teaching staff of our schools at present is as ignorant about sex as were its parents and it possesses quite as many emotional conflicts on the subject," wrote an American superintendent in 1924. "In fact, a majority of teachers suffer from the additional handicap of being unmarried, with whatever disappointments and emotional strain that unnatural condition may have created." Other critics worried that teachers might be *too* experienced in sex. Noting that German university students had the nation's highest rate of venereal disease, local educators fretted that young male teachers—particularly those "beginning their duties in great cities"—would contract and spread the very disease that sex education was designed to interdict. Others charged that unmarried teachers of both genders were often homosexuals, who used their power and cunning to corrupt young students. "Such perverts are not so rare as normal wholesome people would like to believe," wrote Marie Stopes, the British birth-control and sex education advocate, adding that male homosexuals posed an even greater danger than "Sapphos" (that is, lesbians). "With girls the corruption is chiefly mental and evanescent," Stopes wrote, "and even if Sapphoism is practiced ... it does not so profoundly injure the girls' physique as the corresponding physical side of homosexual manifestations may affect the young boy or lad."[49]

Finally, educators charged, even teachers of "sound morals" often did not have sufficient information or skill to address sex in the classroom. Only a fraction of teachers received formal preparation for the profession during these years, and those who did received little or no instruction about sex. The exception was Germany, where at least some states required future teachers to pass an examination in "sex hygiene," including "the pathological and psychological manifestations of sexual life." But most nations had neither the educational infrastructure nor the political consensus to mandate such courses for teachers. Part of the problem lay in the "integrated" or interdisciplinary nature of sex education; depending on the country and school, children might encounter the topic in biology, religion, civics, social studies, health, or physical education. Across the West, then, teacher-training institutions typically tried to include material about sex in one or more of these disciplines rather than requiring a separate course, which crowded the curriculum and might also draw fire from conservative citizens and legislators. In practice, though, many teachers' training was so minimal—and so disjointed—that they misrepresented or simply avoided the subject when they reached the schools. Here was yet another vicious circle, constricting sex education around the world; political and educational obstacles restricted the preparation of teachers, but the obstacles could not be surmounted so long as the teachers remained unprepared.[50]

So sex educators sponsored special lectures for teachers who were already in the schools, hoping to compensate for the poor instruction they had received before they got there. The most elaborate system of "teacher talks" was developed in Sweden, where the national parliament had rejected several bills to require sex education for children. In 1933, the newly formed Swedish Association for Sexuality Education (known by its Swedish acronym, RFSU) resolved to focus instead on teachers, who could then sway students—and public opinion—in favor of the subject. Over the next three decades, its indefatigable founder, Elise Ottesen-Jensen, spoke to an estimated thirty thousand teachers. In Prussia, school authorities organized a course of lectures for 150 teachers on the development of sexual instinct, its "chief perversions," and the "cultivation of self-control"; in the United States, volunteer groups or individual philanthropists often organized similar talks. "There is no subject more difficult to teach helpfully and skillfully than that of sex," wrote John D. Rockefeller, who financed talks for teachers in New York. "Ninety-five out of a hundred men and women teachers would not be favorably disposed to give such instruction." Rockefeller's largesse raised some hackles at Columbia University's Teachers College, where officials told him that their own faculty addressed the subject with more sophistication than his chosen lecturer. But most American schoolteachers did not attend a formal training institution like Teachers College. They heard an occasional talk on sex education, or they got nothing at all.[51]

Some of these "special lecturers" went directly into schools, bypassing the regular teachers altogether. In Canada, for example, a government-appointed lecturer for Ontario went from school to school around the province, speaking on "elements of sexual physiology and anatomy" and "the duty of treating sexual matters with reverence." Most of these speakers were physicians, whose jaundiced view of classroom teachers was underscored in a 1920 article coauthored by the American behavioral psychologist John B. Watson. Interviewing several dozen doctors, Watson found that almost none of them trusted teachers any more than parents to inform children about sex; this was a medical matter, best handled by physicians. "Certainly such instruction should not be left to old maids or to young unmarried male teachers," one doctor declared. "If parents are incompetent, it certainly must be a poor community where there is no upright, well-informed physician who can undertake this task." For their own part, though, educators worried that doctors would bore young students; as one British physician admitted, "some doctors have no talent for teaching" and "the lectures become ... extremely dull." Still others feared that any "special" lecture on sex— even by a competent physician—would draw too much attention to the topic. "The very fact that a doctor comes expressly to speak on the subject means that there is certainly excitement, curiosity and gossip about it, which it is wiser to avoid," a Danish headmistress warned. As always, the problem was to teach children about sex without provoking their interest in it.[52]

## SUFFER, LITTLE CHILDREN?

As best we can tell, however, most students learned next to nothing from sex education. In a 1938 survey of Americans between the ages of sixteen and twenty-four, just 8 percent identified "school" as their central source of information about sex; the two most common sources were peers and parents, in that order. But three-quarters of the respondents said they would support *more* sex education in schools, where brief and vague lessons left them confused instead of enlightened. "Oh, no, nothing, we didn't learn anything," recalled one British woman, recalling the brief sex education she received in the 1930s; another woman from the same era remembered seeing "terrifying" slide shows about venereal disease, even though her school didn't address pregnancy or childbirth. For some children, VD lessons were more puzzling than frightening. Echoing public service announcements, an Australian headmaster told his male students to "seek medical attention" if they got "it," but as one former student recalled, looking back with a laugh, "I never knew what *it* was." Others were perplexed by the ubiquitous—and ambiguous— plant and animal analogies in sex lessons; at a loud children's party in England, for example, one girl worried that the "rough little boys" would "put some pollen on her." To be sure, some teachers were much more honest and direct with their students about sex. By the 1930s, handfuls of American teachers were already using the "anonymous question and answer box," which became ubiquitous in later years as a way to promote inquiry and dialogue; in the United Kingdom, several girls' headmistresses were well known for their simple and straightforward lessons on human reproduction.[53]

As the students' own commentary reveals, however, such openness and clarity were extremely rare in early twentieth-century sex education classrooms. Even students who received more explicit and frank instruction from a teacher noted how most other adults—including teachers—avoided the subject, "so we get the impression that it is not nice to talk about," as one British student wrote. Still others made light of adult reticence about sex. In a much-repeated (and probably apocryphal) story told by Mary Ware Dennett, the American sex education and birth control advocate, a girl asks her mother where she came from. The mother replies, "God sent you," prompting the girl to inquire about the origins of her mother, grandmother, and great-grandmother. Of course, the answer was the same: God sent them, as well. "Do you mean to say," the girl asks, "that there have been no sex relations in this family for over two hundred years?" As Sigmund Freud reminded us, children have always known more about sex than adults care to admit; more to the point, the children also know what they do *not* know. In 1937, a mock "Parliament" of Canadian high school students passed a resolution on behalf of compulsory sex education, noting "widespread ignorance among youth"; a model "City Council" in New York passed a similar measure two years later, complaining that sex education was "not covered clearly enough to be of any use." In Great Britain, finally, students even produced an underground magazine—with the evocative title *Out of Bounds*—that mocked schools' hypocritical messages on sex, "a beautiful shoe whose very latchet you may not loose." Respect sex, the adults said; just don't engage in it, because that would be disrespectful.[54]

Here the students drew on the small group of self-described "sex radicals" in Europe and the Americas. Their numbers included A. S. Neill and Bertrand Russell in the United Kingdom and Magnus Hirschfeld and Wilhelm Reich in Germany, and they coalesced around the World League for Sexual Reform that Hirschfeld helped found in 1921. To these thinkers, sex education was neither a rational project to improve human health and efficiency—as supporters said—nor a radical challenge to modern order and decency, as its critics charged. It was instead part and parcel of that same order, which rested on shame and repression of sex itself. Witness sex educators' refusal to acknowledge sexual pleasure, which would remain a taboo across the West for many years to come. "So far there is only a form of *Education Against Sex*, plus inadequate information on the Mechanism of Reproduction and menacing warnings against 'illicit intercourse,'" underlined the German socialist Max Hodann. "To create and direct a positive Sex Education is a task for the Mental Hygiene of the future." In other words, minds must be changed. A 1933 conference of sex reformers in London heard a message from America's Mary Ware Dennett, who predicted that youth opinion would evolve before adults' did. "Neither you nor I ... will live to see the day when, as a whole, we Anglo-Saxons on both sides of the Atlantic will have fully shed our inner feelings of shame and fear regarding sex," Dennett wrote. "But the younger people will."[55]

Writing four years later, however, the world's most famous tribune of sexual enlightenment expressed strong doubts about sex education in schools. In his younger years, Sigmund Freud was sure that teachers should compensate for parental silence and duplicity surrounding sex; anything less would condemn children to lives of fear, anxiety, and confusion. Yet near the end of his life, exiled from Austria and dying of cancer, Freud wondered whether sex education in schools could make much of a difference. "I am far from maintaining that this is a harmful or unnecessary thing to do," Freud wrote, "but it is clear that the prophylactic effect of this liberal measure has been vastly overestimated." It turned out that young people—the hope of the future, in the eyes of Dennett and others—were much more conservative than Freud had realized; indeed, they were deeply wedded to the fallacies and falsehoods that adults had foisted upon them. Even after receiving sex education, Freud wrote, children "are by no means ready to sacrifice those sexual theories … about the part played by the stork, about the nature of sexual intercourse, and about the way in which children are born." To put it differently, sexually "enlightened" children "make no use of the new knowledge" that they received. "For a long time after they have been enlightened on these subjects they behave like primitive races who have had Christianity thrust upon them," Freud concluded, "and [they] continue in secret to worship their old idols." Using schools to change children's sexual beliefs was far more difficult than even Sigmund Freud had suspected, and expecting schools to change students' sexual behaviors would be more difficult still. But faith in this liberal measure continued, undimmed, among many educators; if anything, it brightened as the century wore on. It would peak after the next world war, when a new global order once again promised to refashion human beings—and their sexuality—around order, reason, and self-control.[56]

# CHAPTER TWO

# A Family of Man?

## SEX EDUCATION IN A COLD WAR WORLD, 1940–64

In 1950, the American Social Hygiene Association published a florid tribute to a long-deceased French nobleman who had become a United States folk hero. When Alexis de Tocqueville visited America in 1831, he recognized "our national genius for organization as expressed in the banding together of private citizens," noted the *Journal of Social Hygiene* (*JSH*), the ASHA's monthly periodical. To Tocqueville, voluntary associations represented the key to American development—and, even more, to American democracy. "Americans of all ages, all conditions, and all dispositions, constantly form associations," he wrote, in a passage the *JSH* quoted. "In aristocratic societies men do not need to combine in order to act.... Among democratic nations, on the contrary, all the citizens are independent and feeble [and] fall into a state of incapacity, if they do not learn voluntarily to help each other." Molding like-minded citizens into a potent political force, organizations like the ASHA had won sex education in most American schools. But most of all, the *JSH* argued, they underscored what was distinctive about America.[1]

The following year, ironically, the ASHA called upon other nations to follow America's supposedly unique example. Addressing the International Union Against the Venereal Diseases (IUAVD), the ASHA's new Committee on International Relations and Activities acknowledged the "great differences" between the various countries represented in the union. But all of them faced problems of "home and family life," which were the "root cause" of "sexual promiscuity"—and, by corollary, of sexually transmitted diseases. "In looking beyond the differences in cultural patterns, we find more and more similarities," the ASHA declared. "A man belongs to the human race, first, and he seeks … membership in a family." Thanks to its historic tradition of citizen engagement and organization, the United States had taken the lead in "promoting education for wholesome and strong family life," the ASHA noted. Now it was time for other countries to do the same, by starting their own civic organizations to spread the gospel of sex education. Here the ASHA could be of special assistance, sharing its deep experience and expertise in pressing for sex-related instruction. In time, another ASHA spokesman predicted, people everywhere would realize "not only benefits to be gained for themselves in their own countries, but for humanity the world round" in sex education.[2]

In some ways, these appeals echoed patterns that had marked sex education since the early 1900s. The subject remained dominated by the United States, which stressed education—not medicine or law—as a solution to the global scourge of venereal disease. As the horrors of World War II yielded to the grim stalemate of the Cold War, however, Americans added two new elements. The first was an emphasis on family relationships; initially in the United States and then around the world, sex education became more commonly known as "family life education." As Alexis de Tocqueville might have predicted, Americans also promoted their archetypal political mechanism—the voluntary association—as a route to winning the subject in schools. Standing between the individual and the state, such organizations allegedly distinguished democracies like the United States from their Communist foes. By starting advocacy groups for sex education overseas, Americans were not simply protecting the world from venereal disease; they were also shielding it from totalitarian dictatorship, or so they thought. Most of all, sex educators said, they were defending the modern family from a host of internal and external threats. As the bedrock of civilized society, the family was also a bulwark against Communism. Indeed, its most devout believers said, sex education would help defeat the Communist menace and unite a polarized world into the "Family of Man."

As always, the day-to-day practice of sex education fell short of these lofty ideals. In the United States and Europe, the same democratic qualities that sex educators celebrated often constrained sex education itself. When "the people" spoke on the subject, they were as likely to oppose it as to support it. To some critics, the entire subject *violated* their democratic rights—as citizens, parents, and religious worshippers. In the so-called developing world, meanwhile, sex education was denounced as a Western or even an American import; despite their efforts to inspire "native" or "indigenous" organizations on its behalf, Americans could never quite shake the impression that *they*—not the natives—were the engines of sex education. Finally, Communist-bloc countries blasted the subject as a bourgeois affectation that was superfluous—or, even, subversive—in their own societies. Communist regimes began to soften on sex education during the political "thaw" of the early 1960s, when a few brave educators introduced pilot programs in the subject. But the only place where it came close to flourishing was Sweden, a quasi-socialist country that became the first nation-state to require sex education in its schools. It also pioneered a new brand of instruction, with different goals and values, which would eventually challenge America's global hegemony over sex education.

## REPRISE: WAR AND VD

Like World War I before it, World War II sparked new demands for sex education around the world. The key factor, as before, was venereal disease. National conscription highlighted the large number of men who were afflicted, while international military assignments multiplied their opportunities to infect others. In 1942, for the first time, the United Kingdom transferred responsibility for sex education from the British Social Hygiene Council—a voluntary organization that began during the prior world war—to the state-run Central Council for Health Education. The following year, the government issued its first official decree on the subject. "The circumstances of wartime ... are liable to break down restraints," the UK Board of Education warned. So it was the job of schools to restore them, via sex education. The board balked at providing "definite methods of instruction or approach," preferring to leave such decisions to local authorities. Some schools would choose to teach the subject as part of biology, while others folded it into their lessons on history, literature, religion, or domestic science. In 1945, as the war came to an end, the United Kingdom's leading sex educator proclaimed that the country had turned a corner. "It is clear that there has been in recent years a radical and widespread change of public opinion," Cyril Bibby exulted. "Probably there will remain with us for many years a few frightened adults who will continue to foster the culture of ignorance; but an increasingly large section of the population is allowing the myths of the gooseberry bush and the stork to fade into oblivion."[3]

In Canada, likewise, reports of a spike in VD—and memories of the previous world conflict—triggered new sex education efforts. "The last war ushered in jazz, women smokers, disregard for authority ... popular profanity and general looseness of behaviour," a Toronto high school journalist wrote in 1940, warning against "a similar decline" on the home front as well as among troops overseas. Four years later a nurses' bulletin blasted the "prevailing hedonism of the day," which gave birth to a "rise in individualism" as well as an increase in venereal disease. The year after that, in 1945, the Ontario Department of Education published its first guide for teachers in addressing the subject. By 1947, when the International Union against the Venereal Diseases passed a resolution in favor of sex education, dozens of nations had enlisted schools in the anti-VD effort. In some countries, like Finland and Romania, ministries of education promulgated new policies and curricula; in others, like Norway and France, citizen groups took the lead. A panel commissioned by the French government in 1947 reported that "no aspect of education is more neglected than sex education"; even in science classes, one observer quipped, "the study of the human body stops in the middle, leaving a great hole between the thighs and below the stomach." Like their British counterparts, however, French officials preferred to leave the matter to local schools—and to local citizens—rather than dictating policy from above.[4]

Just as they did during World War I, finally, federal officials in the United States sought to expand sex education in order to stem sexually transmitted disease. The US Office of Education enlisted prominent sex educator Lester Kirkendall, who visited thirty-six states to promote educational programs aimed at reducing the "wartime venereal disease rate." But US commissioner of education John W. Studebaker remained "very fearful of political repercussions," as Kirkendall later recalled, carefully reviewing Kirkendall's correspondence with state superintendents and elected leaders. Studebaker also balked at publishing the proceedings of a 1944 sex education conference at the federal Office of Education, where Kirkendall pleaded with assembled experts to move sex education beyond disease control and into the realm of "human relations," especially familial ones. Kirkendall was himself a product of the disease-centered model, worrying endlessly as a boy that his "solitary sinning"—masturbation—would lead to shyness, mental illness, and an early grave; later, he fretted about contracting VD. But his experiences as a high school teacher and professor persuaded Kirkendall that sex education should substitute a "positive" model of human relations for the "negative" one of disease prevention. When the war ended and the Office of Education discontinued his position, he also became convinced that "non-governmental agencies"—not the state—held the key to transforming the subject. Working in their own local communities, human beings would reorient sex education around face-to-face interaction and communication. Then they would spread out over the nation and the world, Kirkendall predicted, unleashing a true revolution in human thought and behavior.[5]

## GOING GLOBAL

But that revolution would require new international relationships, dedicated to transmitting these ideas around the globe. As the United States assumed greater powers and responsibilities on the world stage, American sex educators turned their gaze overseas. The key agency was again the American Social Hygiene Association, which established an "emergency committee" in 1946 to provide services to war-torn countries marked by "moral looseness and low standards"—and, especially, by rising VD rates. The following year, ASHA officials announced a more permanent international presence. "The Association, with its wide experience [in] an economically and socially stable country, must be prepared to stay for some years to come," the

ASHA declared. Requests for its assistance "come as frequently from the more fortunate countries," the ASHA added, "which, like our own, were never invaded by panzer units or kamikaze planes, but which are still fighting a war—a long-range battle against venereal disease and prostitution and other enemies of family life and national strength." The ASHA also assumed leadership of the Regional Office for the Americas of the IUAVD, pledging to reorient the office around sex education. It became an official liaison to the newly forged United Nations, which was turning its attention to questions of health. Finally, the ASHA announced the extension of its Committee on International Relations and Activities—formed several years earlier—to areas *beyond* its hemisphere. During the war, one member explained, the committee's efforts were "naturally limited to the Americas." Now that the conflict had ceased, however, it could assist every corner of the globe.[6]

By the following year, the ASHA was already providing information and materials to forty-seven different countries and sixty-one national and international agencies. It also sent staffers on "field visits" to twenty-five different countries, while hosting forty representatives from twenty-one countries at its New York headquarters. To be sure, the ASHA had engaged in international activity earlier in the century, when it sent social-hygiene films to different countries and provided periodic advice to the League of Nations and other organizations. But the postwar era witnessed an entirely different form of overseas American influence, in degree as well as kind. Consider the example of Brazil, which an ASHA officer visited in 1947. He met with state health officials and also with members of Brazil's fledgling social-hygiene community, who subsequently mailed the ASHA further requests for information and guidance. "Please send a small list of some of your leaflets and little booklets on sex education generally and more especially those dealing with the behaviour of young people of both sexes in their social intercourse," one Brazilian wrote. "American productions will interest us very much, the Americans being clever in educational methods." The ASHA received similar requests from media organizations, which were likewise starved for sex-related information. "This type of material is very scarce in our country, and we need it badly, very badly," one journalist wrote in 1950. It also fielded letters from doctors and educators, who often expressed frustration with the slow pace of change in Latin America. "I should like to start a mass erradication [*sic*] for fighting syphilis," wrote one physician, "but the trouble in getting help is so big I believe that it would be easier to start a mass erradication [*sic*] of our politicians."[7]

In response, the ASHA sent thousands of pieces of literature to Brazil. At least some of it was translated into Portuguese; the rest was in English or in Spanish, the most common languages of ASHA international materials. In 1947, for example, Brazilians received ASHA pamphlets on "Suggestions for Organizing a Community Social Hygiene Program" and "Application of Catholic Philosophy to the VD Program"; a decade later, the ASHA provided copies of its leaflets on "Strengthening Family Life Education in Our Schools" and "Suggestions for Preparing Teachers in Education for Personal and Family Living." ASHA international director Josephine V. Tuller also visited Brazil during her "World Trip" of 1954, which took her to twenty-one countries—in the Near East, Far East, Africa, and South America—in just ninety days. In private, Tuller jokingly called herself an "itinerant peddler"; in each country she visited, she told her hosts about the progress that neighboring countries had made. Most of all, though, she helped them with "community organization"— that is, with "ways and means of gaining public interest and support of an educational program in this field," as Tuller explained. In many parts of the globe, she noted, state officials lacked the will or the wherewithal—or, sometimes, both—to institute sex education in schools. So voluntary organizations would have to pick up the slack, providing sex education even as they pressed governments to do the same.[8]

## SPREADING THE VOLUNTARY ORGANIZATION

The first step was to identify willing partners in host countries. Like Brazil, some nations already had nascent sex education or family planning organizations; in others, the ASHA worked with church-based groups or with parent-teacher associations, which one ASHA visitor to Mexico described as "the opening wedge" into government schools. From its New York headquarters, the ASHA sent letters and telegrams advising local organizations on how to proceed, or it might send Josephine Tuller or another representative to work directly with them. Privately, however, Americans wondered whether their hosts possessed the skill and initiative to organize on their own. "The South Americans, on the whole, are less trustworthy than Europeans, and their development and culture is slower," complained one ASHA official, after visiting several Latin American nations. "A successful program ... would require careful consideration [of] the lethargy of the people. Volunteer agencies in this area seem to be weaker than the rest of the field." In a 1945 memo marked "confidential," likewise, an ASHA field worker in Puerto Rico worried that the territory's "tropical climate" inhibited "group planning and participation." But he concluded on a positive chord, noting slow but important changes in the "natives'" behavior. "More and more they are coming to think of themselves as Americans, and have quite a natural desire to show that they, too, can accomplish some of the things that we have done," he wrote. "They have their Rotary Clubs with meetings conducted in English, their Lions Clubs with meetings conducted in Spanish, and other typically American organizations."[9]

In areas that the United States occupied after World War II, meanwhile, ASHA representatives worked closely with American military officials as well as with local citizens to establish new sex education organizations. In "pre-Hitler" Germany, one ASHA official wrote, the German Society for Combating Venereal Disease was "the strongest in Europe and, next to the ASHA, the strongest in the world." But as British sex education pioneer Marie Stopes wrote, following a 1949 tour of Germany, Nazi educators had replaced the society's careful warnings against premarital sex with "immoral teachings" that any woman who bore a child—whether legitimate or not—was "doing a service to the state." In the wake of the war, moreover, there were three times as many young women as young men; without "scientifically accurate instruction," girls would be tempted into "irregular associations" with older and married Germans or with soldiers in the Allied occupation forces. Later that year, the German Society for Combating VD reestablished its first postwar chapter, in

the American Zone of Berlin; by 1951, a new German Fellowship
for Youth and Marriage Guidance boasted chapters in all four occupation zones. Unlike the prewar anti-VD organizations, which had
stressed legal measures, the new groups trained their attention squarely
on "sexual pedagogic education," as one German member told the
ASHA in 1951. Venereal disease rates in Berlin had already plum-
meted to historic lows, he noted. Now was the time to shift education
toward "the American way," which would teach children about proper
human relations—including dating, marriage, and parenthood—
rather than simply warning against improper ones.[10]

In Japan, likewise, Americans helped to revive older anti-VD
groups and to reorient them beyond the question of disease. Occupation officials established a Purity Education Committee in 1947,
with an American chairman but a majority-Japanese membership.
The committee released a statement the following year, warning
that venereal disease "ruins families, their offsprings [sic], and society at large"; if left unchecked, it could "lead the whole race to de-
struction." By the early 1950s, Japanese sex educators had replaced
this emphasis on VD—and its apocalyptic language of eugenics, now
discredited in the West—with American-style paeans to gender relations, family, and community. A December 1948 memorandum
from the US Office of the Commanding General provided a check-
list for sex education in the schools, including:

> Are we giving guidance to both sexes in boy-girl relationships
> as a contributing factor for a wholesome well-rounded life?
>
> Are we giving guidance in sex education as it is related to
> building young people for responsible family living?
>
> Do we encourage wholesome coeducation activities in the
> classroom as well as extra-curricular activities?

Here US officials cited literature provided by the ASHA, which continued to advise the new Japanese government after the Allied occu-
piers left. It also worked to jump-start the Japanese Society against
Venereal Disease, which had fallen moribund during the war. Without a healthy voluntary association pushing for it, Americans warned,

sex education would never survive. "It seems to us ... that techniques of community organization, as a means of enlisting the support of public opinion, is a fundamental necessity," Josephine Tuller told a Japanese visitor to the ASHA's headquarters in 1954. As an American teacher in Japan added, such an organization would help challenge the society's traditional reticence about sex. Even more critically, it would help the Japanese "learn much more about democracy ... than they will from security pacts."[11]

## THE FAMILY OF MAN

The new emphasis on domestic relations—and on democratic ones— echoed important trends in the United States, where postwar prosperity and suburbanization spawned a new celebration of the family as the key to American character, strength, and security. An official in the E. C. Brown Trust, an Oregon-based organization that produced pioneering sex education films for U.S. schools, captured the shift in a 1956 article. "Sex education is like the elephant in the story of the blind men, each of whom described the whole animal in terms of the particular part he had felt with his hands," Curtis A. Avery wrote. "But, whereas the descriptions of the elephant varied with perspective, descriptions of sex education vary with time. That is, sex education in 1911 was one thing; another thing in 1939 and still another in 1950." In Oregon, early twentieth-century educators stressed "the perils of sex, especially with reference to the venereal diseases," Avery noted. But in 1929 retired physician E. C. Brown left an endowment to the state social hygiene association, to promote "a sound and healthy view" of sex, marriage, and family. The association used the funds to produce *Human Growth*, which would become the most commonly shown sex education film in the United States—and, eventually, around the world. Like E. C. Brown's print materials, the movie embodied what Avery called the three central principles of modern sex education. It dispensed "social and psychological" facts about sex, not just physiological ones; it stressed "family climate and child rearing practices"; and it connected sex to "all other aspects of human life and human relationships."[12]

So it would also help steel Americans to shoulder their new international duties, sex educators added. "Never perhaps in our memory is a straight look at life, a belief in humanity, and a faith for living more essential than today," wrote Missouri sex educator Helen Manley, who served as an adviser to American occupation authorities in Japan. "Our hope for permanent peace is being constantly clouded by our fear of war." But America was also under threat from within, Manley claimed, noting recent increases in divorce and out-of-wedlock births. "All homes are not worthy of emulation, and some children have no family life," she cautioned. "The school has a distinct obligation in supplementing the home or substituting for it in such cases." For the past century, another educator added, American schools had been doing just that. "It is an ironical fact," he added, "that the school after audaciously taking over so many functions of the family now is beginning to provide instruction on how to conduct family life itself." Nothing less than the fate of the nation—and of the world—lay in the balance. World peace demanded a strong America; a strong America required stable families; stable families needed sex education; so sex education was the key to world peace. "The gap between 'family strength' and 'world strength' seems at first glance too wide to bridge, even in a slogan," the ASHA editorialized in 1959. "But the gap must be bridged.... The ASHA's slogan, 'The American Home, the American Hope,' may well become 'The World Home, the World Hope.'"[13]

Most of all, Americans urged other countries to rename "sex education" with new euphemisms: social hygiene, human relations, character education, marriage and family education, or—most commonly—family life education (FLE). Around the globe, nascent or revived sex education organizations followed suit. In the same statement where it called for "sex instruction in the schools," a Canadian health group resolved that "the term 'sex' in the name of the school program be avoided"; better to use "more widely accepted names" such as health education, family relations, or family life education. No matter where they taught, sex educators discovered that "centering the teaching on the child and family rather than on the sex organs would also help to take the curse off it," as an observer wrote from Norway, which sent an educator to the United States to study FLE.

So did Pakistan, where a spokesman noted that Americans had pioneered one euphemism for sex education in the early twentieth century—social hygiene—and replaced it with another, FLE. "The term 'Sex-Education' seems to me to offend some people here," a frustrated family planning official wrote from Hong Kong in 1955, "and I am most anxious to take this opportunity to have them correctly informed, and their complex or prudishness dispelled." The first step, Americans advised, was to change the name of the course to emphasize family relations; over time, more families would come to embrace it.[14]

## A DREAM DEFERRED

In many parts of the world, however, sex education stalled. Even in the United States, many students received only minimal sex instruction—or none at all—in the public schools. The problem was not solved by calling sex education Family Life Education, which often allowed nervous school officials to avoid the thorny topic of how families were actually made. "Presumably liberal and enlightened educators recommended temporarily de-emphasizing sex in suggested courses in order to get them approved by allegedly reactionary and unenlightened administrators, parents, and citizens at large," wrote American sex educators Robert and Frances Harper in 1957, reviewing the previous decade of development. "Sex, it was argued, was the kiss of death.... Play up budgets, household management, child care, in-law problems, and how to shop wisely." After a few years, the argument went, sex could be added without controversy. But sex educators were still waiting. "The years have passed," the Harpers quipped. "Family life education has become a relatively common commodity in schools and colleges. But where, pray tell, are the clear and forthright voices on sex?" Some educators were simply "prudes" or "Puritans," the "'neo-Victorian' rejectors [*sic*] of sex as a fit topic for discussion"; others were "rationalizers," the "emotional phonies" who said the public would never stand for it. The Harpers preferred the prudes, who were at least honest about their Puritan predilections. But "the rationalizers are at heart prudes," the Harpers concluded, "who lack the courage to profess their prudery."[15]

Outside of the United States, likewise, the new emphasis on family did little to quell popular opposition to sex education. Part of the problem lay in the rhetorical overlap between "family life education" and "family planning"—that is, between sex education for youth and contraceptive services for adults. The question was sharply debated at postwar international meetings of family-planning advocates, where Americans—led by birth control pioneer Margaret Sanger—argued for avoiding the entire subject of sexual instruction in schools; although she supported such instruction herself, Sanger worried that it would embroil population-control efforts in unneeded controversy. Sanger was opposed by representatives from Sweden and Holland, who argued that family planning would never succeed *without* school-based sex education. "Even the most material problems in organizing birth control can be solved only in the trail of a path-making sex education," a Dutch delegate argued, "that makes mankind conscious of sexuality, as a thing of special importance apart from reproduction." But the Americans won the battle, insuring that the International Planned Parenthood Federation skirted sex education until the 1960s. Meanwhile, at the IUAVD, delegates from France—where a 1920 law still barred dissemination of birth control information—fought to block any mention of family planning from the group's new sex education initiatives. Yet in the developing world, especially, "family life education" and "family planning" were often seen as one and the same. "It would be dangerous to associate birth control methods with this project in social hygiene," wrote an American in Costa Rica, where Catholic critics accused FLE of teaching family planning. "Let's not wave the red flag in front of the Roman Bull."[16]

Most of all, though, critics around the world charged that family life education was too *American*; despite its rhetoric of international values and cooperation, it bore the imprint and biases of the place it was born. Observers in France blasted school-based sex instruction—no matter what it was called—as "an American importation"; in the Virgin Islands, meanwhile, several social workers charged that a new ASHA-minted "personal and family living" curriculum aimed to "impose a different culture" on the islands, even though they were territories of the United States. In Latin America, finally, allies warned American sex educators that "anti-US feeling" would doom the subject if its "Yanqi" flavor were too apparent. "The impetus, or the initiating of the program must come from within the country itself," wrote the ASHA's Josephine Tuller, after consulting with a sex educator in Brazil. "Ours should be a 'hands-off' policy, unless certain specific services are requested." The trick was to help build up local organizations so that sex education always *seemed* to come from indigenous sources, as Tuller told the head of the IUAVD. "The ideal approach ... would be built around strong national organizations which have been spontaneously developed in each country," Tuller wrote. "However, I think the Union can ... point out the need of a voluntary organization and give help [in] techniques of developing such a voluntary organization. In that way, we are not superimposing ourselves and our work would not be initiated from the international angle first."[17]

Try as they might, though, Americans could not escape the impression that sex education had been initiated—and imposed—by *them*. Overseas critics often linked it to rock and roll music and other commercial forms of American popular culture, which were allegedly corrupting the globe with sexual filth. Ironically, Americans promoted sex education as an antidote to obscene films, music, and comic books; in 1955, for example, the US Senate's subcommittee on juvenile delinquency demanded "better sex education for teenagers" to challenge the "deleterious effect" of US-made pornography and highly sexualized literature. Outside of the United States, however, sex education was condemned as an extension of precisely the trends it purported to interdict. As one Ceylonese critic told the ASHA, the family in his own country "remains strong despite Western influence." Why risk harming it, he asked, with another Western import? Such attacks multiplied with the publication of reports by Indiana entomologist Alfred Kinsey, whose data on widespread extramarital sexual relations in the United States made headlines around the world. In yet another irony, Kinsey himself was a skeptic about school-based sexual instruction; echoing Sigmund Freud's late writings, he doubted whether "factual information" on sex could correct for warped attitudes dating to infancy and early childhood. To outside critics, however, the Kinsey reports simply confirmed the filthy state of American sexual culture—including American sex education. As one anti-sex-education minister told a 1953 youth rally in Australia, every teen "had to choose between the Christian and the Kinsey view of life"; likewise, Italians cited Kinsey as another reason why their own schools should not follow the "degraded" example of the United States. "Kinsey," a radio commentator in East Germany surmised, "has revealed the moral bankruptcy of American life."[18]

## SEEING RED: SEX EDUCATION AND COMMUNISM

Predictably enough, as the final comment illustrates, the most vocal and bitter critics of American- or Western-style sex education often came from the Communist East. To the United States and its Cold War allies, sex education promised to "convert the jangle of warring races and nationalities into the 'Family of Man' and the 'Household of God,'" as a Canadian enthusiast wrote in 1945. But to America's Communist foes, the very need for sex education in the West underscored the essential depravity of capitalist societies. Here authorities often cited interwar Soviet educators such as Anton Makarenko, who warned that sexual knowledge and discussion would divert youth away from their revolutionary duty. Even in Italy, where Communists made significant electoral inroads in the 1950s, party officials invoked Makarenko—and joined hands with Catholic conservatives—to block any mention of sex in schools. In the USSR and its Eastern European satellites, meanwhile, educators blasted Western popular culture alongside Western sex education. Soviet authorities reserved special disdain for American rock-and-roll dances like "The Twist," which Russian youth had begun to imitate; alarmed officials even launched a campaign to revive traditional folk dance, which would allegedly stave off the "bourgeois amorality" of the West. In schools, finally, most teachers continued the venerable Soviet doctrine on sex education: least said, soonest mended. Indeed, officials pointed to sex education as the cause—not just the result—of sexual depravity and familial instability in the West. In Denmark, one Soviet author claimed, children "learn everything at a young age"—and adults experienced one of the highest divorce rates on earth.[19]

Yet the growing youth embrace of Western popular culture also contributed to a sex education "thaw" in the early 1960s, when Communist countries began to soften their opposition to the subject. Noting the rise of venereal disease as well as divorce in East Germany, authorities blamed "imperialist psychological propaganda" from capitalist countries—including film, music, and comic books—that "lead young people towards decadent irresponsibility." So Communist nations would have to institute their *own* form of sex education in schools to repel not only sexually transmitted infections but also "the corrupt influence of the West." In the Soviet Union, likewise, reports of youth promiscuity spawned new demands for sex instruction. In 1963, for example, a medical journal demanded that schools address the subject after a fifteen-year-old girl got drunk and pregnant at an event sponsored by the Young Pioneers—the same organization that was dedicated to protecting youth morality in the USSR! The issue sparked several loud public debates, which themselves demonstrated a new openness to sexual knowledge and information. "There are no forbidden subjects! Nothing is shameful or secret!" one critic complained in 1964, condemning sex education; to another Soviet opponent, the entire subject was "pornographic nonsense" aimed at the "seduction of minors." In Communist China, meanwhile, several highly publicized speeches by president Zhou Enlai—a longtime supporter of sex education—led a few schools to introduce brief lessons about it. But even these small experiments ended during the Cultural Revolution, which silenced any public mention of the subject. In Poland, finally, hard-line Marxists joined with Catholic prelates to rebut new calls for sex instruction. In spite of their many differences, one educator quipped, "both were rather puritanical in their attitudes towards sex."[20]

Here the Polish educator echoed critiques in the United States and Western Europe, which often used similar adjectives—prim, prudish, and especially puritanical—to mock sex education in the Communist world. Citing the libertine free-love theories of the early Bolshevik era, some right-wing ideologues in the United States charged that sex education was a Soviet plot designed to drown Western resolve in a sea of licentiousness. More commonly, though, Americans attacked the "iron-fisted prudery" of the contemporary USSR and its Warsaw Pact satellites. Despite its "brief flirtation" with free love in the 1920s, one journalist noted in 1964, the Soviet Union had evolved into a "rigidly puritanical society" that squelched almost all public discussion of sex—especially when children were in the room. "Sex education in the schools is virtually non-existent, and at home the subject is never raised voluntarily by parents," the American reporter wrote. "Little Tanyas and Ivans who ask blunt questions may be told they were purchased in the children's department at GUM," he added, referring to a popular Moscow department store. Nor could citizens get much information from published literature about sex, which was rigidly censored; indeed, the reporter quipped, "a *seks* manual in the Soviet Union is about as hard to find as a Barry Goldwater button in the Kremlin." The most popular resource on the subject was reportedly a sex education manual produced for American servicemen during World War II. A "coveted war trophy," the book had been copied by hand and "passed from one initiate to the other like a translation of Henry Miller." When a female journalist from the United Kingdom told a young Soviet woman that she could walk into any bookshop in the West and purchase sex-related literature, the Russian refused to believe it. "Why, no one would dream of discussing such intimate things," she declared.[21]

## THE SWEDISH ALTERNATIVE

Of course, many people in the West did not "dream of discussing such intimate things," either—particularly not in school classrooms. The major exception was Sweden, which in 1956 became the first nation in the world to require sex education in all of its public schools. Swedes had taught the subject intermittently since the early twentieth century, when socialist and feminist groups pressed for "sex hygiene" as a way to promote birth control—and to ease the burden of working mothers. The subject received a boost from the 1935 Royal Population Commission, which used research by prominent social scientists Gunnar and Alva Myrdal to argue that school-based sex instruction would lower birthrates—and improve living conditions— among the poor. Its other key support came from the Riksförbundet för Sexuell Upplysning (RFSU), the Swedish Association for Sexuality Education, founded in 1933 by the journalist and labor activist Elise Ottesen-Jensen. The seventeenth of eighteen children born into a sprawling Norwegian family, she traced her interest in worker and women's rights to the unplanned pregnancy and suicide of her only younger sibling. She married a Swedish anarcho-syndicalist and moved to Stockholm, where she campaigned for abortion rights and for repeal of a national ban on birth control information. She also pressed for more "honest" and "realistic" sex education, joining Alva Myrdal in attacking a 1944 sex education handbook that denounced all extramarital sexual activity. To Ottesen-Jensen, the manual was overly "moralizing" and "contrary to Swedish culture"; Myrdal complained that it ignored the national tradition of cohabitation before marriage, where Swedish youth "show quite unusual faithfulness in their love." Myrdal added a jab at the church leaders who stood behind the 1944 handbook. "There has been too much bishop and too little of physician and pedagogue," she quipped.[22]

Controversy continued to wrack sex education into the postwar period, pitting Ottesen-Jensen and the RFSU against conservatives in the religious, medical, and teaching communities. Downplaying the population-control goals that had marked its birth, the RFSU began to emphasize sex education as a key to personal happiness, fulfillment, and growth. "The league has no neomalthusian program," an RFSU official declared in 1955. "Its goal is individual welfare." Unlike Thomas Robert Malthus, the British scholar who warned against unchecked population growth, Swedish sex education sought to "make people of all ages relieved of their inhibitions and anxieties," as Ottesen-Jensen explained. The key was to remove the sense of sin and shame that still permeated sexuality, even in a society as proudly "progressive" as Sweden. "Exhaustive and correct sex education at an early age is imperative in order to eliminate ignorance and prejudice, neuroses and sexual disharmonies," the RFSU editorialized. Even more, it noted, such problems were as common inside marriages as outside of them. "Marriage *in et per se* does not elevate the moral quality of a sexual relationship," the RFSU declared. "We cannot acknowledge a sex education which brands all extramarital relations as sinful." A 1956 revision of the national sex education handbook omitted outright condemnation of sex outside of marriage but continued to recommend "continence during adolescence." But that was still too "outdated" for the RFSU, which lobbied authorities to eliminate the passage.[23]

Meanwhile, conservatives rallied to the manual's defense. "Premature sex education ... serves to make our population into sexual idiots," a Pentecostal paper warned in 1962. Two years later, when the Royal Board of Education appointed a committee to revise the sex education handbook yet again, 140 doctors and teachers quickly assembled a petition urging Sweden to slow down. "The advanced pedagogues who now rule Swedish education have bombarded school children with sexual instruction beyond their years," the petition charged. "Sexual education has been unnaturally inflated, producing an obsession among adolescents, and it is the duty of the schools to reduce it to its correct proportions." The issue also caused a rift within the Lutheran Church—the state church of Sweden—when 744 pastors demanded the firing of Carl Boethius, editor of the denomination's journal and a future director of the RFSU. In a country where 80 percent of engaged couples had sex before marriage and one-third of married mothers conceived before their wedding, Boethius argued, it was "pointless" for the church to oppose all extramarital relations; in response, his Lutheran critics asked whether he would countenance theft if most people engaged in that, too. But time—and public sentiment—was on Boethius's side. The country's largest student organization condemned "propaganda for premarital abstinence," arguing that schools should not "take a position" on such a controversial subject. Later that year, the newly revised Swedish sex education handbook agreed. The 1964 edition omitted its old warning against extramarital relations, replacing it with a tepid comment that "sexual norms are necessary, but they may vary from place to place and time to time."[24]

## SWEDES AND THE WORLD

Meanwhile, Elise Ottesen-Jensen and the RFSU were spreading these messages around the world. Starting in the late 1940s, Ottesen-Jensen made dozens of trips to other countries to promote sex education; in Sweden, meanwhile, RFSU officials received hundreds of foreign visitors. Wherever she went, Ottesen-Jensen stressed that she was "presenting the Swedish example to stimulate thinking," as she told a New Delhi audience in 1959; it was "not as a blueprint for effort elsewhere," she added, "since public opinion everywhere was sensitive and varied on this subject." Yet Swedes often implied that their own brand of sex education should be universal, belying their rhetorical paeans to diversity and variation. Addressing an international conference in London in 1948, Swedish sex educator Gunnar Lycander argued that "sexual need ... prevents people from developing into self-controlled, critical beings" and "drives them to hate and cruelty." The solution lay in sex education, of course, which would help them overcome "fear and guilt" and thereafter live in harmony with each other. Unlike American sex educators, who emphasized family stability as the bedrock of world peace, the Swedes stressed individual freedom and happiness. Their vision drew accolades in many corners of the globe, especially from people dissatisfied with the sexual mores of their own nations. "This is a most narrow and puritanical country," one correspondent wrote to Ottesen-Jensen from the United Kingdom. "The whole question of Human Love and Human Sex is still in the grip of the Pharisee and the dark ages of barbarism!" But Sweden provided a different example, he added, along with a ray of hope. "I think that your Country must be a grand and truly human Country in all these human sex matters," the British writer concluded. "You lead the way in HUMANITY— long may you all live."[25]

Likewise, sex educators around the world sent florid notes of praise—plus plaintive pleas for assistance—to Ottesen-Jensen and the RFSU. "I thought it may interest you in your advanced state of affairs to hear how we are still struggling on for a minimum of sex instruction in our schools," an Australian wrote in 1954, noting how a Sydney teacher who tried to introduce the subject was blocked from doing so. Similarly, an American who visited Ottesen-Jensen congratulated Sweden for "developing a much healthier and more rational approach" to sex education than the United States. ("I hope that we will not be too long in catching up," he added.) Ottesen-Jensen's proudest moment was probably her 1954 tour of the United States and Mexico, which began with an award ceremony sponsored by the Planned Parenthood Federation at the Waldorf-Astoria Hotel in New York. It concluded in the same city three weeks later, when she addressed a press conference at the United Nations and met with Secretary General Dag Hammarskjöld. In between, Ottesen-Jensen spoke to dozens of educators, journalists, and community organizations, giving different versions of the famous lecture to teenagers—"Anatomy and Physiology of Sex and Reproduction"— that she had delivered in Sweden thousands of times. She also tried to rebut the myth of Swedes as overly prurient or sex obsessed, which was already apparent in letters to the RFSU from young men around the world seeking pornographic material. The point of sex education was not to encourage promiscuity or deprive sex of romance, she reiterated; if that were true, she often joked, "physicians would not be able to love." To the contrary, it was to "eliminate anxiety" surrounding sex, so that a man could "devote himself completely to another person"—and vice versa.[26]

But the distinction was lost on overseas critics of Swedish sex education, who multiplied during these same years—and invoked the same myths that Ottesen-Jensen tried to dispel. Here, too, Americans took the lead. In 1955, *Time* published an article with a provocative title—"Sex in Sweden"—focused largely on sex education in the country. It drew on an informal dinnertime conversation between two of the magazine's correspondents and Elise Ottesen-Jensen, who later claimed that she was unaware she was being interviewed; nor did she imagine that her off-the-cuff comments would soon appear on the pages of *Time*. "I tell girls it is all right to sleep with a boy— but first they must be in love," Ottesen-Jensen was quoted as saying. "Everybody knows that [teenagers] sleep with each other. Their mothers and fathers know it. What use is there of trying to change human nature?" The article concluded with a flippant remark by a nineteen-year-old, who happily admitted that he had "no real morals" when it came to sex. "I would never marry a girl because I had made her pregnant," he added. "Why should I give up my liberty for the sake of a child?" The piece triggered an angry letter from the Swedish ambassador in the United States to *Time* publisher Henry Luce, whose aide replied with a vigorous defense of the magazine's "energetic and accurate reporting." But it also sparked debate inside Sweden, where conservatives rallied behind the article. "It seems that the sexual radicals do not want to be known by their own fruits," one right-wing newspaper gloated. "Decade after decade they have preached sexual freedom. Does not one believe that this eventually has consequences?" Ottesen-Jensen's allies mounted their own attack upon the *Time* article, blaming its harsh tone on Claire Booth Luce, the publisher's wife and a convert to Catholicism. "Catholic *Time* has deceitfully chosen to come to Lutheran Sweden," one reader wrote.[27]

In a pattern that would repeat itself over the next half century, meanwhile, observers around the world projected their own beliefs and biases onto Ottesen-Jensen and Swedish sex education writ large. "Sex is running amuck with the human race everywhere these days," an appalled South African letter writer told *Time*. "It is the devil's playground, and I really think the world would be a finer place without it." To a correspondent in neighboring Norway, meanwhile, the entire episode showed that Scandinavians "are facing the issue squarely"; Americans, by contrast, were "dodging the sex problems of their own youth" and enveloping the subject in needless shame and mystery. In the United States, finally, critics linked Swedes' sex education—and sexual promiscuity—to the excesses of their "socialist" welfare state, which had allegedly fostered a dreary national ennui and a rising suicide rate. The suicide statistics were a distortion, possibly dating to a speech by outgoing president Dwight D. Eisenhower at the 1960 Republican National Convention. But so were almost all foreign reports about Swedish sex education, which was neither as libertine nor as pervasive as its enemies and allies imagined. Despite the highly publicized national mandate for sex education, about half of Swedish teachers avoided the subject or ignored it altogether; although the national handbook advised instructors who "feel embarrassed" to "pass the task on" to other colleagues, one observer wrote, "many are too embarrassed to confess their embarrassment." Meanwhile, surveys revealed that students receiving sex instruction in school knew barely more about the subject than children whose teachers omitted it. Overall, an RFSU official admitted, many Swedish youth remained "naïve, ignorant, and unsophisticated" about sex.[28]

## GIRLS, BOYS, AND SEX

Around the world, the same problems that had stifled the subject in the prewar period continued into the postwar one: religious objections, parental resistance, poor teacher preparation, and so on. Despite national government initiatives to promote sex education in the United Kingdom, for example, only 16 percent of respondents in a 1953 poll said they had received it; the rest "picked up the facts of life at the street corner, in the factory, or even in the marriage bed." When children did get sex instruction in schools, meanwhile, it often echoed the harsh, hushed tone of previous eras. "Always the tactics were to try to scare you out of it, instead of telling you what it was all about," said one American, recalling brief but terrifying lectures about the perils of VD and masturbation in the late 1950s. In Australia, where special classroom editions of Shakespeare excised references to sex, schoolboys read a treatise warning that VD would bring "delicate, deformed, or weakly children"—whereas "self-abuse" would injure their own health. "Such boys are constantly weak and tired, and rarely excel at either sport or school work," the pamphlet noted, describing chronic masturbators. "They certainly never become leaders, because they kill all those things which go to make leaders: namely, self-control, courage, pride, confidence, will-power, and ambition." Invoking animal metaphors, another legacy of the early twentieth century, such lessons sowed boredom as well as fear in young minds. When a British headmistress delivered a lecture about fish reproduction, concluding with a comment about "how much better the human method was," her female pupils shrugged. "Who wants to know about fishes?" one recalled. "What we needed to know … was boys and what they wanted to do to you."[29]

Other students remembered very clear messages on that point: boys wanted sex, and it was girls' job to rebut and restrain them. With the new accent on familial relations, few textbooks or teachers openly maintained that women "actively dislike" sex or were "indifferent" to it, as a British physician told Oxford students in the early 1900s. (The rare woman who enjoys sex "will always be a harlot," he added.) Instead, sex educators acknowledged female sexuality, as part of marriage, and made women responsible for keeping sex inside of it. "A boy may think the girl expects him to continue as long a she lets him," an American sex education book warned. "Since you cannot be sure your date is under emotional control, it is up to you—boy or girl, to stop while you have control." But that was always easier for the girl than the boy, the book added, because "his desire does indeed become more intense at a more rapid rate than the girl's." A 1959 Japanese textbook—titled, simply, *Sex and Chastity*—put the matter differently: men have an "active" sex drive, while women have a "passive" one. But neither text left any doubt about where the act should occur: in a marital union, between a husband and a wife. Until they assumed these roles, boys and girls should "learn to direct [their] sex drives in a healthy channel," the American textbook advised. "Begin by involving yourself in many activities such as active sports," it added, "leaving you little time to fret and worry about sexual desires and drives."[30]

At the same time, ironically, sports coaches and teachers became the most common instructors about sex. Since the early 1900s, educators had recommended athletics and organized sports as an antidote to "primitive sex urges," as Boy Scouts founder Robert Baden-Powell wrote. As more schools provided physical education, however, they increasingly transferred sex instruction from biology and science classes into PE classes. "The very nature of physical education gives the teacher a better chance to become intimately acquainted with her students," an American educator explained. "She cannot only give the fundamental teaching of reproduction, but can instill higher ideals and attitudes in her students." Science classes mixed boys and girls together, where they might be "shy in the presence of the opposite sex," the educator added. Physical education was sex segregated, by contrast, so "the bug-a-boo of mixed classes is done away with." As more and more high schools grouped students by ability, finally, many children in "nonacademic" tracks did not take a science course at all; but almost all of them took PE, providing another good reason to locate sex education within it. Other sex educators urged schools to teach the subject in new "Marriage" or "Life Adjustment" courses—which became common in the United States and United Kingdom during these years—while others warned against separating it into a special class, which would make it an easy target for hostile parents and media critics. "The understanding and cooperation of all teachers are urgently needed," the Purity Education committee in U.S.-occupied Japan declared. "Each will make a contribution [to] Purity Education which stands like a Pyramid."[31]

## PARENTS, TEACHERS, AND SEX EDUCATION

In practice, though, teaching sex education "across the curriculum" allowed teachers of any given discipline to avoid it. Nor did that strategy insulate them from angry parents, who continued to claim that sex education would promote the same vices it was designed to inhibit. In India, which made ginger forays into sex education in the 1950s, one opponent said the subject would "arouse curiosity where none existed." Indeed, another Indian critic added, plenty of citizens in the West believed the same thing. "It is not in our country alone, that misgivings on sex education exist; the other advanced countries too face similar setbacks," he emphasized. In the United Kingdom, India's former colonial master, a fourteen-year-old unwed mother made national headlines in 1949 when she blamed her pregnancy on the sex education she had received in school. That same year, an angry mother collected over a thousand petition signatures against sex education after her thirteen-year-old daughter came home from school and refused the egg that had been prepared for her; after her teacher told her how eggs were made, she said, she lost her appetite for them. Her mother searched the girl's possessions and discovered graphic drawings copied from sex lessons at school; if such figures were found in her own handbag, the mother noted, she would be called a "dirty woman." She then began to talk to other mothers in the community, who reported that their daughters were discussing "nothing but sex, sex, sex." The reason wasn't hard to find: they were learning about it in school.[32]

Elsewhere, too, parents savaged sex education as an attack on their own prerogatives. "It is our flesh and blood you are gambling with when you put sex instruction in the public schools," an American mother thundered, in testimony before the Los Angeles Board of Education, "and we feel it is the parents' duty, let alone their right, to instruct their children in accordance with their own beliefs." In New York, likewise, a bishop preaching at St. Patrick's Cathedral denounced schools for showing children the ASHA film, *Human Growth*, which he described as "an invasion of the rights of the parents." Catholic sex education critics around the world quoted Pope Pius XI's 1929 encyclical against sex education, which was reaffirmed by Pope Pius XII in 1951. A Catholic physician in Italy condemned sex education as "fit only for Bolshevik schools"; when a women's federation in Jamaica endorsed sex education and family planning, the island's bishop called on Catholic women to withdraw from the organization; Scottish bishops released a statement in 1944 expressing "instinctive distrust of all sex instruction and sex teaching"; and nearly two decades later, in 1962, a well-known London priest and author denounced the British Broadcasting Corporation for putting a sex education segment on the radio. As the priest acknowledged, two of five new Catholic wives in the United Kingdom were pregnant at their weddings. But the solution to that problem lay in religious faith rather than in sex education, which "did not admit the supernatural as a means to control the natural," he concluded.[33]

Many teachers were only too happy to cede the subject to others. "Let the parents explain it!" one French teacher told a researcher. "Aren't they able to?" Often the answer was "no," of course, which provided a key rationale for sex education in the first place; unless teachers intervened in the family, a prominent American author argued, the "vicious circle" of ignorance would continue. But that was often too much to ask of lowly schoolteachers, who risked losing their jobs—and their meager livelihoods—if they flouted community sentiment on matters of sex. A small-town teacher in Norway was fired in the early 1950s when his brief sex education lesson—from an American textbook—triggered a parental strike. Although he was eventually reinstated, after suing his school board, other teachers could not miss the real lesson of the episode: stay away from sex education, particularly in rural areas. Even in nearby Denmark, which had joined Sweden as an international symbol of liberal sexuality, rural teachers introduced the subject at their peril. "An ideal Sex Education throughout the country has proved to be almost an impossibility due to the many variations in local emotional feelings," one observer wrote. "In many small villages and rural districts ... old-fashioned sexual prejudices are strongest." In 1961, an American court upheld the dismissal of an English teacher who led a discussion of prostitution and the "pros and cons" of premarital sex. As the court ruled, the teacher failed to point out that adultery—like prostitution—was illegal in his state; he "transcended the bounds of the standards of propriety of the community"; and, most of all, he exceeded the limits of his own professional skill and training:

> Sex education is a subject matter for which a teacher should be especially competent to teach. A parent and the school authorities have a right to expect that children are not going to be exposed to comments, discussions, and personal opinions of a teacher on sex who had not been certified to teach such subject in classes which do not relate to such subject.... Only one qualified and so certified by the proper authorities should be allowed to undertake to teach this delicate subject and only in a class expressly for that purpose.[34]

In fact, almost no teacher during this era—in the United States or anywhere else—was specially prepared or certified to provide sex education. The American court's demand also ran counter to the popular doctrine of integrating sex education across the curriculum, which would have required every teacher—not just a specialized few—to receive training in the subject. But teachers rarely encountered the topic as part of their professional preparation; the exceptions were mostly preservice teachers in health or physical education, who often took a course from someone scarcely more prepared than they were. "The teachers of teachers are no braver, or any better equipped, than the teachers themselves," an American sex educator complained, "so there exists a circle which up to this point has resisted all efforts to break it." High schools typically assigned the subject to a teacher based not on her academic background, but on her personal characteristics; indeed, one British educator wrote, the "best qualification" for teaching about sex was a "normal married life" at home. "Men must be definitely masculine with that quality which used to be called manly, and women must be feminine with that quality which used to be called womanly," she declared. "It won't do to shade even slightly in the opposite direction." Administrators were warned against assigning sex education not just to "confirmed bachelors"—a code word for homosexuals—but also to "immature" younger women and "maladjusted spinsters": the first group would be too interested in sex and the second one too alienated from it. "*Only wholesome persons can be fine sex educators,*" an American sociologist underlined. "The ultra-conservative, prudish women of the teaching profession cannot be expected to impart healthy attitudes to our school children when the very word sex makes the teachers blush and giggle, or leaves them 'shocked.'"[35]

## REPRISE: SEX EDUCATION, VOLUNTARY ORGANIZATIONS, AND DEMOCRACY

Around the world, voluntary organizations took it upon themselves to compensate for what teachers would not—or could not—do. Following the example of Sweden's RFSU, which offered periodic lectures and summer courses, some organizations worked with teachers to promote and improve sex education. But others went directly into the schools, providing instruction for children and teachers alike. In the United Kingdom, the Alliance of Honour—a purity organization dating to the turn of the twentieth century—sent midwife Annabelle P. Duncan to Scotland, where she visited girls' high schools to teach about sex. Duncan's standard short "course" was three classes, spread across an equal number of weeks. Using several film-strips, Duncan devoted the first two visits to explaining the physio-logical and psychological changes of adolescence; in the third ses-sion, from which other teachers were barred, she fielded anonymous questions from the students. In Ghana, meanwhile, the local Chris-tian Council sent several physicians and other representatives into middle schools in Accra—the capital—to give talks about sex; in 1961, the first year of the pilot project, sixty of seventy-eight middle schools in the region hosted a lecturer. The talks sparked freewheel-ing discussions, as a sample of student questions reveals:

What should we do with boy friends who pester us to have intercourse?

Why is it not good to have more than one husband?

Is masturbation good?

Can woman conceive without having intercourse with a man?

Since pre-marital intercourse is wrong what should people do if they have the sexual urge?[36]

But the Christian Council failed to get public schools to take up this curriculum on their own, as council leaders had hoped. First of all, nobody knew who would teach it on such a broad scale; if the council's syllabus were adopted nationwide, one member admitted, "it would immediately raise questions that existing teachers have not been hitherto trained to teach this subject." Even more, though, government officials proved decidedly cool to sex education in the schools. "I am not sure that Ghanaian boys and girls passing through secondary schools have any 'erroneous myths' about sex," one edu-cation official wrote in a private memo, dismissing the Christian Council's claim that students needed more information on the sub-ject. "I have personally held the view that the sort of 'sex education' being talked about here is only necessary for artificial societies such as we find in Europe and North America. We should be careful of such importations into our natural society." Even in the West, of course, plenty of people regarded sex education as unnatural and unnecessary, if not actively harmful. Hence sex educators' reliance upon voluntary organizations, which played a slightly different role than the American Social Hygiene Association—and, many years before, Alexis de Tocqueville—had imagined. Invoking Tocqueville, the ASHA promoted civil-society groups as a way of "maintaining the democratic principle that the voice of the people must be heard," as one spokesman wrote. But they were also a way to dodge or evade the people's voice, if it was sounding off against sex education.[37]

Some governments preferred it that way, because voluntary organizations could insulate them from popular fire. "It was more convenient for the Authorities to have a separate non-governmental organization specializing in sex education, than to involve themselves in this activity," one Polish sex education advocate noted. Indeed, Catholic critics trained more of their ire on his own organization than they did on state educational officials. In Scotland, similarly, the Education Department partially funded Annabelle Duncan's school lectures but also tried to keep that fact out of the public eye, refusing to put a government representative on her voluntary council; "in this particular respect," one official explained, "the Department must walk warily." Canadian educational officials advised teachers not to send home any material about sex education and even asked students not to make their own notes on the subject in schools; such information could expose schools to public attack and also to scurrilous rumors, officials argued, including a widely circulated story that one district was using a Kinsey report as a textbook. The more democratic a society became, it seemed, the more sex education came under assault. "It can't be taught in school," a West German educator stated flatly in 1960, noting stalled efforts to establish the subject in Berlin. "When a progressive teacher attempted to teach sex education, he ran the risk of losing his job." At least one teacher had already done so.[38]

The German's use of the term *progressive* highlighted a final irony in the story of postwar sex education. Particularly in the United States and the United Kingdom, advocates often touted the subject as an exemplar of progressive education. It was centered on the needs and interests of the student, not the teacher; it addressed real-world concerns, not arid academic ones; and, most of all, it prepared young people for life. "Education is not only a question of imparting knowledge," progressive patron saint John Dewey had written in a passage routinely quoted by sex educators. "More than anything, education is living, experiencing, experimenting." But in his own life experience, a half-joking British miner quipped, he had learned about sex simply by doing it; so would his children, who "have to find out for themselves." And in the real world of democratic politics, citizens often balked at school-based sex education. "Even in America, where 'progressive' education got its start, sex education is so obviously the most neglected area of instruction that the point hardly needs belaboring," two American educators complained in 1961. Of course, they quickly added, America was "not alone" in that respect; except for Sweden, other countries were "equally backward" or even more so. "In most of the world," they conceded, "it is much easier to come by sexual experience than to gain accurate information about sex." The real questions were whose experience counted, what information they needed, and who would decide the difference.[39]

# CHAPTER THREE

# Sex Education and the "Sexual Revolution," 1965–83

In 1968, the eminent anthropologist Ashley Montagu published a hopeful article hailing a recent invention: the birth control pill. A British transplant to the United States, the sixty-three-year-old Montagu had witnessed enormous technological and cultural changes during his lifetime. But most of them paled next to "The Pill," which he called one of a half dozen "major innovations" in the history of mankind. "In its effects I believe that the pill ranks in importance with the discovery of fire, the development of the ability to make and employ tools, the evolution of hunting, the invention of agriculture, the development of urbanism, of scientific medicine, and the release and control of nuclear energy," Montagu wrote. Emancipating women from their second-class status, the Pill would also liberate them—and men—to enjoy the pleasures of sex. But its full potential would not be realized without the guiding hand of teachers, who needed to reorient sex education away from its repressive roots and into the new dawn of freedom. "The sexual revolution should precipitate the educational revolution, which should in turn lead to the human revolution," Montagu predicted. "The dead hand of ugly traditional beliefs (such as the nastiness and sinfulness of sex, the wickedness of premarital sex), which has been responsible for untold human tragedies, will be replaced by a new flowering of human love."[1]

Four years later, another British visitor to the United States confirmed Montagu's sense of an impending sexual and educational revolution. But Mary Whitehouse sounded a cautionary chord, warning that recent changes were eroding essential human traditions—especially family, community, and personal responsibility. For the past decade, Whitehouse had spearheaded a campaign in the United Kingdom to limit sexual imagery on the airwaves as well as sexual information in schools. But "the problems that we face in Britain are international," she told an American audience, so they would in turn require cross-national solutions. In a tour arranged by antipornography crusader Charles Keating, whose name would become synonymous with scandal during the savings-and-loan crisis of the 1980s, Whitehouse met with several other leading activists in America's "New Right" as well as with Herbert Klein, communication director in Richard Nixon's White House. She also gave dozens of speeches and interviews, calling on citizens across the United States—and around the world—to rebuff the "sexual libertarians" threatening children everywhere. "They talk about bigotry, they talk about prejudice," Whitehouse thundered. "But there is *nothing* more bigoted— there is nothing more prejudiced—than the licentious people who are determined that we will go on one path, and one path only.... They're the bigots. They're the ones who are repressive. And not us at all."[2]

Together, these passages underscore the transnational dimensions of both the "sexual revolution" and its growing body of foes in the 1960s and 1970s. Across the West, liberal intellectuals declared a new gospel of sexual freedom and called upon schools to preach the same. At the same time, conservatives in Europe and North America joined hands to defend the old verities: faith, chastity, and authority. In the so-called developing world, finally, the same technology that Ashley Montagu identified as a force of liberation—contraception— spawned a new but narrow form of sex education, centered on the concept of "population." Stressing the social imperative for small families, schools developed "population education" courses that sometimes avoided mention of sex altogether; in the ideal, one pair of educators urged, population education would be completely "sexless." As family planning programs mounted, advocates feared that any discussion of sexual practices among unmarried youth would hamper efforts to alter the behavior of married couples. Most of all, though, sex educators found that Montagu's vision of personal liberation did not resonate in societies stressing communal authority and obedience. "What I miss here is a sex-affirming policy giving space for the individual's sexuality from birth to death," admitted a Swedish official at a 1976 workshop for sex educators in the developing world. "It is hard for people to be autonomous in cultures where autonomy seems to be of such little use." Even as they declared a new era of sexual freedom, Western educators were distressed to discover that large parts of the planet seemed bound by the chains of the past.[3]

## THE TIMES THEY ARE A-CHANGING

In a 1965 speech on "Youth and Sexual Behavior," American sex education leader Mary Calderone quoted a recent hit song by a hugely popular folk artist. "Come mothers and fathers throughout the land, / And don't criticize what you can't understand," Bob Dylan sang. "Your sons and your daughters are beyond your command, / The times they are a-changing." He was right. Across the West—and, it appeared, in many parts of the East—sexual mores and behaviors were in flux. Surveys revealed that growing numbers of young people were having sex; in many places, venereal disease and out-of-wedlock pregnancies were also on the rise. So were pornographic images and literature, which encircled the globe as national censorship laws fell away. Coupled with antiwar protests and other youth-oriented political campaigns, the sexual revolution left young people in a "complicated state of uncertainty ... on a wide international scale," as one British commentator observed in 1969. Indeed, as a Swedish educator confirmed the following year, sexual behavior and standards were "a matter of considerable emotional charge all over the world." So the real task for sex educators was to help develop a new set of mores, as Mary Calderone argued. Here she invoked an older and less contemporary figure in American letters, Walter Lippmann. "We are unsettled, to the very roots of our being," Lippmann wrote, in a passage Calderone quoted. "There are no precedents to guide us, no wisdom that wasn't made for a simpler age."[4]

Calderone's own solution—"each must answer for himself"—simply reasked the question. The daughter of noted photographer Edward Steichen, Calderone attended medical school and became a director in the Planned Parenthood Federation of America. But her experiences in the family planning movement convinced her that Americans needed new attitudes toward sex, not simply new services or technologies. With a large bequest from the Rockefeller family, a key supporter of sex education since the early twentieth century, Calderone founded the Sex Information and Education Council of the United States in 1964 to promote more "rational" and "tolerant" viewpoints. Like other liberal educators around the world, Calderone often pointed to Sweden as a place where children learned about sex in a calm, matter-of-fact manner. But even the Swedes were divided—and confused—about the subject, as American sex educator Howard Hoyman observed. Prizing individual choice and decision making, the Swedes often declared "neutrality" on sexual issues, but they also stressed "mutual commitment and responsibility," denouncing adultery and promiscuity. Around the world, Hoyman wrote, the "central issue" was "sexual permissiveness": how much discretion should young people receive, and how—if at all—should adults try to guide them? Clearly, Hoyman noted, "horse and buggy sex education won't do in the Space Age." But it was far easier to declare a revolution than to decide what should come afterward.[5]

The problem was especially acute in the developing world, where the infusion of Western literature, film, and television challenged long-standing ideas of sexual reticence and continence. "Hippies, Beatles and the like [sic] of them are visiting our country every day," an Indian educator wrote in 1969, shortly after the Beatles' "Fab Four" departed the country. "Most of our young people are now expressing their preferences for the liberalized sex mores and decrying the rigid traditions of our own society." To some observers, such trends merely highlighted the need for sex education as a "preventive measure" against "greater liberty and experimentation," as another Indian wrote; more than ever before, a Kenyan educator added, young people needed instruction about sex "before the damage is done." Echoing sex educators in the West, other commentators urged schools to develop new standards instead of simply shoring up older ones. "*We have to recognize that we are living in an age and in a society in which children are almost indoctrinated with the idea of sexual satisfaction as an ultimate axiom in life*," a principal in Hong Kong underlined. But educators still ignored sex, except for periodic warnings not to engage in it. "It is a world of contradictory attitudes, sexual indoctrination by the mass media on the one hand and a conspiracy of silence by [schools] on the other," the principal wrote. "Can we blame young people if they are confused?"[6]

For their own part, youth around the world demanded more discussion about sex in school. A special session on "Youth and Sex Education" at a 1967 family planning conference in Chile drew over two thousand young people, which was more than the venue could accommodate. Turned away at the door, the overflow crowd waited patiently to meet the speakers as they exited; inside, meanwhile, doctors and educators from four continents "frankly answered questions which doubtless have never before been asked at a public meeting in Latin America," as one observer wrote. Even in the supposedly "advanced" countries of Europe and North America, however, students were alternately astonished, angered, and amused by the information—or, frequently, the mis-information—that they received about sex in their classrooms. In the Netherlands, "provos"—that is, youth rebels—demanded "honest" sex education and free contraceptives in the same breath as they denounced air pollution, South African apartheid, and the war in Vietnam. Likewise, Italian schoolgirls paraded through the streets of Rome to demand sex education alongside abortion rights. In the United States, finally, the New York Student Coalition for Relevant Sex Education demanded that each high school establish a "Rap Room" where students could receive accurate information about abortion, contraception, and other topics that the regular curriculum downplayed or ignored.[7]

In a more radical vein, meanwhile, a German student magazine suggested that schools set aside "Love Rooms" for youth to obtain "practical experience" in sex itself. "Where does one find the peace to really enjoy each other without the permanent fear of being surprised at any minute?" the magazine asked. "At home?" Denouncing the standard curriculum as dated and irrelevant, some German students even stripped to the nude to demonstrate for more explicit sex education as well as contraceptive services in schools; others simply handed out birth control pills on their own. But their philosophy of sex was often less radical—and more romantic—than these agitprop events suggested. "Love should be the only motive for sexual intercourse at the beginning," the German student magazine editorialized. "A girl who sacrifices her virginity should only do so for the sake of love." Most of all, students said, they simply wanted schools to address sex openly and honestly. "Too many teachers give the once-over treatment, if any treatment at all," an American high school student conference resolved in 1966. Fourteen years later, in 1980, another group of American high schoolers confirmed that little had changed. "All they do is show the same movie we've seen every year," one of the students surmised. "You don't learn anything new."[8]

## SEX EDUCATION IN THE WEST: A REVOLUTION DEFERRED

As these comments illustrated, sex education changed much more slowly in the 1960s and 1970s than either the heralds or the critics of the sexual revolution imagined. In the United States and the United Kingdom, the number of children who received instruction in the subject rose steadily. By 1979, at least 90 percent of American schools provided some kind of sex education; the following year, 98 percent of British children reportedly received the same. As one British observer added, school biology courses—still the most common venue for sex education—increasingly focused on "the human reproductive system rather than that of the rabbit"; indeed, the high school biology syllabus included such formerly tabooed terms as semen, ejaculation, and ovulation. Even primary school pupils learned many of these words from sex education filmstrips and television shows produced by the British Broadcasting Corporation, which reached over a quarter-million children in three thousand schools by 1971. But sex education rarely moved beyond these "plumbing" lessons—as critics mockingly called them—to examine the social contexts and dilemmas of sex. Indeed, in most instances, there was no dilemma at all; even as they widened their sexual vocabulary, schools continued to instruct students to avoid sexual activity. The confused spirit of most sex education was vividly captured in American filmmaker Frederick Wiseman's popular 1969 documentary, *High School*, which showed a visiting doctor making crude sex jokes to male students—all in the course of a lecture warning them to steer clear of sex.[9]

Elsewhere in the West, meanwhile, sex education varied with "local socio-cultural conditions," as a 1975 study reported. The "most advanced" instruction took place in "liberal Protestant" nations, especially in Scandinavia and West Germany; the "slowest progress" was found in Catholic countries like Portugal, where high school biology textbooks still depicted human bodies without reproductive organs. French officials explicitly restricted sex education to "biological knowledge," excluding questions of morality or values; here they drew less upon the country's Catholic roots than on its tradition of *laïcité*, or state neutrality on religious matters. But even the supposedly liberal countries in northern Europe placed much more emphasis on pubertal changes and reproduction than on sexual mores and relationships, as the German example illustrates. Sex education received renewed attention with the 1967 release of *Helga*, a government-subsidized documentary aimed at creating a new consensus for the subject across West Germany's different states and regions. The film opened with person-on-the-street interviews, showing adults reminiscing about their sexual ignorance as children. Then it provided the missing knowledge, including detailed descriptions of contraceptive methods and even a short clip of a live birth. As several commentators noted, though, the movie focused almost exclusively upon the biological aspects of sex; so did a subsequently released "Sex Atlas" for schools, which featured still photos from *Helga*. Indeed, a British journalist observed, a "Germanic coldness … ran through the entire film."[10]

Over the next few months, *Helga* became an international sensation; grossing a surprising $4 million in Germany alone, it was also a box office hit in about a dozen other Western countries. So it highlighted contrasts between different nations' approaches to sexuality writ large. "While the French often regard sex as a game, the Danes, as a reality, the Swedes, as poetry," a German observer wrote, commenting on the *Helga* craze, "the Germans seem to regard it as something to be analyzed—and explained and explained and explained." In the United States, where *Helga*'s popularity rivaled blockbusters like *Paper Lion* and *The Boston Strangler*, critics flayed the film—as well as its soft-porn sequel, *Helga and the Sexual Revolution*—as too "intellectual," and too inattentive to social and emotional dynamics.

Responding to such critiques, later editions of the German student "Sex Atlas" showed families playing with a newborn baby; they also discussed the working careers and parenting roles of the child's mother and father. Likewise, courses and textbooks in the United States and United Kingdom gradually began to address "healthy relationships," as one skeptical British author wrote in 1980, fueled by the faith that such instruction would solve everything from rising divorce rates to "football hooliganism."[11]

But almost all countries continued to avoid discussion of the "Big Four" taboos, as sex educators around the world called them: abortion, contraception, homosexuality, and masturbation. Just as "Problems of Democracy" courses generally ignored actual issues of democracy, one American philosopher wrote, so did sex education eschew the "real problems" of sex. Asked by a student which contraception method he would recommend to a sixteen-year-old girl, an American teacher curtly replied, "Sleep with your grandmother"; when the girl brought birth control pamphlets to school the following day, she was told that distributing them was illegal. Meanwhile, at least 80 percent of the world's national educational systems ignored sex altogether, as one expert estimated in 1972. The previous year, the Spanish government blocked children from watching *Adiós, cigüeña, adiós* ("Goodbye, Stork, Goodbye"), Spain's first sex education movie and a hit among adults; even children who acted in the film were barred from seeing it. Three Italian girls were investigated by prosecutors and forced to undergo medical examinations after publishing a 1966 article demanding sex education; eight years later, when another group of Italian students organized their own sex education course, local parish leaders denounced it. "Catholics, let's act and make sure that here things will not be like they are in Denmark," a parish leaflet blared, "where Catholic families no longer send their children to state schools where they only learn immorality."[12]

## SCANDINAVIA: SYMBOL AND REALITY

To friends and foes alike, Scandinavia remained a symbol of progressive, liberal-minded sex education. International attention focused especially on Sweden, which had become the first country to require the subject back in 1956. As in the 1950s, much of this invective reflected right-wing stereotypes of "the typical Swede as a person with a bottle in one hand and a welfare check in another, wallowing in lust and sexual promiscuity, as he or she staggers along the brink of insanity and suicide," as an American visitor quipped in 1971. But liberal sex educators and journalists across the world distorted Sweden and other Scandinavian nations, too, imagining them as united beacons of sexual openness, honesty, and dialogue. The movie *Helga* even included scenes from a sex education class in Sweden, asking German viewers if schools should provide Swedish-style instruction because many parents "did not know enough about their own bodies." For most sex educators in the West, the answer was obvious: yes. American educators were especially prodigious in their praise of Sweden, noting its relatively low rates of rape, divorce, venereal disease, teen pregnancy, and abortion. They also made repeated trips to Sweden to study its sex education system and to meet with its revered leader, Elise Ottesen-Jensen, whom American allies saluted with a revealing nickname: "Great Lady."[13]

Elsewhere, too, liberal correspondents and visitors hailed Swedes and other Scandinavians as the world pacesetters in sex education. A British journalist marveled at the "frankness, confidence, and objectivity" of sex instruction in Denmark, which made the subject compulsory in 1970. In Sweden, meanwhile, the office mail of the RFSU—the Swedish Association for Sexuality Education—groaned with overseas appeals for information and advice. Some correspondents requested pornography, often in the guise of edification; in Japan, for example, a young teacher asked for pictures of female genitalia and a "small model of a woman's waist," so he could "study more harder." But most foreign writers requested more substantial assistance—especially textbooks, pamphlets, and posters—to help bring their own countries up to the Swedish standard. "There is no sex education in our schools due to repressive attitude of Catholic Church," a young Irishman complained, noting the surge of teen pregnancies in Dublin; in England, meanwhile, a biology teacher asked the RFSU to help him combat sexual prudery on his own shores. "We are about 20 years behind you in our educational approach to sex and morality," the teacher wrote. Even a sex educator in the Netherlands—which would soon join Scandinavia as a global symbol of sexual openness—praised Sweden's progressive policies, which stood head and shoulders above Dutch ones. "Our country is too conservative with regard to the sexuality," he groused, requesting RFSU materials. "I am very interested in your way of working ... which is so far with the sexuality."[14]

Scandinavian educators were more detailed and descriptive in their lessons about sex. In Denmark, for example, a junior high school textbook depicted male-female couples performing different sex acts "in softly lighted, decorously posed photographs," as an astonished American reported. In 1965, the revised Swedish National Handbook on sex education included explicit discussions of contraception and abortion; a ninth grade test required students to define "sodomy" and "pedophilia"; and a top sex education official told a British interviewer that schools should provide "facts about sexual stimulation, sexual responses, and techniques of intercourse." In practice, however, Swedish sex education remained far more limited than either advocates or critics assumed. Although the subject had been mandatory for over a decade, a 1967 survey reported that one-third of Swedish teenagers had not studied it; two years later, another scholar estimated that 30 to 50 percent of Swedish children received "inadequate or little or no sex education." Moreover, the minimal instruction that students did get bore little resemblance to the candid, no-holds-barred spirit of the Scandinavian stereotype. A survey in the early 1970s showed that over half of fifteen-year-olds were still uncertain whether masturbation was "dangerous" or not; meanwhile, just over one-quarter of Swedish teachers had shown contraceptive devices to their students, as the national curriculum suggested. "Are we twenty-five years behind the Swedes?" American Lester Kirkendall asked in 1967, in the preface to a book by Swedish sex educator Birgitta Linner. "Or is it that Mrs. Linner and leaders like her are twenty-five years ahead of the rest of Sweden?"[15]

Commonly invoked across the West, the metaphor of the race—with some nations "ahead," and others "behind"—assumed that everyone was running toward the same finish line. So it also distorted the purposes of sex education in Sweden, which focused less on the perils of sex—a leading theme around the globe since the early 1900s—and more on its pleasures. Put simply, sex instruction aimed to help each individual develop a sex life that was personally meaningful and satisfying, and that goal came before broader social ones, including the protection of young people from disease and unwanted pregnancy. Asked by an Irish educator in 1978 how Swedish sex instruction reduced teen pregnancy and gonorrhea rates, RFSU chairman Carl Boethius freely admitted that Swedes "do not *know* if these positive figures are partly due to sex education." But nor was that the purpose of such instruction, Boethius quickly added. "PS. The fundamental reason for sex education is—according to the Swedish view—the right to knowledge, not ideas about special effects," Boethius wrote, in a scrawled note beneath his signature. Indeed, Boethius told another correspondent two years later, "the effects of sex education have never been studied in Sweden." The only effect that mattered was deeply personal, and probably unmeasurable. "The best contribution of sex education is that the sexual act is now more often than previously experienced as a positive factor in the total relationship by both men and women," Boethius explained. In the past, he noted, a well-known joke held that sex was a woman's price for marriage, and marriage was what a man paid for sex. "There is nowadays little left of this deeply unhappy attitude," he added.[16]

Of course, there was no way to know whether this attitudinal change was attributable to sex education, any more than the incidence of teen pregnancy was. But Boethius's comments spoke to the evolving goals of Swedish sex instruction, and also to the tensions between them. On the one hand, Swedes said, schools should help each individual experience sexual pleasure on his or her own terms; on the other, they should teach every individual that pleasure was a legitimate goal—even, a "right"—for all. Discarding the warnings against premarital sex that had marked older editions, the 1965 Sex Education Handbook described Sweden as a "pluralistic society … holding different views about sexual morality"; twelve years later, another revision said schools should aim to promote "sexuality as a source of happiness with another person." But it also underscored the "common value" that everyone needed to share: the sexual sovereignty of each human being. "We do not put a stigma upon sexual relations before marriage," a Swedish sex educator told an American correspondent in 1971. "Of course, we are presenting various kinds of questioning and a wide ideologi [*sic*] in these questions, but we do not press a sexual way of living as a model. The fundamental thing is that nobody should press anyone to do what he or she does not want to do." Asked if schools should teach "a particular set of values or moral viewpoint," another Swedish sex educator answered simply: no. "Who knows what are the right attitudes to develop in the young?" she replied.[17]

## THE CONSERVATIVE COUNTERREVOLUTION

To many adults, in Sweden and around the world, that question also had a simple answer: parents know. From its inception, of course, sex education had tried to supplant parental authority by intervening directly in a matter that was formerly reserved for families. But the sexual revolution of the 1960s and 1970s heightened that tension, bringing more and more citizens into conflict with their schools. Ironically, sex educators often framed their project as a way to tame and discipline the more unseemly aspects of the revolution, especially the growing commercial trade of sexual images in advertising, film, and television; according to one Scottish advocate, school-based sex instruction would "meet the manifest needs of adolescents to be armed against the blandishments of the permissive-acquisitive society." But to its growing cadre of conservative critics, sex education was a product of the same permissive trends it purportedly sought to halt. "Some educators say that we must have sex education because society is over-heated on the subject," an American pastor told his church in a 1969 sermon. "But why are the schools seeking to add more fuel to the fire?" Modern society "already has a preoccupation with sex," he added, so "it would appear to be compounding the problem to install sex in the classroom as well." Indeed, a member of Great Britain's National Viewers' and Listeners' Association (NVLA) averred, sex education reflected "the filthiness of the Permissive Society." Reversing these trends would require nothing less than a worldwide "sexual counter-revolution," the group's founder added.[18]

The founder's name was Mary Whitehouse, who was immortalized in a 1977 song by the British rock band Pink Floyd. "Hey you, Whitehouse / Ha ha, charade you are," the band jibed. "You gotta stem the evil tide / And keep it all on the inside." In the eyes of her liberal detractors, Whitehouse epitomized traditional middle-class British prudery, but she also became a hero to right-wing foes of the sexual revolution, first in the United Kingdom and then around the globe. Whitehouse was a schoolteacher in the 1930s and again in the 1950s and early 1960s, when she noticed that students were mimicking the new sexual banter they heard on the radio and television. She went on to create the NVLA, which focused most of its early fire on the British Broadcasting Corporation; when the BBC began producing filmstrips and TV shows for sex instruction in schools, Whitehouse started campaigning against sex education as well. Critics on the left condemned the BBC series as both too elliptical and too didactic; concealing or omitting important topics, it imposed a singular moral code that ignored human change and complexity. But to Whitehouse and her legions of followers, sex education was too detailed and not moralistic *enough*. "Your organisation is indeed extremely important at this moment of time, as a 'voice' for those thousands of decent folk, bewildered by the crude pressures on our sensibilities," a British physician wrote Whitehouse in 1972. "I feel so sorry for the generation of teen-agers and what has been done to them in the name of 'liberation.'"[19]

Hundreds of similar missives arrived from elsewhere in Europe and North America, illustrating the increasingly cross-national character of the campaign against sex education. "It is like the Battle of Britain all over again," a Canadian correspondent wrote Whitehouse, offering to come to the United Kingdom to assist her. "If England stands and recovers the whole world has a chance of returning to sanity." Just as sex education supporters sought advice from the RFSU in Sweden, meanwhile, so did opponents write to Whitehouse and the NVLA for guidance on how to fight the subject in their own countries. Still others asked to join hands across borders and oceans, noting that a truly international crisis—the sexual revolution—would also require an international solution. "The big thing is that we all compare notes, ideas and thinking, and work as hard as we can to bring sanity to all our countries," American activist Martha Rountree told Whitehouse. She was "*not* talking about one world," Rountree quickly added, echoing the right-wing fear of the United Nations and "one-world government" during these years; nations will always exist, she emphasized, and it was "not realistic or expedient" to imagine otherwise. "But, if the right people in every Nation work together … the voice of the people in the world can bring about miracles," she explained. "And, when I refer to the right people, I mean those who believe in God and their Country, who believe in the family unit, who hold high moral and ethical standards above the temptations that beckon at every turn." Rountree urged Whitehouse to make another voyage to America, where they could "settle the world's problems" together.[20]

Here she alluded to Whitehouse's highly publicized 1972 visit to the United States, sponsored by an American group called Citizens for Decent Literature (CDL) and its energetic founder, Charles Keating. A member of President Nixon's National Commission on Obscenity and Pornography, Keating—like Whitehouse—had entered the political arena to fight sexual imagery in mass media; now he, too, was turning to sex education in the schools. At Whitehouse's request, Keating had given the keynote address at the NVLA's 1970 convention in the United Kingdom. Two years later he returned the invitation, organizing a whirlwind two-week North American tour for Mary Whitehouse. Her schedule for the trip reads like a veritable Who's Who list of the burgeoning American New Right, featuring meetings with antiabortion crusader Phyllis Schlafly, journalist Fulton Lewis, and Catholic archbishop Fulton Sheen. "If 'epistle' is the feminine of 'apostle'—then—you are a great epistle," Sheen told her. Whitehouse also reunited with California congressman and conservative firebrand Robert Dornan, who had already met her during his own trip to the United Kingdom. Compared to Whitehouse's expansive efforts, Dornan complained, the American New Right fell short. "He wonders—as I do—where is the Mary Whitehouse of America?" wrote CDL director Raymond Gauer, after talking with

Dornan. "We sorely need a woman who can speak out intelligently, reasonably, forcibly and articulately against immorality." Gauer added a nod to Carrie Nation, the nineteenth-century American prohibitionist who made her name attacking saloons with an axe. "That's what we need today!" he exclaimed.[21]

Whitehouse also traveled several times to Australia and New Zealand, under the auspices of the Festival of Light (FOL). Founded in London in 1971 by Whitehouse and several conservative compatriots, the FOL lit bonfires around the coastline of England to warn of "moral decay"—just as people did centuries earlier, to alert residents to threats of the Spanish Armada. Building on contemporary left-wing refrains, Whitehouse thrilled Australian audiences with her appeals to "people power" and "participatory democracy"; she also invoked the liberal-leaning environmental movement, calling on citizens around the globe to stamp out "moral pollution" alongside the industrial kind. New Zealand hosted representatives from another British anti-sex-education group, The Responsible Society, who warned listeners against going down "the slippery slope Britain has descended"; in Australia, meanwhile, visiting conservative luminaries from the United States—including Schlafly, Moral Majority founder Jerry Falwell, and Republican strategist Paul Weyrich—assisted in campaigns against abortion, pornography, and homosexual rights as well as against sex education. By the early 1980s, an appalled sex educator observed, right-wing groups in Australia had adopted many of the same "inventive acronyms" and "anything-goes tactics" that marked conservatives in America. Most of all, the campaign against sex education borrowed key conceptual frameworks from the Americans. "He who frames the issues helps to determine the outcome of the debate," Weyrich told an Australian audience.[22]

## POWER TO THE PARENTS?

The most important frame concerned parents' right to educate their children, which had undergirded opposition to sex instruction since the early 1900s. But it assumed a new resonance in the 1960s and 1970s, when several well-publicized disputes about parental rights galvanized foes of sex education around the world. The most important case came out of Denmark, where three sets of parents—including two teachers and two clerics—entered a complaint about sex education before the European Court of Human Rights in 1971. The previous year, Denmark had mandated the subject for all children, as early as age seven but no later than nine; it further specified that sex education should be "integrated" across the curriculum, rather than taught in a separate course. But that feature made it impossible to withdraw children from sex education lessons, which the complaining parents described as "vulgar" and contrary to their "Christian outlook." It also violated Article 2 of the European Convention of Human Rights, the parents said, which held that "no person shall be denied the right to education" and that "the State shall respect the right of parents to ensure such education in conformity with their own religious and philosophical convictions." In reply, the Danish government noted that parents remained free to educate their children at home or at parochial schools, which were heavily subsidized by the state; it also argued that schools took a strictly "factual approach" to sexual matters, providing students with information but allowing parents "to implant their own moral viewpoints in their children."[23]

The European Court ruled against the plaintiffs in *Kjeldsen, Busk Madsen and Pedersen v. Denmark* (1976) by a vote of 8 to 7, the slimmest possible margin. Reviewing the Danish sex education curriculum, the court held that it did not constitute "indoctrination" of a "specific kind of sexual behaviour," nor did it "affect the right of parents to enlighten and advise their children." At the same time, however, the court warned that schools "must take care that information or knowledge is conveyed in an objective, critical, and pluralistic manner" that respects "parents' religious and philosophical convictions." The decision outraged right-wing parents in Denmark, who had previously formed a group called National Protection against the Indoctrination of Children, using the Danish acronym LIBER; after the European court's ruling, members fanned out to other countries to warn about the impending assault on parental prerogatives. In a letter to the queen of England, LIBER chairman Svend Laursen described the decision as "a stunning blow against the parents who believed in human rights"; in New Zealand, he exhibited allegedly "pornographic" European textbooks and lectured on "The Danish middle classes versus sex education"; and he appealed the *Kjeldsen* decision to the United Nations, citing the Universal Declaration of Human Rights' passage that parents have a "prior right" to choose their children's education. "It is clear to us that this issue is not confined to Denmark," a British sex education critic surmised, "but is of prime concern to Christian parents, and to others with traditional family standards, throughout the world."[24]

A few years earlier, Great Britain had been gripped by a similar controversy. In 1970, the parents of four teenaged girls complained about their school's use of a BBC sex education film. After promising the parents that the film would be shown outside of regular class hours, the school proceeded to show it to the entire student body; even worse, the four girls were called to the front of the room, told that their parents disapproved of the film, and sent home. Their father contacted his Member of Parliament, who said British parents did not possess the right to remove their children from disagreeable lessons; educational secretary and future prime minister Margaret Thatcher confirmed that claim, noting her own reservations about BBC's sex education films (which, she said, did not give sufficient attention to "love and marriage") but insisting that "there is no legal right of withdrawal" from the subject. Eventually, the parents decided to remove their four girls from the school entirely. "I submit that teaching captive audiences in schools, during compulsory education, sexual attitudes which are known to be repugnant to [the] conscience of many parents is tyranny, and should be prohibited," the girls' father declared.[25]

The issue eventually worked its way into Parliament, generating several fiery and well-publicized debates. "Have parents no rights? Are they to be ridden roughshod over by the trendy educational fringe?" one member of the House of Lords asked in 1976. "Parents may withdraw their child from religious education, but not from sex education, even though it may be taught in a manner which is repugnant to them." In 1980, another conservative peer proposed a measure requiring head teachers to give parents prior notice of sex education—and allowing parents to withdraw their children from it.

But the amendment was quashed by liberal legislators, who feared that it would put teachers and children alike at the mercy of "ill-judged parents," as one peer noted. "I think it is unrealistic as well as rather unfair to say that parents should deal with this problem," another lord noted, "because often, with the best will in the world, parents are unable to do so." Here she took a page from sex educators themselves, who often cited parental ignorance and inadequacy as the prime reason that schools needed to step into the breach. But that was deeply insulting to many citizens, as a Catholic bishop—and sex education opponent—replied. "The BBC decides that parents are not adult enough to do this," he blared. "It makes a take-over bid, beaming their programme directly to the children." A conservative newspaper columnist—and mother—agreed. "We are mostly quite capable of doing the job perfectly adequately ourselves," she wrote, "in spite of what Auntie B.B.C. and the 'experts' think."[26]

Only in the United States—with its deep-rooted traditions of lay and local school control—did parents win real authority to exempt their children from sex education. By 1980, nine states specifically decreed that parents could withdraw children from the subject; five others required written parental consent before students could receive it. But that still meant that millions of children could receive the subject against their parents' will, as sex education critics pointed out; in New York State, most notably, Governor Hugh Carey vetoed a parental-withdrawal measure because it could "close young people off from the sex information they need," as one educator argued. Critics also lost bids in at least six state courts to declare sex education unconstitutional on First Amendment grounds, as a violation of families' religious freedoms; and twice, in 1970 and 1976, the Supreme Court let stand lower court rulings that rejected such claims. But parents continued to insist that they—not educators—should have the final word on sex instruction for their children. "It's our child, our family," one parent declared, in a typical jeremiad. "My authority comes before the school's authority." Indeed, both sides of the debate acknowledged that it was never just about the birds and the bees. "It is, as our enemies say, more than a matter of sex education," wrote right-wing activist Gordon Drake in 1969. "It is a question of who will run the schools."[27]

## CHILDREN AND SEXUALITY

It was also a question about children, and whether they were naturally sexual beings. The issue had hounded sex education since the early 1900s, when supporters invoked Sigmund Freud's concept of infant sexual instincts; to its critics, meanwhile, sex education would corrupt otherwise sexually innocent youth. But the sexual revolution of the 1960s and 1970s—especially the new frankness about the subject in mass media—underscored the question of child sexuality as never before. "For heaven's sake, don't bombard youngsters with long diatribes about sex at the period in their lives when keeping their ears free from potato crops and their shoes nicely polished is their first priority," wrote a critic of the BBC sex education films in Glasgow, which voted not to show the films in schools; according to the head of a primary school that also rejected the films, they would cause children to take a "morbid introspective interest in their own development." In the United States, likewise, parents complained that a sex education movie disclosed grown-up secrets to previously innocent children. "Now our kids know what a shut bedroom door means," one mother protested. "The program is taking their childhood away." Girls were walking around with apples and oranges under their blouses, another mother grumbled, while a third was appalled when her son said, "Guess what, next week our teacher's gonna tell us how daddy fertilized you."[28]

To sex educators, of course, such episodes simply confirmed children's natural interest in sex—as well as their parents' unnatural anxieties about it. Indeed, they demonstrated the ongoing need for schools to break the "vicious circle" of silence and fear that still surrounded the subject. Several American cities hosted revivals of Frank Wedekind's *Spring Awakening*, the fin de siècle German tragedy of youth sexual anguish that remained "surprisingly undated" in the 1970s, as one theater critic wrote. "The pains of adolescence are still great," he added, "and the horrors of repression, emotional and physical, are still very real." Other educators noted new scientific evidence of sexual arousal from birth and even before, as fetal erections seemed to suggest. Still others pointed to survey data collected from children themselves, who thought and knew much more about sex than many adults imagined. Most of all, educators mocked the continued conservative assumption—reaching back to the early 1900s, but revived in the 1960s and 1970s—that sex education would encourage students to engage prematurely in sexual activity. "How does one persuade irrational people bent on their own irrationality to accept the single fact that concurrence of two happenings does not necessarily indicate causality of or by either?" exasperated American sex educator Mary Calderone asked an Australian counterpart. "If I take an aspirin in the morning and drop dead at noon, surely the aspirin caused my death?"[29]

Especially in the 1970s, finally, some educators started to suggest that children's sexual nature implied a *right* to receive sex education, or even to pursue sexual pleasure. To be sure, the mere mention of pleasure remained taboo in most schools outside of Scandinavia. Not surprisingly, then, Scandinavian and especially Swedish educators took the lead in promulgating the idea of "sexual knowledge as a human right," as a Swedish speaker told a 1970 conference in Austria. Since this instruction was truly a "moral right," another Swede told a London audience the following year, schools did not allow parents to withdraw their offspring from it; "schools are for children," she flatly declared, "not parents." The concept proved irresistible to sex educators elsewhere in Europe and in North America, where parental objections constantly stymied them. It also spawned a set of conferences and resolutions in the late 1970s and early 1980s, all devoted to establishing sexual knowledge—and, increasingly, sexual pleasure—as a basic right. Meeting in 1979, the "International Year of the Child," educators in Mexico City, Tel Aviv, Montreal, and York, England, debated a resolution on the "Sexual Rights of Children"; that same year, an international meeting in Uppsala, Sweden, affirmed that "it is the right of every individual to live in an environment of freely available information, knowledge, and wisdom about human sexuality." In 1983, finally, the World Health Organization (WHO) endorsed a similar set of statements in its "Consultation on Sexuality":

At present, it is not possible to define the totality of human sexuality in a form that would be acceptable to all countries, but every person has a right to receive sexual information and to consider accepting sexual relationships for pleasure as well as for procreation.

Sexuality starts at birth, if not earlier in the foetus. Masturbation and sexual play in children are normal and healthy activities, but children in most countries suffer from sexual repression.... Children as well as adults require support to be able to feel enjoyment as sexual beings.

By 1995, in every country at least 80 percent of the people ... will have an opportunity of leading an emotionally satisfying sexual life in harmony with the needs, beliefs, and values of the individual and society.[30]

In reply, conservatives also invoked the rights of children—to remain sexually innocent. Especially after the *Kjeldsen* decision, which limited parental rights, they often cited the United Nations Declaration of the Rights of the Child (1959): "The child shall enjoy special protection ... to enable him to develop physically, mentally, morally, spiritually, and socially." Sex education allegedly violated that credo by exposing children to material that threatened their well-being. Others rejected the entire concept of a universal "right" to sexual information and particularly to sexual pleasure, noting—correctly—that many cultures and societies around the world simply did not recognize such a thing. Even within European democracies, sex education caused "considerable distress" for "orthodox Muslim and Hindu families," as a British observer wrote; in Sweden, likewise, the burgeoning Yugoslav community often rejected sex education along with "the Swedish pattern of sexuality and sexual relations," as an RFSU official noted. And when Western sex educators left the West, they found similar resistance to their own liberal consensus on sex instruction for children. "The weight of tradition seems oppressive," wrote American Lester Kirkendall in 1972, after a three-month speaking tour in Japan, the Philippines, and Hong Kong. "Many of my suggestions were countered with the argument that 'we can't do it that way in our culture.'" Japan's "Chastity and Purity

Education" (as it was known) preached strict sexual abstinence, while Filipino educators provided only small snippets of sexual information in their "population education" course. In their voyages overseas, especially, Western sex educators would have to confront the enormous diversity of human sexuality—and the limits of any shared approach to the same.[31]

## EXPORTING SEX EDUCATION: AMERICA, SWEDEN, AND THE WORLD

Kirkendall traveled to "the Orient" (as he called it) under the auspices of the Sex Information and Education Council of the United States, which developed several overseas outreach projects in the 1970s and 1980s. So did a handful of other private groups and foundations, continuing the long tradition of voluntary-organization assistance pioneered by the American Social Hygiene Association (renamed the American Social Health Association) in the 1940s and 1950s. The Ford Foundation aided sex education groups in several Latin American countries, including Mexico, Venezuela, Costa Rica, and Colombia; it also funded a trailblazing 1973 conference in Mali on sex education in sub-Saharan Francophone Africa, organized by the American Friends Service Committee (AFSC). The AFSC, meanwhile, advised sex education advocates in Hong Kong, Uganda, and across Latin America. In Honduras, it sponsored a weeklong sex education course for five hundred primary school teachers; it also paid for several Mexican teachers to attend a workshop on the subject at Catholic University in Washington, DC. For the first time, finally, the United States Agency for International Development (USAID) also began to promote and develop sex education abroad. In 1968, most prominently, Chile's Ministry of Education signed an agreement with USAID to train two thousand teachers in the subject by 1971. The pact also paid for several Chileans—including President Eduardo Frei's daughter—to visit the United States and Sweden to observe sex education classes there.[32]

Sweden hosted hundreds of other visitors as part of its overseas efforts, which began with an RFSU-sponsored "International

Symposium on Sexology" in 1969. The event drew 105 applications from educators, physicians, and public officials in twenty-two different countries, who competed for just thirty slots; rejected applicants included Filipino senator and future president Benigno S. Aquino, who received summaries of the conference's lectures after it concluded. The RFSU sponsored a second symposium in 1971, when it also welcomed a delegation of twenty-eight Japanese high school teachers who were "seeking how to diffuse the sex education" in their own country, as their travel agent wrote. "The problem of sex in Japan is still in a very 'Dark Continent,'" a Japanese visitor wrote. "The most useful and helpful way to have a solution in this matter is to go to the European countries to study and research their advanced present conditions and introduce it in Japan." Like USAID, meanwhile, the Swedish International Development Cooperation Agency—the government's foreign-aid arm—developed several overseas sex education initiatives in the 1970s. The agency hosted three seminars for Latin American and Caribbean sex educators, which featured frank discussions with Swedish officials and students. "I know that there are many countries with more restrictive attitudes ... but I cannot believe we are different from people in other parts of the world," a nineteen-year-old Swedish student told the second seminar, in 1972. "We are the same humans I think."[33]

A similarly universalistic spirit marked sex education efforts by international organizations, where Swedes and other Scandinavians often played leading roles. The International Planned Parenthood Federation (IPPF) held its first-ever session on "Youth and Sex Education" in 1967, drawing an overflow crowd to hear talks by RFSU founder Elise Ottesen-Jensen and by Danish educator Agnette Braestrup; countering the idea that sex education was "dangerous," Braestrup noted that students in Denmark received it "with neither the teacher nor the children becoming excited." The key was to discover a "globally common denominator for sex education," as Swedish psychiatrist and IPPF president Thorsten Sjövall told the group in 1970. "Who needs sex education?" asked Sjövall, who also served as the RFSU's president. "All nations and all individuals at all ages need it; there are no developed or developing countries in this particular respect." Associations affiliated with the United Nations also entered the sex education arena during these years, often under the leadership of Scandinavians. "The idea of an education designed to form and set free the individual personality is implicit in the concept of sex education," a UNESCO regional conference for Latin America resolved in 1971, echoing a common Swedish refrain. So did a WHO meeting in 1979, which stressed "the positive aspect of sexuality" rather than "negative" elements like the prevention of pregnancy and VD.[34]

## SEX EDUCATION AND FAMILY PLANNING IN THE "THIRD WORLD"

But sex education took root slowly—if at all—in the "Third World," as Westerners called it, belying their dreams of a truly worldwide educational revolution. Like critics in the West, many citizens in Asia, Africa, and Latin America objected to the public discussion of formerly tabooed topics in schools; others were more specifically repelled by the idea of female sexual independence, as a Ford Foundation official in Senegal noted. In Mexico, similarly, "the entire culture ... is still permeated by attitudes intended to emphasize the role of women as sexual playthings of men or as mothers," a local educator wrote; at its root, she added, sex education threatened the idea that females should be "subservient" to men. Most of all, Third World educators and families rejected the idea of adolescent autonomy—for both genders—in sexual decision making. In Ghana, where a church council introduced public school sex education, curricula stressed teen abstinence above all. "The marriage bed should be without wrinkles," a science teacher wrote in 1965, summarizing the "exhortation and warning" that students received. "Boy and girl should be virgins at the time of marriage." The following year, when a coup toppled Ghanaian independence leader Kwame Nkrumah, his enemies pointed to youth sexual laxity as a central cause of the country's woes. "Morals were so low that adultery and fornication ... became a shameless social practice," a church group told the National

Liberation Council, which replaced Nkrumah. Only the "right type of education" would save youth from "immorality and debauchery," the group added.[35]

In the early 1970s Ghanaian sex instruction shifted from religious to family-planning auspices, reflecting another important global trend. "In most countries, sex education programmes are regarded as an essential part of family planning programmes," declared the Planned Parenthood Association of Ghana in 1971, inaugurating a new "Family Life Education" initiative; by 1975, the group was conducting FLE in forty schools for ten thousand students. Elsewhere, too, some family-planning officials and advocates embraced sex education as one of the keys to defusing the "Population Bomb" that supposedly threatened the planet's future. As an Indian family-planning official explained, successful population-control efforts required "changing the subtle human attitudes," not just "importing contraceptive technology"; and these attitudes would never alter without "sound sex education," as a family-planning proponent in Uruguay added. "When the mechanics of birth control information are introduced to people, it is found they have many questions, hang-ups, nutty or hostile ideas about morality," a Ford Foundation official in Latin America wrote. "Much of this, of course, is rooted in the sniggering or frightening attitudes about sex." Unless children learned new values and perspectives at an early age, he warned, the foundation's population-control efforts would "fall on stony ground."[36]

But when sex education became too closely linked in the public mind with family planning, both projects often descended into disrepute. As their name suggested, "family planning" and "planned parenthood" were "directed only towards married couples," as an Indian government leaflet emphasized; if they became associated with sexual activity *outside* of families, advocates feared, they would lose whatever tenuous public support they had gained. Especially in Asia and Africa, many family-planning organizations sought to "desexualize" themselves—as one American observer quipped—by eschewing sex education altogether. At the same time, sex educators discovered that any visible link to family planning or birth control services could doom their efforts. Korean parents resisted sex education out of fear that it would teach contraception, which they associated with Japanese efforts to control their population—especially via abortion—during and before World War II; educators in West Africa warned that any mention of birth control in classrooms could violate France's 1920 law prohibiting public discussion of the subject, which was still on the books in many former French colonies; and in El Salvador, where a 1972 presidential decree called for training two thousand teachers in "family education," participants warned that any connection to family *planning* would "violate or offend the socio-cultural sensibilities of the Salvadoran people." Especially in heavily Catholic Latin America, another observer wrote from Colombia, such terms bore "a 'North American' label ... which is another cause of resistance."[37]

## POPULATION EDUCATION

So sex educators and family-planning advocates went in search of another phrase, which would avoid both the lascivious, pleasure-seeking tone of "sex" and the coercive, secularizing connotations of "family planning." They found it in *population education*, which became the most common venue for sex education in many parts of Asia, Africa, and Latin America. The concept was actually born in Sweden, where the 1935 Population Commission called on schools to help increase the nation's moribund birth rate by encouraging early marriage and larger families. American demographer Frank Lorimer and military official Frederick Osborn urged a similar educational effort in 1943, fearing that declining fertility rates in North America and Europe threatened economic prosperity and national security. But when population education resurfaced in the 1960s, it had the opposite goal: to stem population growth. Building on the burgeoning environmental movement, American educators urged schools to teach about "overpopulation" and its "disastrous consequences for mankind": pollution, famine, and war. The effort yielded scattered pilot projects in the United States, but little else; instead, it took hold abroad. "We must have experience here before trying to export," a skeptical American observer cautioned in 1971, noting the low level of domestic interest in population education. "If we cannot convince a State Department of Education, how can we convince LDCs?"[38]

The acronym "LDCs" referred to Lesser Developed Countries, where advocates found a much more amenable audience for population education. Indeed, another American asserted in 1971, population education was "unique" insofar as it was "*not* a curricular pattern being exported from technologically developed societies to developing countries." He was only half right. Although population education never took root in US schools, Americans—and, especially, American foundations—played a key role in planting it overseas, fired by a fear of overpopulation. In their public pronouncements, officials from the "Big Three" foundations—Rockefeller, Ford, and Carnegie—warned that unchecked population growth would yield mass starvation and disease; privately, they worried that nonwhite people would overcome white ones. At the same time, though, they realized that population control could not succeed unless it appealed to the very populations whose growth they dreaded. Population education would get Third World people to *want* smaller families, the foundations hoped, even as it protected the West's hegemony over the wider human family. In some countries, one Ford Foundation official wrote, Americans might collaborate with "responsible public sector organizations" to promote population education. But in places where "the public sector is not ready," he added, foundations could partner with friendly private organizations. As in the United States, another Ford representative wrote, "enlightened" people favored sex and population education and "unenlightened" people did not. The key was to locate and cultivate the first group and avoid alienating the second, both inside government agencies and beyond them.[39]

Here the foundations often partnered with American universities, a centerpiece of the "Big Three" vision of global progress and modernization. Funded by two large grants from the Population Council, which had been founded in the 1950s by John D. Rockefeller III, Teachers College (TC) at Columbia University worked with ministries of education in nine Third World countries to develop curricula and train teachers in population education. As the subject became more popular abroad, TC faculty also consulted on it with UNESCO and the United Nations Family Planning Association; closer to home, they hosted dozens of foreign students who came to learn about population education. Harvard's own "pop-ed cadre" (as its members called themselves) designed and evaluated a "population awareness" course in Cali, Colombia, with the support of the Population Council; the University of Michigan sponsored a similar project in Baroda, India, under a Ford Foundation grant; and at the University of North Carolina, which offered the world's first master's degree in population education, scholars developed materials for India, Chile, Nigeria, Thailand, Indonesia, and the Philippines. By 1971, one Indian expert estimated, twenty countries already had an "active programme" in population education.[40]

But other countries resisted the subject, dismissing population education as a "euphemism for sex education." The remark reflected an ongoing dilemma for educators in the Third World, who often tried to teach the benefits of small families while avoiding the question of where families came from, or how they might remain small. Indeed, some advocates warned, "population education would be killed (or even aborted) if it is combined with sex education," as American demographer Edward W. Pohlman and his Indian counterpart K. Seshagiri Rao claimed. Sex education arose in the West to stem venereal disease and out-of-wedlock pregnancy, they argued, which were not large-scale dangers in countries like India; the real peril was the skyrocketing birthrate, a "matter of life-or-death urgency" that could only be arrested by teaching children to limit their fertility as adults. "Music is wonderful, but the man entering a life-boat to escape a sinking ship may miss the boat completely if he insists on taking his grand piano along," Pohlman and Rao explained. "Half a *chappati* is better than no *roti*." When students asked, "If small families are good, how can you stop babies from coming?" teachers could simply reply that they were barred from answering the question; or they could ask the students to discuss it outside of class. "'Sexless' population education is possible," Pohlman and Rao concluded. "The notion that one cannot teach population education without teaching sex is ridiculous."[41]

But to other educators, the idea of separating population from sex was ridiculous—and, even more, duplicitous. "The development of population education exclusive of planned instruction about biology, reproduction, sexual behavior, contraception ... is tomato soup without the tomatoes," wrote a USAID advisor in India, invoking a different culinary metaphor. "'Sexless' population education [is] intellectually dishonest in the first instance and foolhardy in the second." It was hardly clear that Indians would reject sex education, as Pohlman and Rao assumed; indeed, an Indian family-planning advocate reported, one survey found that upwards of 90 percent of high school girls supported instruction about "reproductive physiology" and "family living." In Latin America, meanwhile, the phrase "population education"—like "family life education"—sometimes carried a *greater* stigma than sex education; it was associated with "population *control* education," one observer underlined, which was taboo in the region. Most of all, though, critics argued that population education simply would not work. Even in "developed" countries with high literacy levels, Sweden's Thorsten Sjövall noted, people were not swayed by "demographic tables" showing runaway fertility rates; all that mattered were "concrete human needs," including "sexual harmony" and personal well-being. "The present attempts at introducing so-called 'population education' at the state school level seems to me pathetically euphemistic for the badly needed instruction of more immediate facts of life," Sjövall told the IPPF. "Man has a fundamental right to knowledge about his immediate self."[42]

In reply, some advocates of population education noted that it *did* appeal to students' immediate needs. As Pohlman and Rao argued, population education teaches "the meaning of large or small families, and of later or earlier marriage, to the *individual* .... Here are the effects on *you*." In a very different kind of defense, others argued that population education did not seek to lower family size; it simply sought to "present both sides" of the question, as the Population Council's Stephen Viederman argued, so children could come to their own reasoned judgments. But Viederman also assumed that children who truly reasoned would share *his* judgment, a foible of liberal educators everywhere. "Students are perhaps more likely to make societally correct decisions in open-ended programs, than if they are simply told what is societally correct," he wrote. "Whether this open-ended approach is viable and valuable in the developing world is a matter for each country to decide for itself, depending upon the values and traditions of the educational system." Even in the supposedly "value-fair" United States, another American admitted, such debate "rarely happens" in school, and if the debate was truly "open-minded," he added, some students might end up taking a "pro-natalist position." For exactly that reason, two Filipino educators admitted, most population education openly "indoctrinated" the virtues of small families. "There is a problem, that problem is population growth, and that growth must be curbed," they categorically declared.[43]

Moreover, as the Filipino example also demonstrated, sexual information and discussion was often woven into population education. The Philippines' national population education curriculum included units on human sexuality, which would "favorably affect the future fertility behavior of students," as another pair of educators confidently predicted. In Mexico, likewise, the 1977 Population Law called for sex education—including "explicit information" on bodily changes and functions—as a route to "a more rational and responsible way of facing reproduction." In practice, however, many teachers downplayed or ignored the sexual dimensions of population, for fear of alienating parents and other constituents. Quoting Thorsten Sjövall, an American teacher in Tunisia privately confessed that she wished to "call a cat a cat" and teach sex education. But she ultimately decided to omit it from her "dynamics of population" course, for fear of alienating her conservative hosts. So did many teachers in other places that had adopted population education, if they knew about the subject at all. In a 1976 survey of rural teachers in India, which had instituted population education seven years earlier, 40 percent said they had not even heard of the term. A whopping 88 percent opposed instruction of the subject, which they associated strongly with sex education; indeed, nearly half of the objectors condemned population education on the grounds that "we do not want children to experiment with sex."[44]

## TEACHERS, CAUGHT IN THE MIDDLE (AGAIN)

No matter what it was called, teachers around the world continued to resist sex education in the 1960s and 1970s. Even in the West— and even at the height of the so-called sexual revolution—teachers who addressed sex risked losing their livelihoods, or even their liberty. In France, a twenty-eight-year-old philosophy teacher was charged in 1972 with "outrage against morals" after she shared an evocatively titled pamphlet—"Let Us Learn to Make Love"—with her high school students. Condemning "hypocritical moral authorities" for "the repression of desires," the pamphlet endorsed male-female sexual experimentation as well as masturbation (which "can fill the emptiness of an hour's class or a boring evening"). It made little difference to the arresting authorities that the teacher shared the pamphlet in response to a student's request during a lesson about Sigmund Freud, or that the class voted unanimously to read it. "This is not sex education!" a local official thundered. "This is an invitation to debauchery!" After students went out on strike in support of the teacher, the morals charge against her was dismissed. But other teachers still feared that *they* would be dismissed for teaching about sex. A 1973 government decree that allowed them to address "facts of human reproduction"—but barred them from "moralizing" about the same—did little to quell teachers' worries. Where did facts end and morals begin? Nobody could be sure. In 1976, a nineteen-year-old student teacher was expelled from his teacher-training college when a janitor heard him discussing sex with his high school class. In France, which other nations continued to see as a hotbed of sexual license, the better part of wisdom was to ignore sex education altogether.[45]

The pressures on teachers were probably even greater in the United States and the United Kingdom, where local control of education made them more vulnerable to "small but vocal publics," as a Swedish transplant to the United States observed. A married British student teacher was expelled from her own training college in 1969 for answering a pupil's question about the birth control pill; five years later, a sixteen-year veteran of the New York City schools was placed on administrative leave for showing his class a sex education filmstrip—produced by health educators at New York University—that included pictures of intercourse and oral sex. The teacher was also investigated by the local district attorney, who grudgingly dropped the case when he discovered that the "sex film" was legal in schools; ironically, he argued, showing the same movie to minors in a pornography house would be a crime! But no educator could miss his overall message: when it comes to sex, proceed with the strictest caution. "What shall be taught? Who is to teach it?" a California journalist wrote, examining attacks on sex education in 1975. "Hands off seems to be the wisest approach." After the New Zealand government issued a circular warning that it was illegal to discuss contraceptives in schools—and urging teachers to respect students' "sensitivities" and "ethical and religious beliefs"—a national teachers union advised members to avoid the subject whenever they could. "Adverse gossip, or the slightest innuendo of possible impropriety, could bring professional disaster," a British headmaster wrote, summarizing the sex education situation. "Consequently, many teachers have abstained."[46]

But most teachers did *not* abstain from sex itself, of course, which made teaching about the subject all the more problematic. Although people disagreed about whether children were sexual beings, nobody doubted that teachers were. So anything teachers said about the subject addressed their own erotic behavior and proclivities, at least indirectly. Around the world, sex education teachers were alternately accused of being *too* sexual—or not sexual enough. In Ghana, parents charged that male teachers discussed the subject in order to seduce female students; in India, critics worried that "those who are most enthusiastic may be the least suitable" to teach sex education. "These one-track-mind teachers who cannot raise their minds above their belts should be put right back where they belong—and that isn't teaching in the schools," an outraged Australian conservative complained, after her twelve-year-old granddaughter was asked to draw a penis and vagina for homework. On the left, by contrast, critics feared that teachers lacked the sexual awareness—or, even, the sexual experience—to instruct the subject. They took aim especially at so-called old maids, the "dried up spinstery old things" (as a Swedish teenager complained) who had never married. "Some youngsters have more sex life in one weekend than their sex education teacher has had in a lifetime," warned Dr. David Reuben, author of the bestselling US book *Everything You Always Wanted to Know about Sex, But Were Afraid to Ask*. In the United Kingdom, another physician insisted that "anyone who has not experienced satisfaction or has a distaste of sex is hardly competent to teach it."[47]

Still others worried that sex education teachers had had the *wrong* kind of sexual experience—with members of the same sex. In the United States, Florida and California both considered measures that would have barred gays from teaching in the public schools; in each case, part of the worry was that they would seduce children via sex education classes. Even opponents of such restrictions agreed that homosexuals "may not be the best instructors for sex education," as the liberal *New York Times* suggested in an editorial denouncing the widespread dismissal of gay teachers around the country; in gay-friendly San Francisco, likewise, city supervisor (and future senator) Dianne Feinstein blasted a campaign by homosexual teachers and students to include "gay life and other human diversities" in sex education. "It could open the door to the worst kind of experimentation," Feinstein warned. "Gays should not be harassed (for their sexual preference) but it's reached the point where their lifestyles are imposing on others." In the United Kingdom's House of Lords, meanwhile, one peer likened gay sex educators to homosexual British diplomats who had committed "treason by sodomy" by sharing classified secrets with the Soviet Union. And in New Zealand, finally, right-wing activist Bernard Moran warned that "gay teachers" were "champing [*sic*] at the bit" to teach sex education. But their version of the subject would alienate the nation's Maori minority as well as recent Chinese, Indian, and Vietnamese immigrants, Moran cautioned. "We live in a multicultural and pluralistic society," he added, borrowing a favorite liberal trope. "Classroom persuasion by trendy teachers that human sexuality involves a good time and being responsible through using contraceptives, would be complete anathema to most Asian parents."[48]

### SEX EDUCATION AND THE SEXUAL REVOLUTION: REAPING THE HARVEST?

The final comment spoke to an ongoing dilemma for sex educators, many of whom also fashioned themselves "multiculturalists": how could schools in a diverse society teach about sex in a manner that respected different ethnicities, cultures, and religions? The problem would become more acute in the 1980s and especially the 1990s, when millions of immigrants flowed into Europe, the Americas, and the antipodes. It proved particularly difficult in countries that taught sex education "across the curriculum" rather than as a separate course, as New Zealand's Bernard Moran also noted. "How do parents ... make sure that the teachers are playing the game when the sex education is integrated with other subjects?" Moran asked. "The only sure-fire way [is] to have a separate sex and values education programme with a set text, so that parents know exactly what their children are getting—right across the nation—at each age group." But very few nations did that. In a 1973 survey of seventeen European countries, only two—Finland and Poland—taught sex education as a separate subject; twelve taught it via biology, five in social studies, five in civics, and five as part of religious studies. Even more, countries with otherwise uniform school systems often refrained from standardizing sex education: by 1983, when twelve countries made sex education "mandatory," only four of them set a national curriculum.[49]

So it was difficult to know how much sex education children were receiving, if any, and even harder to measure what it did for them. "It is not possible to determine how many sex education programs there are in the schools, or what is being taught in them," an American scholar frankly acknowledged in 1977. "Most startling of all, no one has the slightest idea what the effects of sex education are or can be." That same year, a study of Muncie, Indiana—the focus of Helen and Robert Lynd's 1924 sociological classic, *Middletown*—confirmed that friends and films had replaced family as the most important source of sexual information in the intervening half century. What had not changed were schools, which were named as the most critical source by only 5 percent of boys (up from 4 percent, in 1924) and 9 percent of girls (up from 5 percent). But that did not stop educators from dreaming, as one did after observing a sex education class in Switzerland in 1969. "I have been witnessing [a] cultural revolution, perhaps the most important of our time," the observer gushed, praising the Swiss instructor's frank, unembarrassed account of sexual intercourse and masturbation. "We will only reap the harvest in 20 or 25 years." A quarter-century later, a new sexual crisis—HIV/AIDS— would indeed bring new expectations for sex education. But it remained unclear what kind of harvest it could reap, and whether it would be bountiful or bitter—and for whom.[50]

# CHAPTER FOUR

# A Right to Knowledge? Culture, Diversity, and Sex Education in the Age of AIDS, 1984–2010

In September 1994, twenty thousand delegates gathered in Cairo, Egypt, for the International Conference on Population and Development (ICPD). Discarding the family-planning model that had marked most such meetings since the 1960s, the conference adopted a new emphasis on "reproductive rights." All human beings should be able to choose when and how they reproduced, the convention resolved; to make informed choices, they also needed access to sex education from the beginning of their reproductive years. "Information and services should be made available to adolescents to help them understand their sexuality," the ICPD declared. "This should be combined with the education of young men to respect women's self-determination and to share responsibility with women in matters of sexuality and reproduction." Scandinavians took the lead in promoting this rights-based approach at the meeting, which heard opening-day speeches from the Norwegian prime minister and from Denmark's minister for overseas development. The resolutions also represented a triumph for American officials at the Ford Foundation, who laid the groundwork for the ICPD by funding local Egyptian groups to "raise awareness" of sex education and especially AIDS. Sex education was "the only available protection" against AIDS, one Egyptian grant recipient noted. It would also help combat "sex perversion," he added, particularly homosexuality.[1]

Yet the final comment also underscored the limits of consensus at the ICPD. Egypt would eventually join with four other majority-Muslim countries in denouncing the idea of "individual" rights to sexual knowledge and self-determination; such a claim "could be interpreted as applying to sexual relations outside the framework of marriage," an Iranian delegate explained, "and this is totally unacceptable." Two mostly Catholic countries (El Salvador and Guatemala) also issued dissents from the resolutions, as did the delegation from the Vatican; earlier in the year, Philippines cardinal Jaime Sin called on Catholics to reject the ICPD along with "the shackles of this new global citizenship." The conference also heard a stinging rebuke from Pakistani premier Benazir Bhutto, who reiterated her support for population control even as she condemned Western leaders for pushing their own libertinism on the conservative East. "This conference must not be viewed by the teeming masses of the world as a universal social charter seeking to impose adultery, abortion, sex education and other such matters on individuals, societies, and religions which have their own social ethos," Bhutto warned. "The world needs consensus. It does not need a clash of cultures."[2]

It got one, anyway, although not the kind that Bhutto imagined. Two years after he declared a "cultural war" in the United States at the Republican National Convention, right-wing columnist Pat Buchanan proclaimed that the ICPD had united conservatives across borders—indeed, across cultures. "While this may be a bold agenda at Washington dinner parties, to traditional societies in Latin America, Africa and the Islamic world, it is the essence of decadent, godless Western materialism," Buchanan wrote, condemning the Cairo resolutions. Prior to the ICPD, Vatican officials met with representatives of the World Muslim League and other Islamic groups; in a joint statement, they condemned the "extreme individualism" and "moral decadence" of the conference. The papal envoy in Teheran also met with Iranian officials, who declared their "full endorsement" for the Vatican in its battle against the ICPD. As an Islamic leader in the United Kingdom wrote three years later, the Cairo controversy generated a "common platform" with "like-minded non-Muslim faith groups." It also emboldened them to challenge school officials, who had stepped up sex education in the face of the AIDS crisis. "Both sides—the authorities as well as the community—speak of promoting 'the moral,'" the Muslim leader wrote. "Whose morals is the child going to subscribe to?"[3]

The same question had surrounded sex education since its inception, of course. But it assumed a new meaning and urgency in the age of AIDS, which made most governments adopt some kind of school-based sex instruction. Suddenly, the question was no longer whether schools would teach about sex; it was what they would teach, and how, and to what end. Abandoning their long-standing opposition to the subject, conservative Christian activists in the West backed new forms of "abstinence-only" sex education. They also made common cause with different faith groups, at home and overseas, belying the popular notion of a "clash of cultures" between them. The real conflict pitted liberal and secular voices against the Global Right, which rallied religious conservatives behind older notions of sexual continence and obedience. For their own part, liberals struggled to respect ethnic and religious "diversity" even as they proclaimed a universal right to sexual choice and information. "How can a sexuality, reproduction and health perspective based on individual rights become a global norm?" a Swedish educator wondered in 2004, on the ten-year anniversary of the Cairo conference. Sadly, the Swede admitted, large parts of the globe still resisted that viewpoint. In an age of diversity, a single shared standard of sex education—or, even a personal "right" to the same—remained a chimera.[4]

## THE AIDS CRISIS AND SEX EDUCATION, I:
## EUROPE AND THE USA

In 1987, US Surgeon General C. Everett Koop traveled to Japan to address a conference on HIV/AIDS. A leader in the effort to combat the disease back home, Koop was shocked when the Japanese Minister of Health raised a glass of sake in honor of his American guest and said, "AIDS, no problem in Japan." Koop bluntly replied that AIDS *was* a problem there, noting that businessmen consorted with prostitutes in Hawaii and then returned to Japan to infect their wives with HIV. And just as in America, he added, the only way to fight AIDS was via education. To be sure, Koop added, "lack of understanding and official denial" hampered AIDS prevention everywhere; in the United States, for example, his 1986 report on AIDS—

calling on schools to start teaching about it in the third grade—had triggered outrage among his fellow conservatives, and even a few death threats against Koop himself. But that was all the more reason to press forward, he argued, citing the Hippocratic oath that was administered to physicians around the world. "We will not abandon the sick or disabled, whoever they are," Koop declared, "or however they got their problem." He added a jab at "homophobia" in Japan, although—as he later admitted—he also feared that his words "were falling on deaf ears."[5]

Koop might have been right. Nearly two decades later, Japanese textbooks took pains to debunk "myths" about AIDS—it wasn't spread by mosquito bites or by shaking hands, for example—but remained silent about how it *was* transmitted, and about who was suffering from it. But even these elliptical remarks represented a much more explicit discussion than what had been taught under Japanese "Purity Education," which had since assumed a more common name: sex education. Elsewhere, the subject continued to appear under older euphemisms—especially family life education and population education—and added a few new ones, including "adolescent reproductive health" and "life skills." As before, many of these names were designed to mask, downplay, or avoid sex-related content. But in the age of HIV/AIDS, such content increased—both in detail and in volume—in almost every corner of the globe. Not surprisingly, much of this instruction simply warned young people against having sex. On the one hand, an American educator wrote in 1996, the spread of HIV/AIDS helped erode "the taboo surrounding sexuality" in schools; on the other, it also reinforced traditional notions about it. Most sex education still focused on "the biology of sexuality" and on "controlling sexual activity through fear," the American educator wrote, reviewing several new initiatives overseas.[6]

The same was true in the United States, where a burst of new sex education laws and policies bore a distinctly conservative flavor. In 1986, when Koop released his AIDS report, just three states and the District of Columbia mandated sex education; by 1992, all but four states required or recommended it. These years also witnessed the rise of so-called abstinence-only sex education, fueled by federal measures that provided funds for the same. By 1999 one in three American school districts was using an abstinence-only curriculum like *Sex Respect*, which touted the idea of "secondary virginity": even if you had already had sex, you could reclaim virgin status by abstaining until marriage. It also issued controversial—and mostly flawed—data about condom failure, insisting that "safe sex" was a contradiction in terms. "There's another good reason not to have sex," the curriculum's creator told an interviewer in a news report she sent to C. Everett Koop. "You can die." Koop himself recommended abstinence outside of marriage but also argued for teaching students about condoms and even anal sex, so they knew how to protect themselves; as he told a reporter, "you can't talk about the dangers of snake poisoning and not mention snakes." His position drove a wedge into the Republican Party and created political headaches for President Ronald Reagan, who blithely announced that he had neither read Koop's HIV/AIDS report nor spoken to him about it. But it also underscored the limits of sex education in the era of AIDS; even in a plea for abstinence, there was only so much sexual information that Americans would allow their children to receive.[7]

In the United Kingdom, likewise, HIV/AIDS sparked a spike in both sex education and the squabbles surrounding it. In 1986, under pressure from Conservatives in Parliament, the government made local education authorities responsible for sex education and also declared that parents could exempt their children from it. When the Education Department issued a pamphlet the following year to guide instruction about AIDS, it emphasized that such instruction remained optional for schools and families alike; in the classroom, meanwhile, many teachers continued to avoid sex education for fear of offending local officials and parents. But it clearly received more attention than ever before; as in the United States, one British educator observed, the question became "how sex education is carried out and not whether it is carried out." A 1996 measure required sex education for all high school students—subject to parental right of withdrawal—but added that it should be taught "in such a manner as to encourage those pupils to have due regard to moral considerations and the value of family life." In 2000, yet another law declared that students should also be "protected from teaching materials which are inappropriate to [their] religious and cultural background." As another educator noted, these mandates made schools "walk a fine line"; stressing the value of family and morality, they also had to respect the varied moralities of different families.[8]

In the more liberal societies of northern Europe, meanwhile, HIV/AIDS brought renewed and often highly explicit attention to safe-sex practices. In the Netherlands, a popular television news program for children staged a condom demonstration on a model of an erect penis; a Danish cartoon book showed "Oda and Ole" making love, using a condom; Finnish authorities sent a sex education leaflet and a condom to all adolescents on their sixteenth birthdays; and in Sweden, teachers passed around condoms in class and urged students to experiment with them. "Take these home and masturbate with them on, so you can see which kinds feel good and what kind you like," one teacher told the boys in her charge. "And girls, you too take some home and open them up and handle them and make sure that you feel comfortable with them, so you won't feel shy when the time comes to put them on your boyfriends." Elsewhere in Europe, finally, countries that had formerly resisted or sharply restricted sex education found that they could no longer do so. Ireland issued its first sex education guidelines in 1987, cautioning that "such education should not be secular and would require religious input"; Poland developed a sex education syllabus to delay sexual debut and promote marital fidelity, which would both allegedly help control AIDS; and in France, minister for education and future presidential candidate Ségolène Royal launched a campaign to distribute a "pocket guide to contraception" in the schools. Across Europe and around the globe, a 1997 United Nations study observed, the spread of HIV/AIDS had "convinced otherwise reluctant governments" to institute—or to expand—sex education.[9]

## THE AIDS CRISIS AND SEX EDUCATION, II: THE DEVELOPING WORLD

The starkest change occurred in the so-called developing world, especially in the epicenter of the AIDS epidemic: Africa. By 2004, 80 percent of people living with AIDS were between fifteen and twenty-four years of age; three-quarters of them lived in Africa, where 70 percent of children entered primary school and two-thirds of those children reached the fifth grade. So schools represented "the single location where the largest proportion of young people can be reached," as two African health specialists wrote. Countries that had formerly taught "population education"—with only a smattering of sex-related information—began to teach much more explicitly about the subject, often supplanting families and other traditional modes of socialization. "In a changing modern world, parents need help with this formidable task," noted one observer in Botswana, where AIDS and divorce had spawned a dramatic increase in single-parent households. "The stable, predictable world is gone." Botswanan schools integrated material about sex and HIV/AIDS into science, home economics, and religious education; so did Kenya, which also taught the subject via geography, history, civics, Swahili, and math. "A hospital had 35 inpatients tested for HIV," one math teacher told his class, in a typical word problem. "Ten percent of these were HIV-negative. How many were HIV positive?" Whatever their subject, almost all such lessons ended with the same advice: abstinence, except in marriage. "If children are 'taught' that it is OK for them to change partners and fall into bed when the emotions move them (provided they use a condom!), what hope is there for that young person ... ever to form a firm lasting relationship based on mutual trust?" asked the minister of health in Zimbabwe, which barred "safe-sex" lessons from schools. "We have to promote *lasting, permanent marriage* since this is the only sound basis for the family, which in turn is the building block upon which the whole structure of the nation is based."[10]

Echoing American abstinence-only organizations, other African countries warned about infertility—a hugely stigmatizing condition in many parts of the continent—and other potentially harmful consequences of sexual activity, particularly illegal abortions and HIV. More often, though, African schools condemned out-of-wedlock sex in moral and religious terms. "The biological aim is to present sex within a creative framework and to vindicate the existence of the Omnipotent and Omnipresent," declared a school textbook in Ghana, where sex education was taught via social studies. "The religious

restrictions are strict but they protect the person from a lot of problems." The textbook went on to cite biblical passages indicting fornication, masturbation, and "homosexuality and lesbianism." To be
sure, sexual relations represented a constant temptation for young
people; quoting a popular Ghanaian proverb, the textbook acknowledged that "there is nothing on this earth which is as sweet as
sex." But that was precisely why schools needed to steel adolescents
against it. Sexually active teens "become disrespectful, indulge in
drug abuse, gambling, stealing, truancy, homosexualism, prostitution or promiscuity leading to contraction of HIV/AIDS, abortion,
and death," another textbook warned. A third text admonished students to resist Internet pornography, urging them to "turn to God
in prayer" if they faltered; yet another book condemned parents
who provided condoms to their children as protection against HIV/
AIDS. "Our children are practicing fornication and we are conniv-
ing at this by giving them every encouragement," the book blared.[11]

Elsewhere in the developing world, sex education was less overtly
moralistic. But nobody could miss its overall moral: no sex out of
marriage. Some of the most sexually explicit instruction occurred
in Iran, where curricula emphasized "the consent and readiness of
the woman" and "the enjoyment of each partner." But Iranians also
stressed that such activity must be restricted to marital unions, echoing educators around the Third World. "By the rules of traditional
religion, law and culture, a girl and boy must be a virgin," a 1994
population education curriculum in the Philippines declared. "There
must be no sex aside from your husband and wife." Schools in India
replaced population education with "Adolescent Education," which
provided more information about sex and especially HIV. But it
also warned against "sexual indiscipline," which educators blamed
for "family and social disorganization, crimes, physical and mental
diseases and widespread discontent, cruelties, miseries, and unhap-
piness." In China, where educators had long ignored or resisted sex,
a 1988 national directive on "Adolescence Education" instructed all
schools to address it. Part of the impetus came from China's one-
child policy and its related effort to delay the age of marriage, which
increased the likelihood of sex *before* marriage. The sex education
initiative also aimed to counter "negative Western sexual culture"—

especially film and video—that flooded China in the 1980s and 1990s, as one educator wrote. Reinscribing abstinence and continence, sex education would provide a timely antidote to "the 'sexual freedom' of capitalism," the educator added.[12]

Around the globe, non-Westerners promoted "corrective sex education"—as one Kenyan called it—as a check on the incursions of Western popular culture. The argument echoed early twentieth-century colonial officials, who promoted school-based sex instruction to challenge the sexual suggestiveness of imported books, magazines, and movies. Now the same cudgel was taken up by postcolonial educators, who feared that the "cultural invasion" of the West had "wreaked havoc on impressionable young minds," as one Indian observer wrote; sex education would "clear misconceptions," he added, and revive the "moral fibre of the child." The danger increased with growing access to satellite television and especially the Internet, which made pornography easily available to millions of young people—even in highly monitored societies like China. "The 'Great Firewall' of Internet supervision is failing to serve its primary stated purpose," a Chinese journalist wrote, noting the growing popularity of digital pornography among the young. But the same report underscored the slow development of sex education in Chinese schools, which continued to evade the subject well after they were directed to provide it. Although its advocates promoted sex education as a "fire extinguisher" against the blazes of "sexual liberation"—as another wry Chinese observer noted—many educators and parents rejected it as a symptom of that same libertine disease. Sex education is "a surrender to the dominance of the corrupt, 'promiscuous West,'" a Lebanese critic wrote, noting that consultants from the United Nations had helped devise curricula for the subject.[13]

## A GLOBAL "RIGHT" TO SEX EDUCATION?

Western and international experts often played key roles in the creation of new sex education programs in the developing world. Nongovernmental organizations (NGOs) from the West had worked closely with local allies since the 1940s to seed "grassroots" sex education groups, even as they tried to disguise the Western role in cultivating them. In the era of AIDS, however, foreign NGOs increasingly offered direct aid and advice to state agencies and officials. With a grant from the Carnegie Corporation, for example, the Washington, DC–based Pan American Health Organization began a project in 1985 to develop curricula and train teachers for family life education in four Caribbean countries. Most of all, the project sought "to help children and young people to develop healthy attitudes and values about their sexuality," as a curriculum guide stated. Prefiguring the 1994 Cairo conference, a 1986 teacher workshop highlighted the shared principle that undergirded this goal: sex as a basic right of every person, to determine and develop as he or she wished. "The individual should be able to see clearly what he wants to do and why and what he wants to avoid and why," the Caribbean workshop declared. "Every human being is a unique individual with rights to freedom privacy, personal fulfillment, and the right to be treated as our equal."[14]

This perspective was especially prominent in projects sponsored by Sweden, which became a global emblem of rights-centered sex education during these years. As in the 1960s and 1970s, the Swedish Association for Sexuality Education (RFSU) hosted trainings and study tours that stressed the right of each individual to a "healthy sexual life," as an appreciative Israeli visitor wrote in 1986. But the RFSU also accelerated its overseas activity, spurred by the murder of the Swedish prime minister, Olaf Palme—a longtime advocate for sex education around the world—as well as the centennial of the birth of RFSU founder Elise Ottesen-Jensen. Borrowing Ottesen-Jensen's nickname, the RFSU launched an "Ottar Fund" to promote sex education in Kenya; over the next several years, the group would also start projects in Tanzania, Zambia, and Lithuania. Here it joined hands with the Swedish International Development Cooperation Agency (SIDA), the government's foreign-aid arm, which matched the private funds raised for Kenya and also sponsored sex education projects in Vietnam and Malawi. In the face of AIDS, Swedish educators stressed, it was not enough to change sexual behavior; the key was to alter sexual *attitudes*. "Whole nations have to be reoriented and retrained," a 2004 SIDA publication declared. "Sex is Good—

Sex is Joy—Sex is Fun—Sex is Love—Sex is Power—Protected Sex is Life!"[15]

Other European countries promoted similar projects via their own NGOs and foreign-aid organizations, emphasizing sexual rights for all. Funded mainly by the German Technical Cooperation Agency, a 1996 "African Youth Conference on Sexual Health" in Ghana called for "comprehensive sexuality education at all levels." Again, the focus was on changing values, beliefs, and attitudes—particularly about gender—so that individuals could determine their own sexual destinies. "On our continent and elsewhere, males are taught to be dominant, controlling, and unemotional, while females are encouraged to be subservient, dependent, and emotional," a participant at the conference observed. "Young people have to change their attitudes and perceptions of each other as males and females." By the mid-1990s, "positive, healthy sexuality for all people"—as a Ford Foundation document called it—had become the standard goal for international sex educators around the world. But in the United States, especially, educators who promoted that ideal overseas were forced to acknowledge that their own country fell far short of it; with the rise of abstinence-only education, America had arguably moved in the opposite direction. So Americans often cited a different country—Sweden—as the prime example of proper sex education, which the United States and the rest of humanity would be wise to follow. "Imagine a world," an American sex educator wrote in 1990,

> where: School sexuality education is compulsory. Contraceptives are readily available. Abortion is free until the 18th week of pregnancy. There is a law that states, "Cohabitation between people of the same sex is entirely acceptable from society's point of view." Teenage births and sexually transmitted diseases among teens are rare. Sound too good to be true? That world exists today in Sweden.[16]

The goal of sex education as a human right reached an apotheosis of sorts in 2008, when the International Planned Parenthood Federation issued its "Declaration on Sexual Rights." Developed with funds from the Ford Foundation, the statement said that sexuality was an "integral part of personhood," and that "the pleasure deriving from it is a central aspect of being human." As one observer noted, the idea of negative rights—that is, freedom from discrimination, violence, and coercion—was easily accepted by the IPPF membership. But positive rights—especially "self-expression and the pursuit of pleasure"—were "more contentious," she added. The controversy would spill across front pages of the world the following year, when UNESCO released a draft report of its "International Guidelines on Sexuality Education." Issued first in Sweden in June 2009, the guidelines echoed the now-standard assumptions that "sexuality extends from birth to death"—and that human beings at every age needed proper information to develop and determine it. Included were brief discussions of masturbation, abortion, and contraception, which drew the ire of conservative foes around the world. "This is like telling our kids not to smoke and yet providing them with cigarette filters," a Singaporean critic complained. He went on to blast the "U.S.-centrism" of the UNESCO guidelines, which were authored by two American educators. In the United States, finally, conservatives blasted the guidelines as "culturally insensitive" toward minorities. "We think it's a kind of one-size-fits-all approach that's damaging to cultures, religions and to children," one critic declared. In this new struggle, conservatives would sound the tocsin of multiculturalism and diversity. They would also join hands across cultural differences, creating a powerful new global force against sex education.[17]

## DIVERSITY AND THE GLOBAL RIGHT, I: INTERNAL FERMENT

Since the 1960s, conservatives like Mary Whitehouse had forged alliances with like-minded critics of sex education across the West. But the new right-wing alliance linked activists around the globe, spurred by unpredicted—and unprecedented—population flows between the developing and developed worlds. Until the 1980s, as envious American educators frequently noted, most countries in Europe remained fairly homogenous. So they had the "luxury" of teaching sex education without inciting major parental or political objections, as one reporter wrote in 1987. The comment understated the degree of dissent within purportedly "united" societies such as Denmark, where parental objections to school-based sex instruction had spawned the landmark *Kjeldsen* case in the 1970s. But it also ignored the fact that European societies were becoming immigrant hubs, rendering sex education far more controversial than it had ever been. This trend was also frequently overlooked by American sex educators, who were eager to contrast the heated controversies of US sex education with the supposed consensus that reigned in less diverse—and more "rational"—European countries. Following a 1998 study tour in the Netherlands, France, and Germany, for example, two Americans jealously reported that "religion and politics have little influence on policies related to adolescent sexuality"; indeed, all three countries regarded sex education as a "health issue," not as a political one. The "overwhelming majority of the people" supported comprehensive sexuality education, including frank discussions of sexual practices and the ways to perform them safely.[18]

The report neglected the long history of parental resistance to sex education in France, especially, where a 2002 survey found that students received a grand total of two hours of instruction in the subject per year. Most of all, though, the Americans failed to notice the astounding growth of ethnic, religious, and cultural diversity in the supposedly "monocultural" societies of western Europe. Resistance to sex education was especially sharp inside Great Britain's burgeoning Muslim community, which skyrocketed from half a million in 1981 to nearly three million in 2011. In 1994, the editor of Britain's *Muslim Education Quarterly* blamed sex education on "the decadence of European civilization"; that same year, the Muslim Parliament of Great Britain resolved that Muslim children would be "better off without the sex education presently offered in state schools." Echoing Islamic critics of the 1994 ICPD resolutions in Cairo, British Muslims complained that sex education violated a core principle of their faith: abstinence outside of marriage. "In Islam extra-marital sex is considered to be a dreadful sin," *MEQ* editorialized in 1996. "Adultery is condemned by stoning to death … and fornication among unmarried people is penalized by whipping." Most of all, though, Muslims objected to the allegedly "value-free" philosophy of modern sex education; by privileging "individual choice" about sex, schools insulted religious communities that did not leave such choices to the individual. Here Islamic critics echoed mainstream sex education opponents like Conservative leader Michael Howard, who noted the "natural ties of friendship, common outlook, and values" between Muslim and Christian conservatives.[19]

Elsewhere in the West, too, growing Muslim communities joined hands with white right-wingers to condemn sex education. In Canada, Somalian refugees argued that sex instruction—like school dances and parties—promoted "promiscuity and corruption"; even as she tried to shield her teenaged children from sex, an Iranian immigrant added, their teachers were explaining it in excessive detail. Australian Muslims were outraged to find schools addressing masturbation and oral sex as well as "the etiquette of dating," which violated the Islamic prohibition on unchaperoned male-female contact; Muslims also blasted schools' emphasis on "personal autonomy," which seemed to privilege students' own desires over communal authority. But the sharpest controversies occurred in Continental Europe, where the Muslim population increase was also the fastest. In Sweden, home to a half million Muslims by 2001, critics said that schools were pushing "free sex"; in Norway, where the Islamic population in the capital city of Oslo rose 34 percent in just two years, Muslims blasted sex educators for providing contraceptives as well as lessons on their use; and in Holland, which had reached a rough modus vivendi on sex education in the 1980s, Muslims mounted energetic new challenges to it. "It is ironic that public sex education became acceptable in the Netherlands at the same time as large groups of Muslim immigrants, with ideals of modesty and obligatory innocence, became resident in the country," one observer wrote. They were now making common cause with Pentecostals in Holland's so-called Bible Belt, home to the last native-born holdouts against sex education.[20]

Eastern Europe also witnessed a spike in religious controversy over the subject, finally, spurred less by immigration than by revolution; with the fall of repressive Communist governments, churches were freed to attack school-based sex instruction. To Catholic leaders in Poland, even the bland, conservative sex curriculum instituted under Communism reflected the "moral decay" of "atheist rule." Quoting numerous Vatican attacks on the subject, Catholics succeeded in revoking Poland's compulsory sex education law in 1993; when the subject was reinstituted a few months later, as part of a strict new antiabortion measure, most schools enlisted priests to teach the "Catholic view" of sex. In Russia, meanwhile, leaders in the Orthodox Church stoked nationalist flames against the alleged "western ideological subversion" of sex education. "Children! The enemies of God, enemies of Russia for hundreds of years have tried to conquer our native land with the help of fire and the sword," the Moscow patriarch declared in a 2000 attack on sex education. "Now they want to annihilate our people with the help of depravity." Most critics trained their fire at a pilot project sponsored by UNESCO to assist sex education in a handful of schools; others hinted at darker forces, accusing "Western secret services" of clandestine efforts to impose it. Yet as several Orthodox priests observed in 1996, even Western nations that had long taught sex education were now facing citizen attacks upon it. So while Russians struggled to rebut this foreign menace, they needed to work with foreigners who were menaced by it as well.[21]

## DIVERSITY AND THE GLOBAL RIGHT, II: UNITING ACROSS BORDERS

Indeed, the work was already well underway. In 1995, two sociology professors at Moscow University invited American sex education opponent Allan Carlson to give an address. Joined by an official from the Russian Orthodox Church, the sociologists and Carlson drew up a plan to bring together conservative activists from around the world. The result was the World Congress of Families (WCF), which held its first conference in Prague in 1997. Meeting again in Geneva two years later, the WCF heard a keynote address by a Kenyan author— dressed in "traditional" African garb—who attacked "worldwide dissemination of a culture of pleasure"; and in 2004, when it met in Mexico City, the group received a letter of praise from the US president George W. Bush. It also heard a speech by Wade Horn, Bush's

key advisor on family issues and a leading advocate of abstinence-
only education. Bush gave the burgeoning Global Right a shot
in the arm, declaring that one-third of US foreign assistance for
HIV/AIDS prevention must be devoted to abstinence programs;
so in Uganda, for example, USAID-funded textbooks were revised
to warn readers that condoms could not prevent the transmission of
HIV because they have "small pores that could still allow the virus
through." Teachers trained via the USAID project were instructed
to avoid all mention of condoms, porous or otherwise, which could
only detract from the schools' abstinence-only message.[22]

But the Global Right's sex education efforts did not stem solely
from Bush and US conservative activists, as some liberal critics have
alleged. The movement galvanized several years earlier, at the 1994
ICPD conference in Cairo; shortly after that, according to American scholar Michelle Goldberg, "the culture wars went global as
never before." The following year witnessed the birth of the WCF
and a bitter controversy at the World Conference on Women in
Beijing, where delegates from the Vatican and Muslim countries
joined with American conservatives to attack the conference's resolutions in support of women's rights and sex education. Two years
after that, a United Nations study found that that "ascension of conservative political opinion" was blocking or restricting sex instruction around the world. In 1999, finally, a UN conference marking
the five-year anniversary of the Cairo meeting confirmed that the
Vatican-Muslim coalition was alive and well. "The Holy See is in an
unholy alliance with reactionary forces deep and unholy," a frustrated British delegate complained, "and I speak as a fully signed-up
ethnic Catholic." Although the UN conference upheld earlier resolutions, including the right of adolescents to receive reproductive
information, it also foretold the struggles that lay ahead. "Cairo provided a blueprint. New York, in the end, endorsed it," one journalist
wrote. "But it is clear that the ways and means ... will remain an
ideological battleground."[23]

Two months later, when the World Congress of Families con-
vened in Geneva, founder Allan Carlson vowed to continue the fight.
Drawing members from many world faiths, not just Muslims and
Catholics, the WCF represented "the most orthodox of each group,

people that are least likely to compromise," Carlson observed. Somewhat paradoxically, it would also connect these hardcore believers across their differences—and against sex education. Funded largely by a donation from Family Voice, a Mormon group based in the United States, the WCF conference was entertained by "Ma and Pa" Osmond of the famous Utah musical family; it also heard a keynote address by Cardinal Alfonso López Trujillo, president of the Vatican's Pontifical Council for the Family and a confidant of Pope John Paul II. A similarly diverse set of opponents converged on New York the following year for the five-year anniversary of the Beijing conference, which became yet another opportunity for the Global Right to condemn sex education. "You will work alongside Catholics, Evangelicals, Jews, Muslims, and Mormons," wrote one activist, rallying protesters to the meeting. "We are the children of Abraham arising to fight for faith and family." Although the conference once again confirmed earlier resolutions, no one could miss the resistance. Protesters included well-coiffed Mormon and Catholic women, wearing "Motherhood" buttons on their power suits, as well as a team of long-bearded friars who arranged themselves in the shape of a cross and prayed for the souls of the assembled delegates.[24]

When George W. Bush entered the White House in 2001, then, the Global Right coalition against sex education was already in full flower. Bush's real contribution was to place the American state—and, sometimes, its resources—behind the campaign. Backing off its previous commitments to the Cairo and Beijing accords, the United States stunned the UN's special session on children in 2002 by opposing any reference to "reproductive health services and education" for youth; other opponents of the resolution were Iran, Iraq, Sudan, Libya, Syria, and the Vatican, leading one wag to suggest that America had actually joined forces with the "Axis of Evil" that Bush accused of fomenting terrorism. In a series of statements, US officials confirmed that American aid to sex education overseas would be limited to abstinence-only instruction. It is unclear how much material support the United States provided to such programs during the Bush years. But the embrace of abstinence-only approaches among conservatives in the West certainly struck a chord in the developing world, where like-minded activists cited the alleged evils of so-called comprehensive sex education in Europe and the United States. "Sex education has failed in America," an Indian observed in 2005, "and the way it is imparted there ... could be blamed for heightened sexual activity, abortions and a high rate of sexually transmitted diseases." Another critic was even more blunt. "One should learn from others," he wrote. "The example of western countries in this regard can be an 'eye-opener' for us.... Let us not repeat the same blunder in India, too."[25]

## THE QUESTION OF CHILDHOOD IN A GLOBALIZED WORLD

Most of all, critics around the world condemned sex education for infringing upon the sexual innocence of children. Since the days of Sigmund Freud, of course, educators had deliberated whether, when, and how young people were sexual beings. But the debate accelerated in the era of AIDS, spurred by the astonishing development of new media technologies: videos, satellite television, and the Internet. Each new advance made sexual imagery more readily available to more and more children and adolescents, which in turn underscored the issue of what—and how much—they should know about the subject. By 1999, even a relatively conservative country like Malaysia reported that nearly half of its teenagers had seen a pornographic video. As one educator predicted, adolescent consumption of pornography would become even more common when the "Multimedia Super Corridor"—soon to be renamed the Information Superhighway, and then the Internet—came to Malaysia. She was right. By 2007, an educator in Ghana warned that the widespread growth of computer technology—one of the keys to the country's economic boom—had also increased students' access to pornography, which in turn "leads to a debased conscience and a perverted character"; in the worst cases, the educator added, children became "addicted" to watching it. Almost all of this sexual content—whether on video, television, or the Internet—came from the West, as a Thai parent emphasized. "I blame the media that allows Western culture to reach Thailand," he charged, noting the rise of premarital sexual activity, pregnancy, and AIDS in the country.[26]

To advocates in the world public health community, of course, these developments simply underscored the need for so-called comprehensive sex education. "Suppose if a couple rides a scooter, both need to wear helmets, as both are vulnerable," an Indian newspaper editorialized, pleading for schools to address contraception, abortion, and other sensitive topics. "Sex education is not at all a liberal thought with strains of western permissiveness; rather, it is borne out of necessity, of the changing times we live in." As the comment's defensive tone suggested, however, more and more critics regarded sex education as a reflection of the "permissive" trends it claimed to control. "Far from being an antidote to today's sexual revolution ... sex education programs are a typical and integral part of it," a conservative Catholic activist in the United States wrote in 1996. "Their real aim is to train the kids to 'get with' today's sexual revolution—*times have changed!*—not to warn them against it." Her rhetoric hearkened back to the 1960s, when Western liberals like Mary Calderone cast sex education as a response to new mores, and conservatives blasted it as an embodiment of the same. Now a similar debate played out around the world, with an added tinge of imperialism; instead of simply corrupting children with sexual ideas and impulses, critics charged, sex education also undermined their "native" or "indigenous" traditions. To one Kenyan, sex education violated "authentic African values"; in India, critics derided it as "a conspiracy by Western bodies" against "Indian culture."[27]

In the worst case, its foes said, sex education led to the actual violation of children's bodies. Ironically, sex educators often promoted the subject as a way to stem the widespread problem of sexual abuse by teachers. The issue was especially acute in Africa, where male teachers coerced female students into trading sex for school fees; such abuse was also a common form of AIDS transmission on the continent, where some countries reported that as many as 30 percent of their teachers were HIV-positive. But to critics, sex education was once again part of the problem, not the solution; by requiring teachers and students to discuss sex, it exacerbated the harm it was designed to prevent. "What has actually happened," one African critic charged, "is that sex education ... has opened doors for many teachers to take advantage of the age and vulnerability of girls to abuse them sexually." On the one hand, an Indian women's leader worried, sex education would make children "more curious about sex"; on the other, it would make teachers more cognizant of the students' sexuality. "Students are constantly complaining about sexual exploitation or harassment by teachers," another Indian warned. "If these sex gurus are appointed, then more girls will be exploited." Some teachers who engaged in sexual abuse even went on to blame sex education, confirming critics' worst fears. "After reading about human reproductive organs and sex education, I was enticed to try it out myself," a male Indonesian teacher told police, after confessing to molesting eight boys in his elementary school.[28]

But it was highly unlikely that the teacher's own sexual instruction made any reference to pedophilia or to homosexuality, other than to condemn both of them—and often in the same breath. To be sure, critics in the Third World often charged sex education with spreading homosexuality alongside other alleged "Western" social ills, including child molestation. In the West itself, however, most schools remained silent about same-sex love. In New York, home to one of the world's largest gay communities, school superintendent Joseph Fernandez was forced out of office in 1993 in a flap over a new multicultural curriculum that included several books about gay families; British parents burned a similar book at a 1986 protest, which set the stage for a Parliamentary law two years later barring "promotion of homosexuality" in schools. The very phrase implied that gay orientation was not "natural" to young people; it stemmed instead from some early trauma or seduction, often at the hands of a teacher or other caregiver. Meanwhile, educators in the developing world continued to insist that homosexuality—like sex education—was an evil import from the corrupt West. As one Kenyan critic noted, quoting national independence leader Jomo Kenyatta, "there's no African word for homosexuality"; according to Daniel arap Moi, the country's ruler in the 1990s, the concept was "against African norms and traditions." So it must originate elsewhere, a Botswanan student added. "These things are from alien countries," he flatly declared.[29]

But in a world of enormous diversity inside borders as well as movement across them, it was becoming difficult to determine what was alien—or "native"—to any given country or community. In a televised debate in Lebanon, for example, a psychoanalyst called childhood sexuality a "scientifically proven fact"; but a medical doctor countered that it did not exist, except in "the perverted Freudian mind" of the West. Likewise, some Chinese educators spoke knowingly of child sexual impulses while others dismissed them as a "foreign" idea, again citing the alleged pathologies of Freud. Some Indian observers called sex education "a crime against the younger generation" and a "form of western aggression," while others warned that Indian youth would suffer—from unwanted pregnancy, early marriage, and especially AIDS—unless they received explicit instruction about it. In the increasingly multicultural West, meanwhile, sex educators discovered that many newcomers simply did not share their assumptions about sexuality, childhood, and much else. "Why should parents allow their children to be taught those values which are destructive of their own family and religious beliefs?" a Muslim immigrant in the United Kingdom asked, decrying discussions of out-of-wedlock sex in schools. But it was even worse in Holland, he added, where a relative reported that his school had required him to make sculptures of "body parts" as part of sex education. The curriculum also included frank descriptions of homosexuality, which was *haram* (forbidden) in Islam.[30]

In the Netherlands, however, gay teachers in Muslim neighborhoods had been "forced back into the closet"—as one scholar wrote—after students harassed them. "The greatest challenge in the Netherlands is to make social life more sexually diverse and to ensure access for young people of all ethnic backgrounds and religious persuasions to the erotic worlds they may be interested in," the scholar added. "The challenge is to add multisexuality to multiculturality." But he gave no indication about how Holland could meet this test, especially if the people providing sex education could not express their own sexual thoughts and identities; he simply called upon schoolteachers to celebrate "difference," even as his own evidence illustrated that many of their students balked at the idea. "Not educational policies, but sexual pleasures ought to be a Dutch concert where every bird learns to sing its own song," he intoned. As always, it would be classroom instructors—not scholars, activists, politicians, or school officials—who had to conduct this cacophonous orchestra.

In a rapidly globalizing world, teachers were charged with harmo-
nizing the dissonant tones and rhythms that human beings assigned
to sex.[31]

## IN THE CLASSROOM, I: TEACHERS

Most of all, teachers were supposed to talk with—not just talk at—
their students. Especially after the AIDS crisis began, "discussion"
became the key pedagogical mantra for sex educators around the
world. To be sure, earlier generations of school officials had also
called for "free, frank enquiry and discussion," as a British teachers'
union resolved in 1944; at the 1973 Ford Foundation conference for
African educators in Mali, likewise, organizers sponsored small-
group conversations to dispel teachers' "subconscious fears" about
sex. But the 1980s and 1990s brought a renewed accent on *student*
discussion. It was not enough to give students information about
HIV and other diseases, educators said; schools had to alter their
attitudes, which could only come from free-ranging dialogues about
the context and meaning of sex in their lives. One Swedish foreign-
aid worker even suggested that HIV/AIDS was "a blessing in a ter-
rible disguise," insofar as it would "force people to start speaking
openly about sex and sexuality"; anything less would be a "recipe for
disaster," a Dutch educator added, citing high adolescent AIDS and
pregnancy rates in the United States. In fact, growing numbers of
American teachers were already using "participatory activities" in sex
education, as an impressed Turkish visitor reported in 2000. Upon
his return home, he instituted similar methods in the school where
he worked. "We have joined the universal educational mission of
talking openly abut sexuality in our schools," he declared.[32]

Yet in most classrooms, in Turkey and around the world, the mission went unmet. The teacher acknowledged that his school was
"not typically Turkish"; as a private institution affiliated with a national university, its teachers were better prepared—and its patrons
more open-minded—than the norm. For the most part, teachers
lacked both the pedagogical skills and the parental support to engage in the type of freewheeling, interactive instruction that inter-

national aid organizations envisioned. Even in Sweden, 92 percent of classroom instructors in a 2006 survey reported that they had "little or no preparation" for teaching the subject. Only four of the sex education measures passed by American states in the wake of the AIDS crisis included a teacher-training requirement, yielding "situations where unprepared teachers are, in effect, *sitting ducks* for ... antisexuality education factions which continue to plague this field," as one worried health educator underlined. Both problems were even more acute in the developing world, of course, where many teachers had little formal training of any kind. Teaching a new and unfamiliar subject to classes as large as eighty or one hundred, instructors often had no choice but to engage in the didactic, teacher-centered pedagogy that aid groups and educational experts denounced. "My teacher stands in front of the class and writes on the board what HIV stands for," a South African student reported, "then we repeat." Around the world, an Irish sex educator noted, many teachers knew little else. "They're trained to walk in, stand in front of the class and act like dictators," she lamented. "It's talk and chalk, still."[33]

To be sure, some brave teachers did attempt to provide sex education via games, role-plays, and other interactive methods. But even these isolated efforts often revealed the teachers' lack of preparation for the task. In Uganda, for example, one instructor led a debate about whether men or women spread the HIV virus more often in their society. The correct answer was men, but the male students in the class won the debate "because the women were few and ladies are not assertive," the teacher recalled. A South African teacher leading a discussion about sex asked students to imagine that a girl in the class was sexually active, rendering her the butt of vicious jokes; another student who participated in a role-play about AIDS was nicknamed "Virus," which caused the confused boy to ask a researcher if he was indeed infected with HIV. Other teachers were hampered by shortages of up-to-date textbooks, which in turn highlighted their own ignorance—especially about sexually transmitted diseases. "People like me do not clearly understand HIV/AIDS and the ways of protection," a Vietnamese teacher admitted. "We know using the condom but how to use it we really do not know." In Tanzania, likewise, a teacher trainee frankly admitted that he lacked enough knowledge to teach about AIDS. "Some people say that the origin of HIV is from gays, so it is difficult to convince students on this," he noted, "I do not have answers for my students on this and I will teach as I am taught."[34]

For many teachers, of course, that meant teaching nothing at all; having learned little in school about sex, they avoided the topic whenever they could. In Hong Kong, over half of the schools reported in 1994 that their teachers were unwilling to instruct sex education; in Russia, three-quarters of teachers said that parents—not schools—should provide it. Most of all, teachers around the world feared that parents would revile them for teaching the subject. In the United States, one-third of teachers said their schools were "nervous about possible adverse community reaction" to sex education; meanwhile, roughly one-fifth reported that they had refrained from discussing sensitive topics—including AIDS, abortion, and gays—for fear of provoking such opposition. "Sex education seems to incorporate everything from scientific information about reproduction to child abuse prevention, from abstinence to contraceptive use, from postponing involvement to rational and informed decision making," one educator explained. "Teachers are on the front line, asked to resolve the conflicts. Is it any wonder that teachers feel uncomfortable?" Self-censorship was also common among British teachers, particularly after Parliament issued a ban on "promoting" homosexuality. "It takes not so much courage as madness for a teacher to teach sex education these days," one British instructor surmised. "After every lesson I just cross my fingers—there's bound to be at least one parent who would complain if they knew what was being discussed in class."[35]

But the biggest risks were in the developing world, where teachers were truly caught between a rock and a hard place. If they avoided sexual topics, especially AIDS, they were disobeying national policy and failing to protect young people from a cruel disease, but if they complied, they were corrupting minors with lurid ideas and images. "Anyone who talks about sex is regarded as a bad person," noted a teacher in Lesotho, where a tribal chief disciplined another instructor for addressing the topic. "It is even worse when you talk about sex with children." The problem was especially delicate for female teachers, and even more so if they worked in coeducational settings. "I cannot teach the boys all these things. I feel ashamed," a Bangladeshi teacher worried. "And what will the community say if they find out?" In Kenya, women who taught the subject were called prostitutes; in Nigeria, vulgar; and in Thailand, promiscuous. Yet Thais also complained that women assigned to instruct the subject were nuns or "old maids," who lacked the sexual experience to teach sex education! No matter their gender, people who taught about sex in schools could not avoid questions about their own sexuality. In Dominica as well as Thailand, parents complained that "effeminate" teachers—that is, suspected gay males—were providing sex education. And in classrooms around the world, students wondered what their teachers did outside of class, and with whom. During lessons on HIV/AIDS, African children asked teachers if they had been tested for it; they also inquired about which contraceptive methods the teachers used. Asked if she had tried the female condom, a Botswanan teacher replied that students "should not become personal when we talk about these things."[36]

## IN THE CLASSROOM, II: STUDENTS

But sex *was* personal, in every respect, and the students knew it. Around the world, they complained that teachers and schools avoided or downplayed the subject because of its intimate implications. Even as teachers worried about instructing such a delicate subject, students said they were too worried—and too delicate—in their presentation of it. "If I want to know about sex, I look at magazines or ask my friends," a fifteen-year-old girl in Hong Kong said. "My teachers are too embarrassed to tell me." To be sure, many teachers dutifully explained the merging of sperm and egg and other mechanics of reproduction. "All they told us in school was what goes where," complained a teenager in England, who was also fifteen. "But we wanted to know was how to do it and how to make it nice." Most of all, she explained, adolescents wanted to understand the social dimensions and consequences of sex. Why, for example, was a boy who had sex regarded as a "hero," whereas a girl who did the same thing received a "bad reputation"? But when students raised real-life issues of this sort, they were often met with a steely silence—or, worse, with a harsh reprimand. "Some teachers are conservative and view sexual communication as a disgusting thing," a Thai high school student noted. "This makes us feel uncomfortable when we want to ask questions. Or, sometimes we ask but get very out-of-date answers."[37]

Indeed, students recognized, a good deal of teachers' reticence on sexual matters stemmed from the teachers' ignorance about them. Some instructors in Namibia actually hid when it was time for sex education class, lest the youth discover how little their teachers actually knew. Others tried to disguise their lack of preparation by lashing out. When a Tanzanian boy asked whether you could contract AIDS from a rusted nail, his teacher brusquely replied that he would not answer "stupid questions"; in Nigeria, meanwhile, a student who insisted that the proper name for female external genitalia was "vulva"—not "private parts," as her teacher said—was denounced by the same teacher as a "nasty girl." Students often responded to such ridicule in kind, eroding classroom discipline and making teachers even more reluctant to address sex at all. Understandably, students reserved their greatest derision for teachers who had sex with students—often, in exchange for school fees or other material goods—even as they preached the evils of sex outside of marriage. But any teacher who engaged sexual topics risked losing students' respect, especially in the developing world. "They think they know more than we do," a South African teacher said. "They'll laugh at us and will think we are going insane." Sex education teachers in India faced "teasing" and "absurd questions"; in neighboring Nepal, students mocked a teacher assigned to the subject as "Reproductive Sir." A Chinese cartoon showed a teacher displaying a picture of a condom and declaring, "Today, we are going to talk about sex." But the boy seated in front of him was laughing, symbolizing sex education's ongoing threat to teachers' authority and control.[38]

Nor did the subject typically affect students' academic outcomes or their teachers' professional trajectories, which were mostly determined by the students' performance in "major" classes: science, math, history, and so on. Educators called these disciplines "testing subjects" because they appeared on national standardized examinations, the sine qua non of assessment and advancement in most parts of the globe; by corollary, anything that wasn't tested didn't matter. "What most parents perceive as a good teacher is one who pushes as many students as possible into better and higher high schools," noted an educator in Japan, which put an especially high accent on test performance. "Of course, human sexuality education falls outside the rubric of 'examination hell' study subjects, and it tends to be ignored by both parents and teachers." Realizing that their instructors rarely took sex education seriously, many students followed suit. "Anything that doesn't have an exam at the end of it is going to be a doss as far as students are concerned," an Irish teacher explained, using the local slang (doss) for an easy course. "It's the class where they can go in and chat." As per the mantra of "discussion," of course, many educators *wanted* students to "chat" in the class. So some of them opposed extending standardized tests to sex education, even as they acknowledged students' minimal investment in a nontested subject. If there was a national examination of it, another Irish educator argued, teachers would ignore "personal development" in favor of test preparation. Sex education remained "the only subject that is only about the students," he added, and not about their scores.[39]

But the students were often reluctant to discuss sexual issues in school, just as their teachers were. In the West, some students demanded a more "comprehensive" approach than the clinical, sperm-and-egg lessons in their textbooks. In the United Kingdom, most notably, over two thousand adolescent girls signed a 2006 petition for realistic, dialogue-based sex education. When they got to class, however, students often balked at the same. "I didn't want a teacher thinking, 'Oh, my gosh, she's having sex,'" a Canadian adolescent said, explaining her own reticence during sex education. In the developing world, meanwhile, many students—but especially female ones—were mortified by the entire topic. Girls in Ghana complained that boys teased them during sex education discussions, which diverted the girls from their studies; they preferred to learn the subject at home, where they could "concentrate much more." In Nepal, meanwhile, students of both sexes were embarrassed to mention the subject in the presence of teachers. "They are like our parents, not friends with whom we feel comfortable," one student said. "How can I discuss these things!" The student had stitched together the sex-related pages in the class textbook, so that nobody could see them; teachers reported doing the same in Egypt, to fend off attacks from parents as well as embarrassing questions from students. Most commonly, teachers lacked access to any books or other instructional materials about sex. So they put a few notes on the blackboard and left the room, leaving students to "learn" the subject on their own.[40]

Predictably, most of them learned little to nothing. In Nepal, for example, only 43 percent of high school students could name a contraceptive used by men and just 37 percent could identify one used by women; and while almost all of them had heard of AIDS, just half knew how it was spread. Most alarmingly, 80 percent of Nepali girls were not aware that a person who looked healthy could be infected with HIV and could transmit it to others; in nearby India, meanwhile, 80 percent of young women seeking an abortion did not know that sexual intercourse causes pregnancy. Similarly dismal statistics could be found among adolescents across the developing world, where myths and misunderstandings frequently substituted for sexual knowledge. Sixty percent of fourteen-year-old girls in China believed they could contract AIDS from kissing or from a toilet seat; the same fraction of teenagers in Zimbabwe said that birth control would lead to infertility; and a similar percentage of male Korean university students said that urination after sex could rid them of a sexually transmitted disease. Adolescents in India and Africa said that showering after intercourse would protect them from AIDS; in Taiwan, that they would be infected by sitting next to an HIV-positive person; and in Ghana, that mosquito bites could transmit the virus. To be sure, adolescents in the West continued to maintain their own fair share of myths and falsehoods. Poles believed that masturbation caused physical and mental illness, that vinegar could act as a contraceptive, and that the withdrawal method was 100 percent effective; in Latvia, meanwhile, over one-third of teens said that HIV could be spread via coughs and other airborne routes. And around the world, of course, youth held on to the most timeless sexual folk wisdom of all: you couldn't get pregnant the first time you had intercourse, or during your menstrual period.[41]

To sex educators around the world, of course, these attitudes simply demonstrated the need for *more* sex education. But it was unclear just how much schools could affect student beliefs—and, even more, student behavior—on matters related to sex. Nor was it clear that "discussion" of the subject would yield the salutary consequences—in belief or behavior—that educators imagined. In 1993, the Chilean government received a grant from the Ford Foundation in support of "Conversations," an innovative program to bring students, teachers, parents, and community leaders into dialogue on questions of sex. Instead of creating more space and independence for youth sexuality, however, the discussion galvanized conservatives who wanted to *limit* such autonomy. As a Ford report admitted, "school authorities could not control the process"; once "discussion" began, there was no telling where it would end. To the advocates of "Conversations," young people had a basic human right to make their own sexual choices. But the program's critics said that parents and religious leaders should rightly control these decisions; indeed, it was wrong to assume otherwise. Eventually, under pressure from the Catholic Church, the government was forced to modify the program's emphasis on student decision making with a more didactic approach. "There are values at stake," a leading right-wing politician explained. He was right about that, and about the value-laden dimension of sexual "rights" overall. A century after modern sex education started, its dilemmas remained largely the same: whose values were right for children and adolescents, who would decide, and why.[42]

# A Mirror, Not a Spearhead:
# Sex Education and the Limits of School

In 1976, the British psychologist Rex Stanton Rogers replied to an angry letter from T. J. Proom, who had withdrawn his four daughters from their public school in the south east of England to protest its allegedly "pornographic" sex education lessons. The editor of a recent collection of essays on sex education, Rogers made it clear that he did not share Proom's views on the subject. At the same time, though, Rogers was sympathetic to his plight. "There are arguments both ways about the distribution of power and about parental rights in education," Rogers wrote. "In the specific area of sex education schools vary vastly in policy both over the topic and the role of parents—again I'd hate to say what ought to happen." On other controversial educational questions, Rogers noted, the "conventional answer" was to expose children to a "plurality of opinion" so that they could form their own. But adults were reluctant to do that on matters of sex, Rogers told Proom, because the stakes were so high:

A lot of sex educators have a "health" orientation. They sex educate for the same reasons that others tell us to wear seat-belts, give up smoking or get our children vaccinated/immunized. In the process a few people die in car fires, survive to 90 smoking like chimneys, or get brain damage from vaccines. But many more forms of suffering are avoided—or so the argument goes. You are among the "unlucky" in this argument. Your children may have been "saved" from unwanted pregnancies, sexual "guilt," etc. There isn't much direct evidence that this is true, in the end sex educators are working on hypotheses. If they are wrong they will get hammered like the planners that put people into high-rise, if they are right they will be hailed as new Pasteurs.[1]

Rogers's remarks neatly encapsulated both the broad ambitions and the dashed hopes of sex education in the modern world. From the dawn of the twentieth century, advocates imagined that schools could transform the sexual lives of young people. Some of these visions focused on changing their behavior, to minimize "unwanted pregnancies" and especially sexually transmitted diseases; others emphasized changing their minds, so they could be liberated from "guilt" and other unhealthy ideas. But sex educators were stymied at every turn by dissident parents and communities, who wanted schools to teach *their* ideas about sex—or nothing at all. "We are not against sex education—quite the reverse—but we do not want modesty, chastity, and fidelity to be undermined in our child," T. J. Proom wrote, in a revealing follow-up letter to Rex Rogers. Nor did he want schools to present a wide array of "opinions" on the subject, as Rogers had suggested. "How do those who believe in reticence counteract the effect of those who impose pornography on children?" Proom asked. "Surely to subject children to a Babel of dissonant voices is to invite cynicism and a myriad of excuses for self-indulgence." As he correctly sensed, even a curriculum oriented toward sexual autonomy and decision making expressed a set of values, about sex and reason and—most of all—about individuality. Whether sex education spawned sexual "self-indulgence" or not, there was no mistaking its focus on the self.[2]

That emphasis echoed the proclaimed values of state-run schools, of course: order, rationality, and individuality. In the twentieth century, for the first time in human history, schools became truly universal institutions; most of the world's people entered their doors, for at least a part of their lives. And wherever they appeared, schools ostensibly taught people to view themselves as rational and purposeful actors who can make their own choices and construct their own lives.[3] More often than not, as many chroniclers have noted, the day-to-day demands and constraints of schools inhibited or squashed this individualist ideal. But as the history of sex education reminds us, the ideal is hardly shared; instead, it is one of the most hotly contested questions of modernity. Examine almost any sex education document—in almost any part of the globe—and you will find statements exalting the conscience and choice of the rational individual, just as you do in the rest of the curriculum. Sex is a highly personal matter, the story goes, so schools should equip each person with the skills and knowledge to navigate its perilous shores. To many people around the world, however, that idea offends *their* conscience; they want schools to map proper sexual behavior, not to liberate individuals to explore it on their own. "The scheme took what it called 'reason' as the basis for morality," a British conservative wrote in 1972, condemning a new sex education project. "What is called didactic teaching about right and wrong was to be abandoned in favour of the child's 'self-evolved solutions.'" The writer's use of quotation marks punctuated his own skepticism. When it came to sex, many adults believed, there was no good reason to let children come to their own reasoned conclusions.[4]

Nor did they believe that expert authority should trump their own, a central theme of campaigns against sex education—and, more largely, of political conservatism—in the modern West. Since the 1970s, sex educators have linked their opponents to antievolutionists and (more recently) to climate-change deniers; in each case, the argument goes, the right wing mobilized its populist legions to counter established scientific truth. But sex education simply lacks the scientific basis or consensus that marks topics like evolution and human-made climate change. To be clear, no credible research has ever sustained the conservative claim that sex education makes young people more likely to engage in sex. Yet there is also scant evidence to suggest that it affects teen pregnancy or venereal disease rates, either, as pioneering American sex researcher William H. Masters acknowledged in a 1968 interview with *Playboy* magazine. "We have no scientific knowledge as to whether it's worth a damn," admitted Masters, whose studies (with Virginia Johnson) of "human sexual response" made them both household names. "There are a lot of people who climb on the sex education bandwagon and say it's great. But somebody is going to take the time and effort to find out whether there is any real value in the entire concept of formally disseminating sexual information to youngsters." Since then, scholars around the world have struggled in vain to show *any* significant influence of sex education upon youth sexual behavior. As a British scholar observed in 2009, the three European countries with the lowest teen pregnancy rates—Italy, Switzerland, and the Netherlands—all took very different tacks on sex education. Italy's approach was particularly "haphazard," the scholar noted: sex education provision was "sparse," parents retained the right to withdraw their children from it, and one survey showed that half of eleven- to fourteen-year-olds believed they could acquire AIDS from a toilet seat. Yet the incidence of teen pregnancy was about the same as in Holland, where youth received much more extensive sexual instruction at school.[5]

Given how sporadically most countries taught sex education, we should not be surprised by the lack of strong data about its behavioral effects. Nor was it clear whether the subject altered individual attitudes, another avowed goal of some—not all—sex educators. This ambition sat uneasily next to educators' repeated claim that they merely sought to disseminate "science" or knowledge, not to change children's minds. But they inevitably taught values, too, whether they admitted it or not. "Most forms of education (like teaching French rather than Cantonese) involve value judgments about what is useful to the child, good for society, and so on," Rex Rogers noted in his letter to T. J. Proom. "Even an apparently neutral subject like mathematics has this characteristic." There was nothing even nominally neutral about sex education, of course, which addressed one of the most intimate dimensions of the human experience. Some educators stressed changed values as a route to improved behavior, insisting that youth would never become sexually continent or responsible until they altered their confused and repressed attitudes about sex. To others, however, fighting repression was an end in itself. "I want these children to learn to experience pleasure without feeling guilty," declared the radical Brazilian educator Paulo Freire, praising a São Paulo pilot project in sex education in the 1980s. "School has to sweep away taboos and sexual prejudices because sex is one of the most important sources of pleasure known to human beings."[6]

But many human beings did not see it that way, in Brazil or around the world. For some, the goal of individual freedom insulted religious or communal prescriptions about sex and sexuality; to others, it violated their own individual rights to raise children as they saw fit. Over the past three decades, as a host of scholars have documented, human rights have become a kind of lingua franca for the modern world. Sex education supporters frequently employed human-rights language, insisting that children's rights—as codified in a growing series of international treaties and conventions—guaranteed the right to receive sexual knowledge and information. But opponents invoked the rights of *parents*, especially as encoded in what Michael Ignatieff has called the "sacred text" of the twentieth century: the 1945 Universal Declaration of Human Rights. "Parents have a prior right to choose the kind of education that shall be given to their children," the declaration states. It also calls the family "the natural and fundamental group of society," entitled to "protection by society and the State." As the 1976 *Kjeldsen* case in Europe illustrated, conservative efforts to harness human rights principles against sex education sometimes fell short of their mark. But they also spoke to the "globalization of the 'family values' movement," as an Australian observer noted in 2007. The first "family values" campaign came out of the American New Right, of course. But it had become thoroughly internationalized, drawing on worldwide networks—and, increasingly, on worldwide human rights doctrines—to mount a global attack on sex education.[7]

When it came to sex, however, the most influential global force was never the school. Starting with magazines and films and culminating in television and the Internet, mass media had a much more profound effect on children's sexuality in the twentieth century than any set of formal educational institutions. Indeed, sex educators often designed their curricula as an explicit challenge to crass media images and ideologies. To an American educator, writing in 1914, "youth is subjected by our civilization [to] aggressive sex stimuli and suggestiveness oozing from every pore"; a French physician worried in 1959 that "theater, film, pornographic publications and posters ... cause a state of sexual over-excitement," which he compared to "a poisoning gas"; and in 1971, a Japanese educator warned that her country was "flooded" with obscenity and pornography from overseas. "Much of what is produced in the mass media today is 'Sexy' in the extreme," she complained. "How best can it be counteracted?" The question became even more urgent in the era of the Internet, when millions of sexual images could be accessed with a few clicks of a mouse. In China, the popularity of Japanese porn stars—and the weakness of the Chinese "Great Firewall," which technology-savvy adolescents could scale with ease—prompted officials to insert sex education for the first time into the national health curriculum. As a New Zealand journalist surmised, after observing several sex education classes in 2006, "schools are being forced to play catch-up with popular culture."[8]

*Could* schools ever "catch up"? History suggested the opposite: try as they might, schools would always be a step—or three—behind the sexual curve. "A 12-minute filmstrip is hardly a match for two years of 'R'-rated films every weekend," wrote Scott Thomson, director of an American principals' association, in a bold 1981 article. "A few chapters of a textbook on marriage and family cannot really compete with *Hustler, Oui* and *Playgirl* and Masters and Johnson. The school marching band plays 'Stars and Stripes Forever' but the students listen to 'Afternoon Delight' on their cassettes." Indeed, Thomson continued, "schools are a puny David without even a sling-shot against the media Goliath." But they pretended that they could slay the giant, nevertheless, perpetuating a kind of "educational fraud" on the entire nation. "As long as one set of values is taught in the larger society, it is absurd to ask schools to neutralize those values in a few weeks of classroom instruction," Thomson concluded. "Even more absurd, however, is the expectation that any significant outcomes will come from that instruction." He was probably right. Even in Sweden, as a 1969 observer wrote, sex education "tended to follow rather than lead social trends"; two decades later, Sweden's leading sex educator agreed. "Sex education will not be really accepted before a profound change of attitudes in broad groups of the society has occurred," wrote Carl Gustaf Boethius, the longtime head of the Swedish Association for Sexuality Education, summarizing a set of reports about the subject in different European countries. "Things must happen first in society and only then in schools.... The school is not a spear head, it is a mirror."[9]

That is not to say that schools have failed entirely in this realm. Surely, across the twentieth century, many teachers and schools have helped children gain more insight, understanding, and knowledge about their sexual lives and selves. When he taught high school social studies in Colorado in the 1930s, for example, the future bestselling author James A. Michener designed and cotaught a pilot sex education class with a science instructor. Boldly mixing boys and girls in the same classroom, the freewheeling course covered such controversial subjects as birth control and masturbation. Students raved about the class, and—most notably—not a single parent complained. "The bogey-man of parental interference ... is grossly over-exaggerated," Michener wrote. "We believe that most American communities will eventually react in this same way if sane teachers teach those fields." He was wrong, obviously, about America and the rest of the world. Over the past hundred years, there is probably no subject that has posed greater headaches to teachers than sex education. However "sane," to borrow Michener's dated metaphor, some teachers obviously lacked the skills and preparation to teach the subject; others were hampered by community pressures from every side, which accelerated—not abated—after Michener's time. But they were most of all stymied by sex itself, which resisted most efforts to rationalize and systematize it in the modern school. "To the theoretical teacher eager to reform the world on paper the introduction of sexual education into the curriculum of our schools may appear a very simple step," a British author and former headmistress wrote in 1920. "Are we really being honest with ourselves? For in sex we have yet learnt very little, and this is true even of the wisest among us; and indeed, I doubt sometimes if we can ever learn very much except each one of us for ourselves out of our own experience."[10]

"Experience" was a hallmark of twentieth-century educational reform movements around the world, which sought to make schools more "practical" and relevant to students' day-to-day lives. Sex educators seized eagerly on this idiom: like health and vocational classes, the argument went, instruction about sex would prepare young people for real-world activities and decisions. "In this day of progressive education," an American school official wrote in 1939, "when schools teach children … habits of healthful living; what foods they should eat; how to use carpenters' tools; how to cook, sew, manage a household, dress, and prepare themselves to earn a living, it is hard to believe that our boys and girls are still left to acquire sex instruction in the gutter." He should not have been surprised. For millions of people around the world, the so-called 3 R's—reading, writing, and arithmetic—remained the sine qua non of proper education; "practical" or "experiential" learning was second rate or superfluous, best obtained outside of schools rather than within them. It also seemed especially pernicious in the realm of sex, where it conjured precisely the behaviors that most adults wanted to prevent. "Modern educational experts believe in 'learning by doing,'" an American conservative wrote in 1970, "and we all know what explorations can take place … stimulated by film strips and class discussions about sex." That same year, but an ocean away, a British critic issued a nearly identical warning. "Children are always eager to put their knowledge into practice," he wrote. "Where would their experimentation end?" Rooted in the modern doctrine of learning via experience, sex education alienated parents and other citizens who did not want students to experience sex.[11]

For the world's children, for the past hundred years, most of this experience has taken place far from the classroom. The rise of near-universal education in the late twentieth century made schools into sexual spaces; indeed, sex education was often designed to purify their erotic atmosphere. But children learned much more about sex from their peers—and from mass media—than they did from teachers, parents, or any other authority figures. In a much-told joke from Mexico, a father informs his son that they need to have a "frank, heart-to-heart talk" about sex. "OK, Dad, what is it you want to know?" the son replies. The joke was on adults, of course, who like to pretend that their children are sexual innocents. But so do schools, which have never influenced sexual knowledge or behavior to the extent that they wanted, or believed. In Sweden, another popular joke described an eight-year-old boy whose teacher announces that his class is about to receive its first sex education lesson. "Miss, couldn't

we who already know how to fuck be allowed to go out to play football?" the boy asks. For the most part, on matters of sex, schools
"taught" the world's students what they already knew. Sex education
was neither a modernist monstrosity like high-rise public housing
nor a "new Pasteur" of scientific triumph, to quote Rex Rogers. It
was instead a mirror, reflecting all the flux and diversity—and the
confusion and instability—of sex and youth in our globalized world.[12]

# NOTES

## INTRODUCTION

1. Ellen Key, *The Century of the Child* (1900; New York: G. P. Putnam, 1909), 204, 243–44.

2. John W. Meyer et al., "The World's Educational Revolution, 1950–1970," *Sociology of Education* 50, no. 4 (1977): 244; John W. Meyer, Francisco O. Ramirez, and Yasemin Nuhoglu Soysal, "World Expansion of Mass Education, 1870–1980," *Sociology of Education* 65, no. 2 (1992): 128.

3. Key, *Century of the Child*, 7; Dagmar Herzog, *Sexuality in Europe: A Twentieth-Century History* (Cambridge: Cambridge University Press, 2011), 2. Over three decades ago, Michel Foucault rejected the idea that modernity "liberated" individuals to develop their own sexual beings; instead, via a "veritable discursive explosion," it inscribed sexuality as a central *part* of their beings. I hope it is possible to acknowledge the power of this insight—which calls our attention to what was liberated, and what was not—while still insisting upon important real changes in the way that people thought, acted, and felt across the twentieth century. Michel Foucault, *The History of Sexuality*, vol. 1, *An Introduction* (New York: Vintage, 1978), 17; Anthony Giddens, *The Transformation of Intimacy: Sexuality, Love, and Eroticism in Modern Societies* (Stanford, CA: Stanford University Press, 1992), esp. 27–28.

4. Key, *Century of the Child*, 11.

5. S. van der Doef, "Why Is Sex Education Necessary?" in *Contraceptive Choices and Realities: Proceedings of the 5th Congress of the European Society of Contraception*, ed. R. H. W. van Lunsen, V. Unzeitig, and G. Creatsas (London: Parthenon, 2000), 56. The subject of sex education has recently received a great deal of careful attention from historians, whose work I have liberally quoted and cited in the pages that follow. But most of their interpretations remain firmly rooted in one nation or another; by contrast, I have tried to tell a story that takes nations seriously while also emphasizing transnational forces, connections, and tensions. An excellent set of essays

about sex education in a dozen European countries, by the best scholars of the same, is Lutz D. H. Sauerteig and Roger Davidson, eds., *Shaping Sexual Knowledge: A Cultural History of Sex Education in Twentieth Century Europe* (London: Routledge, 2008). The standard history of sex education in the United States is still Jeffrey P. Moran, *Teaching Sex: The Shaping of Adolescence in the 20th Century* (Cambridge, MA: Harvard University Press, 2000); more recently, see Susan K. Freeman, *Sex Goes to School: Girls and Sex Education before the 1960s* (Urbana: University of Illinois Press, 2008); Robin E. Jensen, *Dirty Words: The Rhetoric of Public Sex Education, 1870–1924* (Urbana: University of Illinois Press, 2010); and Alexandra M. Lord, *Condom Nation: The U.S. Government's Sex Education Campaign from World War I to the Internet* (Baltimore: Johns Hopkins University Press, 2010). Most other nations still lack full-length historical monographs devoted to their experiences with sex education. But I have benefited especially from the country-specific and comparative insights about the subject in Igor S. Kon, *The Sexual Revolution in Russia: From the Age of the Czars to Today* (New York: Free Press, 1995); Dagmar Herzog, *Sex after Fascism: Memory and Morality in Twentieth-Century Germany* (Princeton, NJ: Princeton University Press, 1995); Roy Porter and Lesley Hall, *The Facts of Life: The Creation of Sexual Knowledge in Britain, 1650–1950* (New Haven, CT: Yale University Press, 1995); Dennis Altman, *Global Sex* (Chicago: University of Chicago Press, 2002); Sabine Frühstück, *Colonizing Sex: Sexology and Social Control in Modern Japan* (Berkeley: University of California Press, 2003); Claudia Nelson and Michelle H. Martin, eds., *Sexual Pedagogies: Sex Education in Britain, Australia, and America, 1879–2000* (New York: Palgrave, 2004); Matthew Guttmann, *Fixing Men: Sex, Birth Control, and AIDS in Mexico* (Berkeley: University of California Press, 2007); Kristen Luker, *When Sex Goes to School* (New York: W. W. Norton, 2007); Matthew Connelly, *Fatal Misconception: The Struggle to Control World Population* (Cambridge, MA: Harvard University Press, 2008); Amy T. Schalet, *Not Under My Roof: Parents, Teens, and the Culture of Sex* (Chicago: University of Chicago Press, 2011); Nancy Kendall, *The Sex Education Debates* (Chicago: University of Chicago Press, 2012); and Colleen McLaughlin et al., *Old Enough to Know: Consulting Children about Sex and AIDS Education in Africa* (Cape Town: HSRC Press, 2012).

6. Hans L. Zetterberg, *Sexual Life in Sweden*, trans. Graham Fennell (New Brunswick, NJ: Transaction, 2002), 162; "Swedes to Scan Teaching on Sex," *New York Times*, April 26, 1964, p. 34; J. Robert Moskin, "Sweden's New Battle over Sex," *Look*, November 15, 1966, "Sex Education (Sweden)" file, Vertical Files Collection, Kinsey Institute Archives, Bloomington, Indiana; Stine H. Bang Svendsen, "Elusive Acts: Pleasure and Politics in Norwegian Sex Education," *Sex Education* 12, no. 4 (2012): 400; "No Sex Please, We're in School," *South China Morning Post*, February 10, 2001, p. 7; Corinne Nativel, "Teen Pregnancy and Reproductive Policies in France,"

in *When Children Become Parents: Welfare State Responses to Teenage Pregnancy*, ed. Anne Dagueree and Corinne Nativel (Bristol, UK: Policy Press, 2006), 125; "Chile's Precocious Teens Cast Aside Sexual Taboos," *International Herald Tribune*, September 13, 2008, p. 1; Alan Guttmacher Institute, "Sex Education Widespread in the United States but Teachers Say, 'Too Little, Too Late,'" press release, May 2, 1989, "AIDS Education" folder, box 101, AIDS History Project Collection, One: National Gay and Lesbian Archives, Los Angeles; "A Sexual Timebomb," *Guardian*, June 9, 1992, p. 60; "Population, Sex Teaching Found Not Widespread," *International Family Planning Digest* 2, no. 1 (1976): 7.

7. Jane Addams, *A New Conscience and an Ancient Evil* (New York: Macmillan, 1912), 102–3; Pierre Pradervand, "Excerpts from the Letters of Pierre Pradervand from West Africa, 1971–1973, Regarding Sex Education, Local Beliefs, Western Approaches" (MS, n.d. [1973]), p. 10, General Collection, Kinsey Institute Archives.

8. Barbara Lombardi, Dina Lombardi, and Francisco Masellis, "Sexual Education in Italian Schools: Past, Present, and Future," in *Medical Sexology: The Third International Congress*, ed. Romano Forleo and Willy Pasina (Amsterdam: Elsevier, 1980), 532; "Social Hygiene Bulletin," *Journal of Social Hygiene* 9, no. 3 (1923): 183; Mrs. C. Neville Rolfe, "The Social Hygiene Delegation to India," *Health and Empire* 2, no. 2 (1927): 79; Dr. J. Sandell, Dr. J. S. Mathur, and Dr. B. K. Trivedi, "Sex Education and the National Family Planning Programme," *Journal of Family Welfare* (India) 22, no. 4 (1976): 62.

9. Lena Lennerhed, "Taking the Middle Way: Sex Education Debates in Sweden in the Early Twentieth Century," in Sauerteig and Davidson, *Shaping Sexual Knowledge*, 57; *Responsible Parenthood and Family Life Education. Proceedings of the Seminar of the Western Pacific Region of the International Planned Parenthood Federation* (Hong Kong: International Planned Parenthood Federation, 1972), 35; Rebecca Firestone, "Mapping the Policy Environment for Sexuality Education in Thailand" (MPH thesis, University of Washington, 2003), 11; UNICEF, *The Situation of Families and Children Affected by HIV/AIDS in Viet Nam: A National Overview* (Hanoi: n.p., 2005), 40, National Library of Vietnam, Hanoi; Agnes Repplier, "The Repeal of Reticence" [1914] in *Counter-Currents* (Freeport, NY: Books for Libraries Press, 1971), 140–41, 145; "Note and Comment," *Social Hygiene* 6, no. 3 (1920): 434–35; Sherry Martschink, "Somewhere, Somehow, Children Must Get an Education in Sex," *News and Courier* (Charleston, South Carolina), August 2, 1986, "South Carolina Sex Education Clippings" folder, box 250, James T. Sears Papers, Rare Book, Manuscript and Special Collections Library, Duke University, Durham, North Carolina.

10. *Report by Miss Martindale on Some Papers on Sex Instruction for Children and Adolescents Submitted from Six Countries to the Medical Women's*

*International Association for the Paris Congress* (Paris: Imprimerie George Petit, 1929), 5–6, folder SA/MWF/N.1/12, Medical Women's Federation Papers, Wellcome Library, London; Joseph S. Darden Jr., "Mandated Family Life Education: A Rose Is a Rose Is a Rose Is a Rose," *Journal of School Health* 51, no. 4 (1981): 294; "AIDS Lecture, January 23, 1987" (MS, 1987), folder 33, box 148, C. Everett Koop Papers, National Library of Medicine, Bethesda, Maryland; *Review of Sex, Relationships, and HIV Education in Schools* (n.p.: UNESCO, 2007), 9.

11. Mikolaj Kozakiewicz and Norman Rea, *A Survey on the Status of Sex Education in European Member Countries* (London: International Planned Parenthood Federation, 1975), 22; T. A. Storey, "General Summary of the Work of the United States Interdepartmental Social Hygiene Board" (MS, n.d. [1919]), p. 16, "Exec Secy: Gen'l Cor. File 1919–21" folder, box 4, General Records of the Interdepartmental Social Hygiene Board, 1918–1921, Records of the Public Health Service, Record Group 90, National Archives II, College Park, Maryland; Agneta Nelson and Birgitta Sandstrom, *"The Best Thing Is Getting to Know What Others Think": A Summary of Quality Assessment of Sex Education in 80 Swedish Schools* (Stockholm: National Agency for Education, 2001), 10; Pam Alldred and Miriam E. David, *Get Real about Sex: The Politics and Practice of Sex Education* (Berkshire, UK: Open University Press, 2007), 57.

12. Howard S. Hoyman, "Sweden's Experiment in Human Sexuality and Sex Education," *Journal of School Health* 41 (April 1971): 177; "The Role of Parents in Sex Education," in *Second Seminar on Sex Education and Social Development in Sweden, Latin America, and the Caribbean, April 1972*, ed. Margareta Holmstedt (Stockholm: Swedish International Development Authority, 1974), 96; "Sex Education—Whose Responsibility?" *BBC News*, March 22, 2000, www.bbc.com/news/ (accessed January 2, 2013); Paula Maycock et al., *Relationships and Sexuality Education (RSE) in the Context of Social, Personal, and Health Education (SPHE)* (Dublin: Crisis Pregnancy Center, 2007), 138.

13. Wolf Bleek, *Sexual Relationships and Birth Control in Ghana: A Case Study of a Rural Town* (Amsterdam: Universiteit van Amsterdam, 1976), 56; McLaughlin et al., *Old Enough to Know*, 72.

14. Roland Robertson, *Globalization* (London: Sage, 1992), 8; Chang Ching-Sheng, *Sex Histories: China's First Modern Treatise on Sex Education*, trans. Howard S. Levy (Yokohama: n.p., 1967), 1–4; "News from Other Countries," *Journal of Social Hygiene* 19, no. 5 (1933): 287; Thomas Dawes Eliot, "Welfare Fares Well: A Chronicle from Norway," *Social Service Review* 26, no. 1 (1952): 46; "Slant in Sex Education," *New York Times*, November 17, 1955, p. 43.

15. Irving R. Dickman, *Winning the Battle for Sex Education* (New York: Sex Information and Education Council of the United States, 1982), 42; "Statement by Rev. W. B. Woodard, General Secretary of the American

Council of Christian Churches, before a Committee Appointed by the San Marino, California School Board" (MS, n.d. [1969]), folder 3752:9, Department of Education Records, California State Archives, Sacramento, California; Paromita Chakravarti, "The Sex Education Debates: Teaching 'Life Style' in West Bengal, India," *Sex Education* 11, no. 4 (2011): 389; Igor S. Kon, "Russia," in *The Continuum Complete International Encyclopedia of Sexuality*, ed. Robert T. Francoeur and Raymond J. Noonan (Bloomington, IN: Kinsey Institute, 2004), online edition; Igor S. Kon, "Sexual Culture and Politics in Contemporary Russia," in *Sexuality and Gender in Postcommunist Eastern Europe and Russia*, ed. Aleksandar Stulhofer and Theo Sandfort (New York: Haworth Press, 2005), 119–20; Jay Friedman, "Cross-Cultural Perspectives on Sexuality Education," *SIECUS Report* 20, no. 6 (1992): 9.

16. Odette Leather, "Think about Those Sex Talks," *Sunday News* (Auckland, New Zealand), November 4, 1973, "MW 1973 visit" folder, box 128, section 1, Papers of the National Viewers' and Listeners' Association, Albert Sloman Library, University of Essex, Colchester, UK; John MacInnes and Julio Perez Diaz, "Transformations in the World's Population: The Demographic Revolution," in *The Routledge International Handbook of Globalization Studies*, ed. Bryan S. Turner (New York: Routledge, 2010), 154; Marcelo Suarez-Orozco and Carola Suarez-Orozco, "Globalization, Immigration, and Education: Recent U.S. Trends," in *Globalization and Education*, ed. Marcelo Sánchez Sorondo et al. (Berlin and New York: Walter de Gruyter, 2007), 96.

17. Michel As-Sabaa, "Our Contribution to Ideological Globalization," *As-Safir Daily*, July 22, 1999, quoted in Azzah Shararah Baydoun, "Sex Education in Lebanon: Between Secular and Religious Discourses," in *Deconstructing Sexuality in the Middle East*, ed. Pinar Ilkkaracan (Hampshire, UK: Ashgate, 2008), 89; "That's Not Faith, That's Provocation: Catholics and Muslims Are Uniting in a Pernicious New Alliance," *Guardian*, November 12, 1999, p. 22; Shaikh Abdul Mabud, "An Islamic View of Sex Education," in *Sex Education and Religion*, ed. Michael J. Reiss and Shaikh Abdul Mabud (Cambridge: Islamic Academy, 1998), 100.

18. G. Stanley Hall, *Educational Problems*, vol. 1 (New York: D. Appleton, 1911), 390; Marcel Fournier, *Émile Durkheim: A Biography*, trans. David Macey (2007; Cambridge: Polity, 2013), 585–86.

## CHAPTER ONE: THE BIRDS, THE BEES, AND THE GLOBE

1. Mrs. C. Neville Rolfe to Secretary, Advisory Committee for the Suppression of Traffic in Women and for the Protection of Children, February 9, 1928; "Outline of a Scheme of Enquiry into Standards of Sex Conduct

in Relation to Biological Education and Adolescent Recreation. Scope and Method of Enquiry" (MS, 1928), both in file ANVA/4/104 10B, box FL098, National Vigilance Association Papers, Women's Library, London; Dame Katherine Furse, "Part of the Social Work of the League of Nations," *Health and Empire* 3, no. 2 (1928): 134.

2. Furse, "Part of the Social Work of the League of Nations," 134–37; F. Sempkins, "Extract of Letter to Dr. Ninck" (MS, March 18, 1929); Sempkins to M. Brifaut, May 28, 1929, both in file ANVA/4/104 10B, box FL098, National Vigilance Association Papers.

3. G. Bernard Shaw, "The Need for Expert Opinion in Sexual Reform," *Journal of Sex Education* 2, no. 1 (1949): 25–26.

4. On these comparative points, see especially Tracy L. Steffes, *School, Society, and State: A New Education to Govern Modern America, 1890–1940* (Chicago: University of Chicago Press, 2012).

5. "The Educational Motion Picture," *Journal of Social Hygiene* 10 (February 1924): 107.

6. Jay Cassel, *The Secret Plague: Venereal Disease in Canada, 1838–1939* (Toronto: University of Toronto Press, 1987), 107, 109; Upton Sinclair and Eugène Brieux, *Damaged Goods* (Project Gutenberg, EBook 1157, 2008 [1913]), http://www.gutenberg.org/files/1157/1157-h/1157-h.htm. The Sinclair/Brieux book was a novelized version of the play, published for American audiences, but the themes hewed closely to the original.

7. Jennifer Burek Pierce, *What Adolescents Ought to Know: Sexual Health Texts in Early Twentieth-Century America* (Amherst: University of Massachusetts Press, 2011), 65; Cassel, *Secret Plague*, 110–11.

8. Peter Gay, *The Bourgeois Experience: Victoria to Freud*, vol. 1 (New York: Oxford University Press, 1984), 319; Jeffrey P. Moran, *Teaching Sex: The Shaping of Adolescence in the 20th Century* (Cambridge, MA: Harvard University Press, 2000), 32; *Health Education and the Preparation of Teachers* (New York: Child Health Organization, 1922), folder 3, box 125, White House Conference on Child Health and Protection Papers, Hoover Institution Archives, Stanford, California.

9. See, e.g., "Sex Education Movement in New Zealand," *Journal of Social Hygiene* 9, no. 3 (1923): 182.

10. Testimony of Miss Norah March, October 1, 1920, in National Birth-Rate Commission, *Youth and the Race* (London: Kegan Paul, 1923), 31.

11. "Abstracts of Periodical Literature," *Journal of Social Hygiene* 7, no. 4 (1921): 471; Newell W. Edson, "Some Facts Regarding Sex Instruction in the High Schools of the United States," *School Review* 29, no. 8 (1921): 594.

12. Steffes, *School, Society, and State*, 201; W. S. Richardson to John D. Rockefeller Jr., November 6, 1918, folder 121, box 15, series K; Rockefeller to Julia Richman, February 19, 1912; Rockefeller to Richman, February 1, 1912, both in folder 81, box 10, series O, all in Record Group 2, Rockefeller Family Archives, Rockefeller Archive Center, Tarrytown, New York.

13. Allan M. Brandt, *No Magic Bullet: A Social History of Venereal Disease in the United States since 1880* (1985; New York: Oxford University Press, 1987), 38–39, 48; M. J. Exner to John D. Rockefeller, December 19, 1918, folder 250, box 24, series R, Record Group 2, Rockefeller Family Archives.

14. Jonathan Zimmerman, "Uncle Sam at the Blackboard: The Federal Government and Education," in *To Promote the General Welfare: The Case for Big Government*, ed. Steven Conn (New York: Oxford University Press, 2012), 44–64; T. A. Storey, "The Work of the United States Interdepartmental Social Hygiene Board," *Social Hygiene* 5, no. 4 (1919): 443, 454–55; Thomas A. Storey, "A Summary of the Work for the United States Interdepartmental Social Hygiene Board, 1919–1920," *Social Hygiene* 7, no. 1 (1921): 64; Thomas C. Stowell to Walter Clarke, "Exec Secy: Gen'l Cor. File 1919–21" folder, box 4, General Records of the Interdepartmental Social Hygiene Board, 1918–1921, Records of the Public Health Service, Record Group 90, National Archives II, College Park, Maryland; "Social Hygiene Bulletin," *Journal of Social Hygiene* 11, no. 1 (1925): 52–53.

15. Otto May, *British Social Hygiene Council, Its Origin and Development* (Shrewsbury, UK: Wilding and Sons, n.d. [1947]), 4, 1, "Great Britain Ephemera (British Social Hygiene Council)" folder, box 203, American Social Health Association Papers (hereafter "ASHA Papers"), Social Welfare History Archives, University of Minnesota, Minneapolis; Lesley A. Hall, "Birds, Bees, and General Embarrassment: Sex Education in Britain, from Social Purity to Section 28," in *Public or Private Education? Lessons from History*, ed. Richard Aldrich (London: Woburn Press, 2004), 102; Simon Szreter and Kate Fisher, *Sex before the Sexual Revolution: Intimate Life in England, 1918–1963* (Cambridge: Cambridge University Press, 2010), 81; Steve Humphries, *A Secret World of Sex: Forbidden Fruit: The British Experience, 1900–1950* (London: Sidgwick and Jackson, 1988), 48.

16. See, e.g., Theodore F. Tucker and Muriel Pout, *Sex Education in Schools: An Experiment in Elementary Instruction* (London: Gerald Howe, 1933); Charles Macalister, "Social Hygiene Teaching in a Rural Area: A Gloucestershire Experiment," *Health and Empire* 9, no. 2 (1934): 134–36.

17. Virginie De Luca Barrusse, "The Concerns Underlying Sex Education for Young People in France during the First Half of the 20th Century: Morality, Demography, and Public Health," *Hygiea Internationalis* 10, no. 1 (2011): 37, 40; Mary Lynn Stewart, "'Science Is Always Chaste': Sex Education and Sexual Initiation in France, 1880s–1930s," *Journal of Contemporary History* 32, no. 3 (1997): 393; Frederick William Roman, *The New Education in Europe* (New York: E. P. Dutton, 1930), 401–2.

18. René La Bruyerè, "Germany from a Motor Car," *The Living Age* 382 (January 15, 1927): 156; Sterling Fishman, "Suicide, Sex, and the Discovery of the German Adolescent," *History of Education Quarterly* 10, no. 2 (1970): 180.

19. "The Sexual Enlightenment of Children (An Open Letter to Dr. M. Furst) [1907], in *Complete Psychological Works of Sigmund Freud*, vol. 9 (London: Hogarth, 1959), 138–39.

20. "Sexual Enlightenment of Children," 139; Helmut Gruber, "Sexuality in 'Red Vienna': Socialist Party Conceptions and Programs and Working-Class Life, 1920–34," *International Labor and Working-Class History* 31 (Spring 1987): 56; G. Stanley Hall, *Educational Problems*, vol. 1 (New York: D. Appleton, 1911), 397; Albert Moll, *The Sexual Life of the Child*, trans. Eden Paul (1913; New York: AMS Press, 1975), 292; Ann Taylor Allen, *Feminism and Motherhood in Western Europe, 1890–1970: The Maternal Dilemma* (New York: Palgrave, 2005), 96; Ann Taylor Allen, "Mothers of the New Generation: Adele Schreiber, Helen Stocker, and the Evolution of the German Idea of Motherhood, 1900–1914," *Signs* 10, no. 3 (1985): 429.

21. Lutz D. H. Sauerteig, "Sex Education in Germany from the Eighteenth to the Twentieth Century," in *Sexual Cultures in Europe: Themes in Sexuality*, ed. Franz X. Eder (Manchester: Manchester University Press, 1999), 19–20; *Report by Miss Martindale on Some Papers on Sex Instruction for Children and Adolescents Submitted from Six Countries to the Medical Women's International Association for the Paris Congress* (Paris: Imprimerie George Petit, 1929), 9–11, folder SA/MWF/N.1/12, Medical Women's Federation Papers, Wellcome Library, London; I. L. Kandel, "Education in Nazi Germany," *Annals of the American Academy of Political and Social Sciences* 182 (November 1935): 159; Hans Peter Bluel, *Sex and Society in Nazi Germany*, trans. J. Maxwell Brownjohn (New York: J. B. Lippincott, 1973), 192–93; Romano Forleo and Pietro Lucisano, "Sex Education in Italy," *Journal of Sex Education and Therapy* 6, no. 1 (1980): 15; Angus McLaren, *Twentieth-Century Sexuality: A History* (Malden, MA: Blackwell, 1999), 134–35.

22. Salomon M. Teitelbaum, "Sex Education in the Soviet Union," *Harvard Educational Review* 16, no. 2 (1946): 87; Albert P. Pinkevitch, *The New Education in the Soviet Union*, ed. George S. Counts (New York: John Day, 1929), 337–38.

23. Pinkevitch, *New Education in the Soviet Union*, 337–38; Lynne Attwood, "Confronting Sexuality in School and Society," in *Education and Society in the New Russia*, ed. Anthony Jones (Armonk, NY: M. E. Sharpe, 1994), 264–65; Eric Naiman, *Sex in Public: The Incarnation of Early Soviet Ideology* (Princeton, NJ: Princeton University Press, 1997), 115, 121–23.

24. Teitelbaum, "Sex Education in the Soviet Union," 86–87; Catriona Kelly, *Children's World: Growing Up in Russia, 1890–1991* (New Haven, CT: Yale University Press, 2007), 576–77; Ann Livschiz, "Battling 'Unhealthy Relations': Soviet Youth Sexuality as a Political Problem," *Journal of Historical Sociology* 21, no. 4 (2008): 401–2.

25. Eunice Blackburn to Dear Family, March 12, 1922, folder 4, box 1, Eunice R. Blackburn Papers, Presbyterian Historical Society, Philadelphia;

John A. Britton, "The Mexican Ministry of Education, 1931–1940: Radicalism and Institutional Development" (PhD thesis, Tulane University, 1971), 97–98, 105–6; Anne Rubenstein, "Raised Voices in the Cine Montecarlo: Sex Education, Mass Media, and Oppositional Politics in Mexico," *Journal of Family History* 23, no. 3 (1998): 313–15; "Students Riot in Mexico against Sex Education," *Chicago Daily Tribune*, April 8, 1934, p. 20.

26. Rubenstein, "Raised Voices in the Cine Montecarlo," 315; Britton, "The Mexican Ministry of Education," 100, 106, 110–11; Alan Knight, "Popular Culture and the Revolutionary State in Mexico, 1910–1940," *Hispanic American Historical Review* 74, no. 3 (1994): 423; "30,000 Catholics Protest on Mexico," *New York Times*, February 25, 1935, p. 1; "Catholics to Pray for Turn in Mexico," *New York Times*, June 24, 1935, p. 5; "The Mexican Persecution," *Irish Monthly* 63, no. 746 (1935): 528; Herbert Ingram Priestly, "The Contemporary Program of Nationalization in Mexico," *Pacific Historical Review* 8, no. 1 (1939): 67.

27. Canadian Social Hygiene Council, *Introductory Studies in Social Hygiene* (Toronto: CSHC, n.d. [1922]), 18, "Canada: VD pamphlets" folder, ASHA Papers; Ben E. Lindsey, "The House of Human Welfare," *Forum* 78 (December 1927): 813.

28. "Miss Edith Cooper on 'Sex Education'" (MS, 1921), folder DC/UWT/129/2, National Union of Women Teachers Collection, Institute of Education Archives, London; C. E. Silcox, "The Interest of the World's YMCA in Problems of Sex," *Journal of Social Hygiene* 13, no. 2 (1927): 83, 72; "Is Seeing Believing?" *Journal of Social Hygiene* 12, no. 3 (1926): 159–60.

29. Alice B. Van Doren, *Christian High Schools in India* (Calcutta: YMCA Publishing House, 1936), 135; "British Social Hygiene Council, Imperial Conference, September 27th, 1928," *Health and Empire* 3, no. 4 (1928): 281; Bronisław Malinowski, "Syllabus on the Problems of Sex Life and Morality among Peoples of a Non-European Culture. Professor Malinowski of the London School of Economics and Political Science" (MS, n.d. [1931]), enclosed with Malinowski to "Miss Grant," February 21, 1931, folder 14/120, Bronisław Malinowski Papers, Hall-Carpenter Archives, London School of Economics, London; Margaret Read, "The Contribution of Anthropology to Social Hygiene," *Health and Empire* 8, no. 4 (1933): 289.

30. James W. C. Dougall, ed., *Christianity and the Sex-Education of the African* (London: Society for Promoting Christian Knowledge, 1937), 31, 12; John Norman Hostetter, "Mission Education in a Changing Society: Brethren of Christ Mission Education in Southern Rhodesia, Africa, 1899–1959" (EdD diss., State University of New York at Buffalo, 1967), 58; Louis Franklin Freed, *Sex Education in Transvaal Schools* (Johannesburg: Central News Agency, 1940), 6, 9.

31. Lucien Viborel, "The Teaching of Social Hygiene in Schools by Means of the Film," *International Review of Educational Cinematography* 5,

no. 9 (1933): 595; A. Cavaillon, "The Cinema and Educational Propaganda against Venereal Risks," *International Review of Educational Cinematography* 3, no. 2 (1931): 146; Kurt Thomalla, "The Development of the Medical Film and of Those Dealing with Hygiene and General Culture in Germany," *International Review of Educational Cinematography* 1, no. 4 (1929): 449; Andre Cavaillon, "The Cinema and the Campaign against the Danger of Venereal Diseases," *International Review of Educational Cinematography* 6, no. 12 (1934): 793; Laura Dreyfus-Barney, "Public Hygiene and the Cinema," *International Review of Educational Cinematography* 6, no. 3 (1934): 162; "The Educational Motion Picture," *Journal of Social Hygiene* 10 (February 1924): 106; Asunción Lavrín, *Women, Feminism, and Social Change in Argentina, Chile, and Uruguay, 1890–1940* (Lincoln: University of Nebraska Press, 1995), 139; Wendell Cleland, "'The Gift of Life' in Egypt," *Journal of Social Hygiene* 11, no. 4 (1925): 219.

32. Havelock Ellis, *Studies in the Psychology of Sex*, vol. 6 (Philadelphia: F. A. Davis, 1913), 58; Leslie Brewer, *The Good News: Some Sidelights on the Strange Story of Sex Education* (London: Putnam, 1962), 105; Tucker and Pout, *Sex Education in the Schools*, 70; Cate Haste, *Rules of Desire: Sex in Britain, World War I to the Present* (London: Pimlico, 1992), 72; Magda Gawin, "Dispute over the Sex Education of Children and Young People during the Interwar Years," *Acta Poloniae Historica* 79 (1999): 204.

33. H. L. Mencken, "Hiring a Hall: Crabbed Age and Youth and the Sex Hygienist," *New York World*, n.d. [1925], enclosed with William H. Zinsser to John D. Rockefeller Jr., September 19, 1925, folder 130, box 16, Series K, Record Group 2, Rockefeller Family Archives; Zinsser to Rockefeller, ibid.; Cynthia R. Comacchio, *The Dominion of Youth: Adolescence and the Making of a Modern Canada* (Waterloo, ON: Wilfred Laurier University Press, 2006), 87.

34. Chicago Society of Social Hygiene, *Education against Venereal Disease a Need of the State* (n.p., n.d. [1907?]), folder 18, box 21, Veranus A. Moore Papers, Division of Rare and Manuscript Collections, Cornell University, Ithaca, New York; "How Shall We Teach?" *Journal of Social Hygiene* 2, no. 3 (1916): 436; Ruth Topping, "Miss Wood's Lecture at a Special Assembly of the Junior and Senior High School Girls, West Haven High School Connecticut, February 4" (MS, February 15, 1932), folder 201, box 10, series 3, Bureau of Social Hygiene Papers, Rockefeller Archive Center.

35. Nancy Leys Stepan, *"The Hour of Eugenics": Race, Gender and Nation in Latin America* (Ithaca, NY: Cornell University Press, 1991), 130; Britton, "The Mexican Ministry of Education," 96; Lavrín, *Women, Feminism, and Social Change*, 141–42; Marie Carmichael Stopes, *Sex and the Young* (London: Gill Publishing House, 1926), 113. See also Julian B. Carter, *The Heart of Whiteness: Normal Sexuality and Race in America, 1880–1940* (Durham, NC: Duke University Press, 2007), esp. chap. 4.

36. Sabine Frühstück, *Colonizing Sex: Sexology and Social Control in Modern Japan* (Berkeley: University of California Press, 2003), 55; B. P. Kolhapure, *Sex Education* (n.p., 1928), 25–26, folder UWT/D/121/1/23, National Union of Women Teachers Collection; Paromita Chakravarti, "The Sex Education Debate: Teaching 'Life Style' in West Bengal, India," *Sex Education* 11, no. 4 (2011): 391; David Mace and Vera Mace, *Marriage: East and West* (Garden City, NY: Doubleday, 1960), 96, 93; Myrtle Law and Gordon Law, "Gandhi in Jail," *Outlook*, April 19, 1922, p. 649.

37. Hugo Rolling, "The Problem of Sex Education in the Netherlands in the 20th Century," in *Cultures of Child Health in Britain and the Netherlands in the 20th Century*, ed. Marijke Gijswijt-Hofstra and Hilary Marland (Amsterdam: Rodopi, 2003), 248; Allen, *Feminism and Motherhood in Western Europe*, 93.

38. American Federation for Sex Hygiene, *Report of the Sex Education Sessions of the Fourth International Congress on School Hygiene and of the Annual Meeting of the Federation* (New York: American Federation for Sex Hygiene, 1913), 65, 72–73; Jeffrey P. Moran, "'Modernism Gone Mad': Sex Education Comes to Chicago, 1913," *Journal of American History* 83, no. 2 (1996): 502–6; "Sex Education as Its Friends and Foes View It," *Current Opinions* 55 (October 1913): 261.

39. See, e.g., Sauerteig, "Sex Education in Germany," 17, 23; Gawin, "Dispute over the Sex Education of Children," 211; Barrusse, "The Concerns Underlying Sex Education for Young People in France," 41; Britta McEwen, *Sexual Knowledge: Feeling, Fact, and Social Reform in Vienna, 1900–1934* (New York: Berghahn, 2012), 75–76.

40. Gawin, "Dispute over the Sex Education of Children," 186–87.

41. Hugo Münsterberg, *Psychology and Social Sanity* (Garden City, NY: Doubleday, 1914), 6, 17; Rosemary Auchmuty, "The Truth about Sex," in *Australian Popular Culture*, ed. Peter Spearritt and David Walker (Sydney: George Allen and Unwin, 1979), 172–73; C. M. McGeorge, "Sex Education in 1912," *New Zealand Journal of Educational Studies* 12, no. 2 (1977): 137.

42. "Washington Schools and Sex Education—A Protest from a Mother," *Washington Post*, January 30, 1930, p. 6; London City Council, *Report of the Education Committee on the Teaching of Sex Hygiene* (London: London City Council, 1914), 5; Hall, *Educational Problems*, 401; Frank Mort, *Dangerous Sexualities: Medico-Moral Politics in England since 1830* (London: Routledge and Kegan Paul, 1987), 160; Hera Cook, "Emotion, Bodies, Sexuality, and Sex Education in Edwardian England," *Historical Journal* 55, no. 2 (2012): 476.

43. "Pontiff Condemns New Naturalism Taught in Schools," *New York Times*, January 12, 1930, p. 1; Robert H. Scott, "Shall Sex Be Taught in Our Schools?" *Los Angeles Times*, August 29, 1937, p. 26; McEwen, *Sexual*

*Knowledge*, 76; Barrusse, "The Concerns Underlying Sex Education for Young People," 41.

44. Allen, *Feminism and Motherhood in Western Europe*, 95; "What to Teach the Child, Whitehall against Sex Instruction," *Daily News*, April 20, 1923, folder DC/UWT/129/2, National Union of Women Teachers Collection; "Sex Education Held Unwise in Schools," *New York Times*, February 8, 1939, p. 19; "Sex Education for the Home," *Los Angeles Times*, July 9, 1914, p. 16.

45. Ellis, *Studies in the Psychology of Sex*, 40–42; Chang Ching-Sheng, *Sex Histories: China's First Modern Treatise on Sex Education*, trans. Howard S. Levy (Yokohama: n.p., 1967), 111; Humphries, *A Secret World of Sex*, 40, 43; Hall, "Birds, Bees, and General Embarrassment," 21.

46. Brandt, *No Magic Bullet*, 25–26; *Report by Miss Martindale on Some Papers on Sex Instruction*, 25; Carleton Washburn, *A Living Philosophy of Education* (New York: John Day, 1940), 88; Freed, *Sex Education in Transvaal Schools*, 10.

47. Ellis, *Studies in the Psychology of Sex*, 57–58; Catherine Gasquoine Hartley, *Sex Education and National Health* (London: Leonard Parsons, 1920), 53–54; Thomas M. Balliet, *Introduction of Sex Education into Public Schools* (New York: American Social Hygiene Association, 1928), 5, "Introduction of Sex Education into Public Schools" folder, box 2, Thomas M. Balliet Papers, New York University Archives; *Sex Education in Schools and Youth Organisations* (London: Her Majesty's Stationery Office, 1943), 9, folder SA/FPA/NK234, Family Planning Association Papers, Wellcome Library.

48. Hanne Riser, "School Sex Education: Structure and System in Denmark," in *The Other Curriculum: European Strategies for School Sex Education*, ed. Philip Meredith (London: International Planned Parenthood Federation, 1989), 115; Max Hodann, *History of Modern Morals*, trans. Stella Brown (London: William Heinemann, 1937), 245; Sauerteig, "Sex Education in Germany," 19; "Cautions Schools on Sex Education," *New York Times*, November 7, 1938, p. 21; "Minutes. Sex Education Committee Meeting. November 30, 1939" (MS, 1939), p. 3, folder 21, box 9, United Federation of Teachers Records, Robert F. Wagner Labor Archives, Tamiment Library, New York University; Geraldine Courtney, "Immorality in Our Schools," *Forum and Century* 98 (September 1937): 132.

49. Hartley, *Sex Education and National Health*, 65; Willard W. Beatty, "Sex Instruction in Public Schools—I," *Journal of Social Hygiene* 20, no. 5 (1934): 233; Hall, *Educational Problems*, 401; Stopes, *Sex and the Young*, 53.

50. *Report by Miss Martindale on Some Papers on Sex Instruction*, 9–10, 28; Kenneth M. Gould, "Progress, 1920–21," *Social Hygiene* 7, no. 3 (1921): 313–14.

51. Carl Gustaf Boethius, "Swedish Experiences—An Historical Perspective," in Meredith, *The Other Curriculum*, 333–35; Ellis, *Studies in the*

*Psychology of Sex*, 83; John D. Rockefeller to Julia Richman, December 13, 1911; James Russell to Rockefeller, January 14, 1913, both in folder 81, box 10, Series O, Record Group 2, Rockefeller Family Archives.

52. Havelock Ellis, *The Task of Social Hygiene* (Boston: Houghton Mifflin, 1913), 252; John B. Watson and K. S. Lashley, *A Consensus of Medical Opinion upon Questions Relating to Sex Education and Venereal Disease Campaigns* (New York: National Committee for Mental Hygiene, 1920), 58, "ISHB Publications" folder, box 5, General Records of the Interdepartmental Social Hygiene Board; *Report by Miss Martindale on Some Papers on Sex Instruction*, 27, 20.

53. Howard M. Bell, *Youth Tell Their Story* (Washington, DC: American Council on Education, 1938), 87–88; Angela Davis, "'Oh no, nothing, we didn't learn anything': Sex Education and the Preparation for Motherhood, c. 1930–1970," *History of Education* 37, no. 5 (2008): 671; Josephine May, "Secrets and Lies: Sex Education and Gendered Memories of Childhood's End in an Australian Provincial City, 1930s–1950s," *Sex Education* 6, no. 1 (2006): 11; Brewer, *The Good News*, 112; "Ch. V. Conclusions and Recommendations" (MS, n.d. [1939]), p. 2, "Michigan Curriculum Study— Sub-Committee on Sex Education 2" folder, box 3, Mabel Rugen Papers, Bentley Historical Library, Ann Arbor, Michigan; Hodann, *History of Modern Morals*, 243–44.

54. Hodann, *History of Modern Morals*, 244; Cassel, *The Secret Plague*, 244; "Boys and Girls Show City Council How to Legislate without Tumult," *New York Times*, April 15, 1939, p. 21; Claudia Nelson and Michelle H. Martin, "Introduction," in *Sexual Pedagogies: Sex Education in Britain, Australia, and America, 1879–2000*, ed. Nelson and Martin (New York: Palgrave, 2004), 3.

55. Ralf Dose, "The World League for Sexual Reform: Some Possible Approaches," *Journal of the History of Sexuality* 12, no. 1 (2003): 1–15; Hodann, *History of Modern Morals*, 261; *Experiments in Sex Education* (London: Federation of Progressive Societies and Individuals, 1935), p. 4, folder DC/UWT/129/7, National Union of Women Teachers Collection.

56. Sigmund Freud, "Analysis Terminable and Interminable" [1937], in *Collected Papers*, vol. 5, ed. James Strachey (London: Hogarth Press, 1950), 336.

## CHAPTER TWO: A FAMILY OF MAN?

1. "The Art of Pursuing in Common," *Journal of Social Hygiene* 36, no. 6 (1950): 338.

2. "Progress and Trends in Sex Education in the United States: A Statement Prepared by the Staff of the American Social Hygiene Association"

(MS, May 1951), folder 5, box 224, American Social Health Association Papers (hereafter "ASHA Papers"), Social Welfare History Archives, University of Minnesota; *Social Hygiene, the Citizen, and the United Nations* (American Social Hygiene Association, 1950), enclosed with "United States Participation in a Delegation to the Congress of the International Union for the Prevention of Venereal Disease" (MS, July 13, 1950), p. 4, "Venereal Disease, Cong. Of the Int. Union for the Prevention of. Zurich. July 29 to Aug. 1, 1950" folder, box 380, Records of International Conferences, Commissions and Expositions, Record Group 43, National Archives II, College Park, Maryland.

3. Board of Education, *Sex Education in Schools and Youth Organisations* (London: Her Majesty's Stationery Office, 1943), 1, 8; Cyril Bibby, *Sex Education: Aims, Possibilities, and Plans* (n.p., 1945), 1–2, both in folder SA/FPA/NK234, Family Planning Association Papers, Wellcome Library, London.

4. Mary Louise Adams, "Sex at the Board, or Keeping Children from Sexual Knowledge," in *Sex in Schools: Canadian Education and Sexual Regulation*, ed. Susan Prentice (Toronto: Our School/Our Selves Foundation, 1994), 61–62, 67; International Union against the Venereal Diseases, *Summary Report of the Proceedings of the 1st Postwar General Assembly. Paris, France, October 20–25 1947* (New York: Regional Office for the Americas, IUAVD, n.d. [1947]), 36; Osmo Kontula and Elina Haavio-Mannila, "Finland," in *The Continuum Complete International Encyclopedia of Sexuality*, ed. Robert T. Francoeur and Raymond J. Noonan (Bloomington, IN: Kinsey Institute, 2004), online edition; Polish Family Planning Association, *Family Planning and Sex-Education in Socialist Countries. Proceedings of a Seminar Held in Warsaw, Poland, December 1976*, ed. Mikolaj Kozakiewicz (Warazawa, Poland: Polish Family Planning Association, 1977), 101; Thomas Dawes Eliot, "Family Life Education in Norway," *Marriage and Family Living* 15, no. 1 (1953): 5; Michele Guimelchain, "Sex Education as a Factor in the Process of Renewal of Education" (UNESCO: n.p., November 13, 1974), p. 7, at http://unesdoc.unesco.org/images/0001/000107/010714eb.pdf (accessed July 26, 2013); Nina Epton, *Love and the French* (Cleveland: World Publishing, 1959), 350; Nicholas Beattie, "Sex-Education in France: A Case-Study in Curriculum Change," *Comparative Education* 12, no. 2 (1976): 116–17.

5. Lester A. Kirkendall, "The Journey toward SIECUS, 1964: A Personal Odyssey," *SIECUS Report* 12, no. 4 (1984): 1–3; Lester A. Kirkendall, "Sex Education in Nine Cooperating High Schools," *Clearing House* 18, no. 7 (1944): 390.

6. American Social Hygiene Association, *World-Wide Service. Report of the Association's Committee on International Relations and Activities for the Year 1947* (New York: ASHA, n.d. [1947], p. 3, folder SA/SMO/R.28/13, Society of Medical Officers Papers, Wellcome Library; "Thirty-Fourth Annual

Meeting. American Social Hygiene Association," *Journal of Social Hygiene* 33, no. 3 (1947): 132.

7. "Thirty-Fifth Annual Meeting. American Social Hygiene Association." *Journal of Social Hygiene* 34, no. 4 (1948): 179, 182; Bruce Webster, "Statesmanship in Social Health," *Social Health News* 36, no. 5 (1961): 2; Jean B. Pinney to Clark H. Yeager, May 2, 1947; M. H. Lisboa to ASHA, June 1, 1947, both in folder 10; M. da Nobrega to ASHA, May 5, 1950, folder 11; Edgar Barbosa Ribas to Josephine V. Tuller, August 20, 1954, folder 12, all in box 216, ASHA Papers.

8. "Publications for the Institute of Inter-American Affairs. For Use in Brazil" (MS, 1947), folder 10; Elizabeth F. Force to Louis F. James, July 30, 1957, folder 12; Josephine V. Tuller, "Report to the IUVD and T on J.V. Tuller's world trip 1954" (MS, n.d. [1954]), folder 2; Tuller to John C. Cutler, June 3, 1954, folder 2, all in box 216, ASHA Papers.

9. Mary B. Bigelow to Conrad Van Hynig, February 9, 1955, folder 12, box 222; "For Discussion" (MS, October 31, 1951), folder 5, box 224; Philip R. Mather, "Social Hygiene Possibilities in Puerto Rico and the Virgin Islands, 1945" (MS, 1945), folder 8, box 112, all in ASHA Papers.

10. Charles Walter Clarke to W. R. Deforest, November 28, 1950, folder 4, box 219, ASHA Papers; "Sex Education Held Need of German Girls," *Indianapolis Star*, February 28, 1949, "Sex Education (Federal Republic of Germany)" file, Vertical Files Collection, Kinsey Institute Archives, Bloomington, Indiana; Erich D. Langer to William F. Snow, December 20, 1949, folder 4; Elisabeth Hagemeyer to American Association of Social Hygiene, March 13, 1951, folder 5; Langer to Josephine V. Tuller, June 18, 1951, folder 5; Langer to Tuller, October 5, 1951, folder 5, all in box 219, ASHA Papers.

11. Ministry of Education memorandum, February 5, 1947, "Sex Education" folder, box 5728; "A Draft of Principles Purity Education (by the Committee of Purity Education)," p. 1 (MS, n.d. [1948], "Sex Education" folder, box 5247; Francis C. Park to Education Section, December 16, 1948, "School Hygiene" folder, box 2840, all in Civil Information and Education Section, Supreme Commander for the Allied Powers Records, Record Group 331, National Archives II; William Neufeld to ASHA, June 24, 1948, folder 9, box 221; Carol V. Reynolds to Mary F. Jones, May 29, 1952, folder 1, box 222; Josephine V. Tuller to Kane Iwashita, October 21, 1954, folder 1, box 222; Jones to Tuller, March 9, 1952, folder 1, box 222, all in ASHA Papers.

12. Curtis A. Avery, "Toward an Understanding of Sex Education in Oregon," *The Coordinator* 5, no. 1 (1956): 1–2, 8.

13. Helen Manley, "Sex Education in the Schools," *Journal of School Health* 21, no. 2 (1951): 62, 67, folder 9, box 3, Helen Manley Papers, Missouri Historical Society, Saint Louis; Office of Family Education Research,

Presbyterian Board of Christian Education, "The Church Faces a Changing Family" (MS, 1959), "BCE—Office of Fam. Ed Research—Folder 1" folder, box 2, Presbyterian Board of Christian Education Records, Presbyterian Historical Society, Philadelphia; "Family Strength Is World Strength," *Social Hygiene News* 34, no. 4 (1959): 4.

14. "Progress and Trends in Sex Education in the United States," 3; Health League of Canada, "6 Resolutions on V.D. Control" (MS, 1945), folder 4, box 217, ASHA Papers; Thomas D. Eliot, "Sex Instruction in Norwegian Culture," *Social Problems* 1, no. 2 (1953): 47; *Problems of Social Vice and Social Diseases: A Report of the Proceedings and Recommendations of a Three-Day Seminar on "Social and Moral Hygiene" (Problems of Social Vice and Social Diseases) Held by the Social Services Coordinating Council, Karachi, in March 1961* (Karachi: Social Services Coordinating Council, 1961), 18, 24; Family Planning Association of Hong Kong to Elise Ottesen-Jensen, November 8, 1955, volume 3, Foreign Correspondence, Papers of Riksförbundet för Sexuell Upplysning (RFSU), Labour Movement Archives and Library, Stockholm, Sweden.

15. Robert and Francis R. Harper, "Are Educators Afraid of Sex?" *Marriage and Family Living* 19, no. 3 (1957): 240–41.

16. Doris H. Linder, *Crusader for Sex Education: Elise Ottesen-Jensen (1886–1973) in Scandinavia and on the International Scene* (Lanham, MD: University Press of America, 1996), 175, 179; W. F. Storm to Vera Houghton, September 1, 1951, folder 9, box 5, Abraham Stone Papers, Francis A. Countway Library of Medicine, Center for the History of Medicine, Harvard University, Boston; Irving J. Fasteau to Department of State, March 31, 1951, "Venereal Disease, 28th General Assembly of International Union Against. Paris May 21–25, 1951" folder, box 380, Records of International Conferences, Commissions, and Expositions; David Richards to Josephine V. Tuller, October 10, 1948, folder 9, box 217, ASHA Papers.

17. "Slant on Sex Education," *New York Times*, November 17, 1955, p. 43; Katherine Rahl, "Report on Conferences in the Virgin Islands of the U.S.A." (MS, June 1956), p. 16, folder 8, box 112; Josephine Tuller memorandum to International Division, June 15, 1956, folder 12, box 216; Tuller to E. E. Hermans, April 26, 1956, folder 6, box 223, all in ASHA Papers.

18. "Big Racket Seen in Pornography," *New York Times*, May 21, 1956, p. 26; Robert A. Frumkin, "Should Public Schools Teach Sex Education?" *Sexology* 23, no. 5 (1956): 305; Josephine V. Tuller memorandum, April 15, 1958, folder 2, box 216, ASHA Papers; "Age Worries over at 16, Kinsey Says," *Washington Post*, May 2, 1956, p. 46; Alfred Kinsey et al., *Sexual Behavior in the Human Male* (Philadelphia: W. B. Saunders, 1948), 443; Bruno P. F. Wanrooij, "Carnal Knowledge: The Social Politics and Experience of Sex Education in Italy, 1940–1980," in *Shaping Sexual Knowledge: A Cultural History of Sex Education in Twentieth Century Europe*, ed. Lutz D. H. Sauerteig

and Roger Davidson (London: Routledge, 2008), 117; Lisa Featherstone, *Let's Talk about Sex: Histories of Sexuality in Australia from Federation to the Pill* (Cambridge: Cambridge Scholars Publishing, 2011), 271; "Kinsey Attacked by Communists," *Social Hygiene News* 28, no. 10 (1953): 1.

19. C. E. Silcox, "The Moral and Social Factors of VD Control," *Journal of Social Hygiene* 32, no. 1 (1946): 56; Wanrooij, "Carnal Knowledge," 111; "Sex in Russia," *Newsweek*, October 19, 1964, 106; V. N. Kolbanovskii, "The Sex Upbringing of the Rising Generation," *Soviet Education* 6, no 11 (1964): 8; Catriona Kelly, *Children's World: Growing Up in Russia, 1890–1991* (New Haven, CT: Yale University Press, 2007), 577.

20. Mark Fenmore, "The Growing Pains of Sex Education in the German Democratic Republic (GDR), 1945–69," in Sauerteig and Davidson, *Shaping Sexual Knowledge*, 82, 84–85; Waltraud Muller-Dietz, "Sex Education in the Soviet Union," *Review of Soviet Medical Sciences* 2 (1965): 3; Lynne Attwood, "Confronting Sexuality in School and Society," in *Education and Society in the New Russia*, ed. Anthony Jones (Armonk, NY: M. E. Sharpe, 1994), 269; "Appendix 2: Development of Sex Education in China," in *Sexual Behavior in Modern China*, ed. Dalin Liu et al. (New York: Continuum, 1997), 553; Alessandra Aresu, "Sex Education in Modern and Contemporary China: Interrupted Debates across the Last Century," *International Journal of Educational Development* 29 (2009): 534–35; Mikolaj Kozakiewicz, "Sex and Family Life Education through the Polish School System," in *The Other Curriculum: European Strategies for School Sex Education*, ed. Philip Meredith (London: International Planned Parenthood Federation, 1989), 196.

21. "The Red Underground," *Herald Tribune*, November 18, 1951; Jonathan Zimmerman, *Whose America? Culture Wars in the Public Schools* (Cambridge, MA: Harvard University Press, 2002), 194; Ruth Daniloff, "Sex? Nyet? Not in Soviet School System," *Louisville Courier-Journal*, July 19, 1964, "Sex Education (Union of Soviet Socialist Republics)" file, Vertical Files Collection, Kinsey Institute Archives; "Sex in Russia," 106.

22. Carl Gustaf Boethius, "Sweden's Way to Sex Education and Birth Control," in *Sex Education in Schools: Proceedings of an Expert Group Meeting. IPPF Middle East and North Africa Region. December 1974. Beirut, Lebanon*, ed. Isam R. Nazer (Tunisia: IPPF Middle East and North Africa Region, 1976), 24–25; Carl Gustaf Boethius, "Sex Education in Swedish Schools: The Facts and the Fiction," *Family Planning Perspectives* 17, no. 6 (1985): 276; untitled MS (1951), pp. 3–4, folder 57, box 4, Stone Papers; Lena Lennerhed, "Taking the Middle Way: Sex Education Debates in Sweden in the Early Twentieth Century," in Sauerteig and Davidson, *Shaping Sexual Knowledge*, 62–63.

23. Nils Nielsen, untitled MS (1955), p. 4, folder 58, box 4, Stone Papers; "Background on Elise Ottesen-Jensen. Supplied by National League

for Sex Education, Sweden" (MS, 1954), p. 6, folder 11, box 205, Planned Parenthood Federation of America II Collection, Sophia Smith Collection, Smith College, Northampton, Massachusetts; *The National League for Sex Education* (Stockholm: Tryckeriaktiebolaget Federative, 1949), p. 4, "Sex Education Organization (Sweden). Swedish Association for Sex Education" file, Vertical Files Collection, Kinsey Institute Archives; *Handbook on Sex Instruction in Swedish Schools*, trans. Norman Parsons (Stockholm: Royal Board of Education in Sweden, 1956), 2032.

24. Stewart E. Fraser, *Sex, Schools, and Society: International Perspectives* (Nashville: Aurora Publishers, 1972), 12; "Swedes Debate Sex Hysteria," *Washington Post*, February 23, 1964, p. E4; "Swedes to Scan Teaching on Sex Education," *New York Times*, April 26, 1964; J. Robert Moskin, "Sweden's New Battle over Sex," *Look*, November 15, 1966, both in "Sex Education (Sweden)" file, Vertical Files Collection, Kinsey Institute Archives; Robert M. Bjork, "An International Perspective on Various Issues in Sex Education as an Aspect of Health Education," *Journal of School Health* 39 (October 1969): 532.

25. Linder, *Crusader for Sex Education*, 228; M. A. Hai, *"Sex Education": A Social Problem of the Mid-Twentieth Century* (n.p.: Modern Press and Publicity, n.d. [1955]), p. 9, folder 2, box 221, ASHA Papers; R. L. Humphris to Elise Ottesen-Jensen, February 18, 1956, volume 4, Foreign Correspondence, RFSU Papers.

26. Lotte Fink to Elise Ottesen-Jensen, May 19, 1954, volume 3; Richard B. Gamble to Ottesen-Jensen, August 22, 1952, volume 1, both in Foreign Correspondence, RFSU Papers; Linder, *Crusader for Sex Education*, 194–95; "Mrs. Ottesen-Jensen Schedule of U.S. Visit, 1954" (MS, 1954), folder 11, box 205, Planned Parenthood Federation of America II Collection; Awad Al-Najim to RFSU, December 12, 1954, volume 3, Foreign Correspondence, RFSU Papers; "Background on Elise Ottesen-Jensen," 6–7.

27. Frederick Hale, "Time for Sex in Sweden," *Scandinavian Studies* 79, no. 3 (2003): 354–55, 357, 359–60, 363, 367.

28. Hale, "Time for Sex in Sweden," 365–66; "Sex and Suicide in Sweden Aren't the Rage after All," *Wall Street Journal*, April 6, 1990, p. A1; Howard S. Hoyman, "Impressions of Sex Education in Sweden," *Journal of School Health* 34 (May 1964): 215; Moskin, "Sweden's New Battle over Sex"; Fraser, *Sex, Schools, and Society: International Perspectives*, 16–17.

29. Leonard England, "A British Sex Survey" in *Sex, Society, and the Individual*, ed. A. Pillay and Albert Ellis (Bombay: International Journal of Sexology, 1953), 363; "What Teen-Agers Think," in *Sex Education and the Teen-Ager*, ed. Seymour M. Farber and Roger H. L. Wilson (Berkeley, CA: Diablo Press, 1967), 133, 135; Norman Haire, "Sex Education for Adolescents," *New Horizons in Education* 3, no. 3 (1943): 16–17; "How Girls Find

Out about Sex," *Intro*, October 21, 1967, folder SA/FPA/A17/120, Family Planning Association Papers.

30. Nina Epton, *Love and the English* (London: Cassell, 1960), 327; Helen Manley, *A Curriculum Guide in Sex Education* (Saint Louis: State Publishing, 1964), 39, 47, folder 10, box 3, Manley Papers; Genaro Castro-Vázquez, *In the Shadows: Sexuality, Pedagogy, and Gender among Japanese Teenagers* (Lanham, MD: Rowman and Littlefield, 2007), 30.

31. Leslie Brewer, *The Good News: Some Sidelights on the Strange Story of Sex Education* (London: Putnam, 1962), 19; "Ch. V. Conclusions and Recommendations" (MS, n.d. [1940?]), pp. 1–2, "Michigan Curriculum Study—Sub-Committee on Sex Education 2" folder, box 3, Mabel Rugen Papers, Bentley Historical Library, Ann Arbor, Michigan; Lester A. Kirkendall, *Sex Education as Human Relations* (New York: Inor, 1950), xiv, 158; "Sex Teaching," *Times Educational Supplement*, March 4, 1944, p. 111; "A Draft of Principles Purity Education," 3.

32. *The First All-India Conference on Moral and Social Hygiene* (New Delhi: Association for Moral and Social Hygiene in India, n.d. [1950]), 1, 13, "India—Ephemera" folder, box 203, ASHA Papers; *Seventh All-India Conference on Moral and Social Hygiene* (Delhi: Neelkamal Printers, n.d. [1959]), 161; untitled clipping, *Daily Herald*, February 2, 1949, folder DC/UWT/129/2, National Union of Women Teachers Collection, Institute of Education, London; "Education," *Time*, February 21, 1949, 73.

33. "Sex Education in Schools Plan Fought by Mother," *Los Angeles Times*, March 9, 1945, p. A1; "Catholic Boycott of Sex Film Urged," *New York Times*, December 5, 1949, p. 20; Wanrooij, "Carnal Knowledge," 111; George W. Cadbury, "Outlook for Government Action in Family Planning in the West Indies," in *Research in Family Planning*, ed. Clyde V. Kiser (Princeton, NJ: Princeton University Press, 1962), 324–25; Roger Davidson, "Purity and Pedagogy: The Alliance-Scottish Council and School Sex Education in Scotland, 1955–1967," in Sauerteig and Davidson, *Shaping Sexual Knowledge*, 93; "Education in Sex Vital, Says Priest," *Sunday Telegraph*, April 8, 1962, folder SA/FPA/A17/117, Family Planning Association Papers.

34. P. Chambre, "Sex Education at Home and in the School," in UNESCO Institute for Education, *Health Education, Sex Education, and Education for Home and Family Life: Report on an Expert Meeting, February 17–22, 1964* (Hamburg: UNESCO Institute for Education, 1965), 86; Sidonie Matsner Gruenberg, "Must We Change Our Methods of Sex Education?" in *Sex Habits of American Men*, ed. Albert Deutch (New York: Prentice-Hall, 1948), 218; Thomas Dawes Eliot, "Welfare Fares Well: A Chronicle from Norway," *Social Service Review* 26, no. 1 (1952): 65; Eliot, "Sex Instruction in Norwegian Culture," 46; J. Bach, "Health, Sex, and Family Education," in UNESCO Institute for Education, *Health Education*, 42; John C. Davis,

"Teacher Dismissal on Grounds of Immorality," *Clearing House* 46, no. 7 (1972): 421; John B. Lewis, "Freedom of Speech and Expression in the Public Schools: A Closer Look at Teachers' Rights," *High School Journal* 63, no. 4 (1980): 138.

35. Lester Kirkendall, "Sex Education in Nine Cooperating Schools Part II: Methods of Teaching for the Individual Schools," *Clearing House* 18, no. 8 (1944): 460; Mary Louise Adams, *The Trouble with Normal: Postwar Youth and the Making of Heterosexuality* (Toronto: University of Toronto Press, 1997), 127; Dollie R. Walker, "The Need of Sex Education in Negro Schools," *Journal of Negro Education* 14, no. 2 (1945): 180; Frumkin, "Should Public Schools Teach Sex Education?" 304.

36. "Fear or Happiness," *Journal of Sex Education* 3, no. 3 (December 1950–January 1951), 104; Linder, *Crusader for Sex Education*, 152; Davidson, "Purity and Pedagogy," 95; Christian Council of Ghana, Committee on Christian Marriage, "Account of an Experiment in Sex Education among Middle School Leavers in Accra Area. July 1961" (MS, 1961), pp. 1–2, 4, enclosed with C. F. Paton to Principal Education Officer, September 29, 1961, folder 3/1/35, Ghana Education Service Records, Record Group 3/1, Ghana National Archives, Accra, Ghana.

37. Christian Council of Ghana, Committee on Christian Marriage, "Conclusions and Recommendations Arising from an Experiment in Sex-Education in Accra Middle Schools in July 1961" (MS, n.d. [1961]), p. 1; M. L. Quist to Miss Addison, November 24, 1965, both in folder 3/31/35, Ghana Education Service Records; "International Union against the Venereal Diseases. History and evaluation" (MS, 1952), folder 4, box 224, ASHA Papers.

38. Kozakiewicz, "Sex and Family Life Education through the Polish School System," 199; Roger Davidson and Gayle Davis, *The Sexual State: Sexuality and Scottish Governance, 1950–1980* (Edinburgh: Edinburgh University Press, 2012), 192; Adams, "Sex at the Board," 76, 65; International Planned Parenthood Federation, *Proceedings: Second Conference of the Region for Europe Near East and Africa* (Amsterdam: Excerpta Medica Foundation, 1960), 53.

39. "Introduction," in UNESCO Institute for Education, *Health Education*, 8; Liz Stanley, *Sex Surveyed, 1949–1994: From Mass-Observation's "Little Kinsey" to the National Survey and the Hite Reports* (London: Taylor and Francis, 1995), 88; Phyllis Kronhausen and Eberhard Kronhausen, "Sex Education—The Orphan Annie of American Schools," *Phi Delta Kappan* 43, no. 3 (1961): 128.

## CHAPTER THREE: SEX EDUCATION AND
## THE "SEXUAL REVOLUTION," 1965–1983

1. Ashley Montagu, "The Pill, the Sexual Revolution, and the Schools," *Phi Delta Kappan* 49 (May 1968): 480, 483.

2. "Mrs. Whitehouse Crusades towards the White House," *Sunday Times*, October 29, 1972; Lee Edwards to Raymond Gauer, December 14, 1972; Mary Whitehouse, "Address at a Luncheon, December 14, 1972, at the Home of Mr. and Mrs. Patrick Frawley" (MS, 1972), all in "MW U.S. visit" folder, box 126, section 1, Papers of the National Viewers' and Listeners' Association (hereafter "NVLA Papers"), Albert Sloman Library, University of Essex, Colchester, United Kingdom.

3. Edward W. Pohlman and K. Seshagiri Rao, "Population Education *versus* Sex Education," in *Population Education: A Panel Discussion*, ed. B. Kuppuswamy et al. (Delhi: Institute for Social and Psychological Research, 1971), 5; *Final Report on the Third Seminar on Sex Education and Social Development* (Stockholm: Division for Population, Health, and Nutrition of the Swedish International Development Authority, 1977), 127.

4. Mary Calderone, "Youth and Sexual Behavior," *Sixth Annual Greater Hartford Forum* (n.p., 1965), p. 53, folder 237, box 14, Collection 179, Mary Calderone Papers, Arthur and Elizabeth Schlesinger Library, Radcliffe College, Cambridge, Massachusetts; International Union of Family Organisations, Commission on Marriage and Marriage Guidance (Paris), "Report of the Meeting Held in Edinburgh (2–4 June 1969)" (MS, 1969), p. 5, "Sex Education" folder, box PC-S101, Accession II, Population Council Papers, Rockefeller Archive Center, Tarrytown, New York; International Planned Parenthood Federation, Europe and Near East Region, *Regional Council Sex Education Seminar, Baden/Vienna, 6–8 October 1970* (London: IPPF Europe and Near East Region, 1970), 1; Mary Calderone, "Sexual Attitudes and the Regulation of Conception," *Emphasis '65: A Report from the Boston University Symposium on Population Growth and Birth Control* (New York: Siecus, n.d. [1965]), p. 52, folder 42, box 2, Collection 83-M184, Calderone Papers.

5. Jonathan Zimmerman, *Whose America? Culture Wars in the Public Schools* (Cambridge, MA: Harvard University Press, 2002), 191–92; Howard S. Hoyman, "Our Most Explosive Issue: Birth Control," *Journal of School Health* 39, no. 7 (1969): 459, 464–65; Howard S. Hoyman, "Sex Education and Our Core Values," *Journal of School Health* 44, no. 2 (1974): 63.

6. S. P. Ruhela, *Sociology of Sex Education in India* (Delhi: Dhanpat Rai and Sons, 1969), 13; Dr. (Miss) J. Sandell, Dr. J. S. Mathur, and Dr. B. K. Trivedi, "Sex Education and the National Family Planning Programme,"

*Journal of Family Welfare* 22, no. 4 (1976): 62; J. Mugo Gachuhi, *Sex Education Controversy [sic]: Views of Youth and Teachers in Kenya* (Nairobi: Institute for Development Studies, 1975), 16; *Responsible Parenthood and Family Life Education. Proceedings of the Seminar of the Western Pacific Region of the International Planned Parenthood Federation* (Hong Kong: International Planned Parenthood Federation, 1972), 85.

7. Beryl Sutters, *Be Brave and Angry: Chronicles of the International Planned Parenthood Federation* (London: International Planned Parenthood Federation, 1973), 365–66; Eighth International Conference of the International Planned Parenthood Federation (Santiago, Chile), "Daily Bulletin" (MS, 1967), folder 8, box 202, Planned Parenthood Federation of America II Collection, Sophia Smith Collection, Smith College, Northampton, Massachusetts; "Swinging Holland: Riots Every Week," *Washington Post*, July 16, 1966, p. A12; "Girls March," *Guardian*, February 19, 1976, p. 2; "Student Coalition for Relevant Sex Education, Birth Control, and Venereal Disease Information and Referral Project in New York City Public Schools" (MS, January 1972), pp. 6–7, enclosed with Jules Kolodny to Harvey B. Scribner, July 21, 1972, folder 11, box 89, United Federation of Teachers Records, Robert F. Wagner Labor Archives, Tamiment Library, New York University.

8. "Women Winning the Sex War?" *Gloucester Citizen*, May 10, 1968, folder SA/FPA/A17/121, Family Planning Association Papers, Wellcome Library, London; Dagmar Herzog, *Sex after Fascism: Memory and Morality in Twentieth-Century Germany* (Princeton, NJ: Princeton University Press, 1995), 147; "Sex Education in the Schools Is Approved by the Following National Organizations" (MS, n.d. [1969?]), p. 2, "Sex Education" folder, box PC-S101, Accession II, Population Council Papers; Judy Mann, "Sex Education Fails to Address the Issues," *Washington Post*, February 8, 1980, p. B1.

9. "Sex Education: The Forbidden Topics," *Washington Post*, December 4, 1979, p. C1; "Is It Time to Teach a New Lesson in Sex?" *Now!* June 20, 1980, pp. 63–64, enclosed with Antony Grey to the Editor, "Now!," July 5, 1980, folder HCA/ALBANY TRUST 2/7, HCA/Albany Trust Collection, Hall-Carpenter Archives, London School of Economics, London; British Broadcasting Corporation, *School Broadcasting and Sex Education the Primary School* (London: BBC, 1971), 3; "Wiseman's New Film," *Christian Science Monitor*, May 19, 1969, p. 7; Frederick Wiseman, *High School* (Cambridge, MA: Zipporah Films, 1968).

10. Mikolaj Kozakiewicz and Norman Rea, *A Survey on the Status of Sex Education in European Member Countries* (London: International Planned Parenthood Federation, 1975), 1, 81, 62; International Union of Family Organisations, "Report of the Meeting Held in Edinburgh," 10; Nicholas Beattie, "Sex-Education in France: A Case-Study in Curriculum Change," *Comparative Education* 12, no. 2 (1976): 118, 121–22, 124; Uta Schwarz,

"*Helga* (1967): West German Sex Education and the Cinema in the 1960s," 200–201; Lutz D. H. Sauerteig, "Representations of Pregnancy and Childbirth in (West) German Sex Education Books, 1900s–1970s," 144–45, both in *Shaping Sexual Knowledge: A Cultural History of Sex Education in Twentieth Century Europe*, ed. Lutz D. H. Sauerteig and Roger Davidson (London: Routledge, 2008); Mary Redliffe, "Is This Teutonic Study of Sex the Best We Can Offer?" *Morning Telegraph* (Sheffield), November 20, 1968, folder SA/FPA/AIP/121, Family Planning Association Papers.

11. Schwarz, "*Helga* (1967)," 198; Adolph Schalk, *The Germans* (Englewood Cliffs, NJ: Prentice-Hall, 1971), 331–32; Sauerteig, "Representations of Pregnancy and Childbirth," 146; Katherine Whitehorn, "How to Turn Off Sex on Tap(e)," *Observer*, November 16, 1980, p. 33.

12. "Sex Education: The Forbidden Topics"; Michael Scriven, "Putting the Sex Back in Sex Education," *Phi Delta Kappan* 49 (May 1968): 485; Stewart E. Fraser, "Introduction to Part IV," in Stewart E. Fraser, ed., *Sex, Schools, and Society: International Perspectives* (Nashville: Aurora Publishers, 1972), 231; "High Schools Are Urged to Assist Birth Control," *New York Times*, September 29, 1971, p. 33; Hariette Surovell, "Most Girls Just Pray," *New York Times*, October 1, 1971, p. 41; "Spanish 'Stork' Film Off Limits to Youth," *Los Angeles Times*, November 25, 1971, p. G16; Bruno P. F. Wanrooij, "Carnal Knowledge: The Social Politics and Experience of Sex Education in Italy, 1940–1980," in Sauerteig and Davidson, *Shaping Sexual Knowledge*, 119.

13. Howard S. Hoyman, "Sweden's Experiment in Human Sexuality and Sex Education," *Journal of School Health* 41 (April 1971): 183; Schwarz, "*Helga* (1967)," 201; "Sex Education Workshop Started," *Northwest Missourian* (Maryville, MO), July 17, 1970, folder 8, box 3, Helen Manley Papers, Missouri Historical Society, Saint Louis; Emily de Forest White, "Family Planning Report on Trip around the World. August 29–November 7 1964" (MS, 1964), p. 1, folder 46, box 203; Alan F. Guttmacher to Elise Ottesen-Jensen, May 18, 1964, folder 11, box 205, both in Planned Parenthood II Collection.

14. A. C. Vaigo, "Denmark: Getting Sex in Perspective," *Times Educational Supplement*, September 3, 1971, p. 13; Toshimi Inaba to Elizabeth Wettergren, March 31, 1971, volume 3; Andrew Phelan to RFSU, December 22, 1971, volume 10; James Pilbeam to RFSU, April 18, 1969, volume 8; J. W. Korstman to RFSU, November 1, 1969, volume 8, all in Foreign Correspondence, Papers of Riksförbundet för Sexuell Upplysning (RFSU), Labour Movement Archives and Library, Stockholm, Sweden.

15. Tom Buckley, "Oh! Copenhagen!" *New York Times*, February 8, 1970, p. 217; J. Robert Moskin, "Sweden's New Battle over Sex," *Look*, November 15, 1966, "Sex Education (Sweden)" file, Vertical Files Collection, Kinsey Institute Archives, Bloomington, Indiana; David Barnard, "Most Swedes

Want Sex in Curriculum," *Times Educational Supplement,* July 30, 1971, p. 8; "Study of Sex Education Programs," *School and Society* 97 (Summer 1969): 271; Hans L. Zetterberg, *Sexual Life in Sweden,* trans. Graham Fennell (New Brunswick, NJ: Transaction, 2002), 162; Hoyman, "Our Most Explosive Sex Education Issue," 464; Carl-Gustaf Boethius, "The Battle for Sex Education in Sweden," in *Second Seminar on Sex Education and Social Development in Sweden, Latin America and the Caribbean, April 1972,* ed. Margareta Holmstedt (Stockholm: Swedish International Development Authority, 1974), 82; Lester A. Kirkendall, "Preface," in Birgitta Linner, *Sex and Society in Sweden* (New York: Random House, 1967), ix.

16. Carl Gustaf Boethius to Ruarc Gahan, June 14, 1978, volume 15; Boethius to Rosa Castella, June 5, 1980, volume 16, both in Foreign Correspondence, RFSU Papers; Boethius, "The Battle for Sex Education in Sweden," 83.

17. Hoyman, "Sweden's Experiment in Human Sexuality and Sex Education," 174; Swedish Association for Sexuality Education, "'Open House' Youth Clinic" (MS, n.d. [1984]), p. 1, enclosed with Kerstin Strid to W. Haddad, February 2, 1984, volume 17, Foreign Correspondence, RFSU Papers; Maj-Briht Bergstrom-Walan to Martin S. Weinberg, March 4, 1971, "Bergstrom-Walan, Maj-Briht" folder, Gebhard Era Correspondence Collection, Part II (1970–79), Kinsey Institute Archives; Barnard, "Most Swedes Want Sex in the Curriculum," 8.

18. Roger Davidson and Gayle Davis, *The Sexual State: Sexuality and Scottish Governance, 1950–1980* (Edinburgh: Edinburgh University Press, 2012), 199; Kirby Kinman, *Sex Education Examined* (n.p., 1969), 12, folder 35, box 22, Institute for Sex Education Records, Special Collections and University Archives, Richard J. Daley Library, University of Illinois at Chicago; Michael Tracy and David Morrison, *Whitehouse* (London: Macmillan, 1979), 132; Paul Ferris, "Sex: What to Tell the Children?" *Observer,* May 29, 1977, p. 13.

19. Pink Floyd, "Pigs," in *Animals* (London: Harvest Records, 1977); Elizabeth M. Elliott to Mary Whitehouse, June 28, 1972, box 80 [no folder], section 1, NVLA Papers.

20. Mary M. Robson to Mary Whitehouse, October 24, 1969, "MW U.S. visit" folder, box 126; Martha Rountree to Steven Stevens, November 7, 1973, "Martha Rountree" folder, box 127, both in section 1, NVLA Papers.

21. "CDL Sponsors Whitehouse Visit," *National Decency Reporter* 10, nos. 1–2 (1973): 1; Raymond P. Gauer to Charles H. Keating Jr., December 18, 1972, both in "CDL Inc" folder, box 127; Gauer to Mary Whitehouse, August 30, 1972, "MW U.S. visit" folder, box 126, all in section 1, NVLA Papers.

22. "Festival of Light People Have Big Plans," *Advertiser* (Adelaide, Australia), October 29, 1973; "Mary, Mary Not Quite Contrary (and How's the

BBC?)" *Woman's Day*, October 8, 1973; Bernard Boucher, "A Talk with Crusader to Clear the Air," *Advertiser*, October 18, 1973, all in "MW 1973 visit" folder, box 128; "Mr. Kurt Kempf President Canterbury Branch SPCS with Mrs. V. Riches and Her Husband in Timaru," *Society for Promotion of Community Standards Newsletter* (New Zealand), no. 48 (December 1983), p. 1; "Combating the Forces Arrayed against the Family," *New Life* (Australia), May 5, 1983, both in "Australian Festival of Light" folder, box 131, all in section 1, NVLA Papers; Thea Mendelsohn, "Getting Sex, Sex Education, and the Opposition into Perspective," in *Teaching about Sex: The Australian Experience* (Sydney: Australian Federation of Family Planning Associations, 1983), 108.

23. Hanne Riser, "School Sex Education: Structure and System in Denmark," in *Preparation for Family Life*, ed. Klaus Schleicher (Strasbourg: Council for Cultural Co-Operation, 1982), 126–27; Mike Duckenfield, "Denmark: Sex Education Protest Goes to Human Rights Court," *Times Educational Supplement*, October 17, 1975, p. 14.

24. Duckenfield, "Denmark," 14; Danish Family Planning Association and the Swedish Association for Sexuality Education, RFSU, *Sexual Rights of Young Women in Denmark and Sweden* (Stockholm: RFSU, 1995), 10; Svend Laursen, "Open Letter to Her Majesty the Queen, London" (MS, January 3, 1977); Therese Brondum to Philippe Schepens, n.d. [1977], both in box 38 [no folders], section 5; "Sex Education and Parental Rights in International Law" (MS, June 1980), p. 3, "Sex Education" folder, box 14, section 2, all in NVLA Papers.

25. T. J. Proom, "BBC Education Spelt Disaster to Our Family: A Personal Report to the Annan Inquiry" (MS, October 1974); "No Legal Right for Parents on Sex Classes," *Daily Telegraph*, March 10, 1971; Proom to Rex Stanton Rogers, March 4, 1976, all in box 80 [no folders], section 5, NVLA Papers.

26. "Lord Clifford of Chudleigh, Continued" (MS, January 14, 1976), "Sex Education" folder, box 14, section 2, NVLA Papers; *House of Lords Official Report* Vol. 407 No. 103 (3/24/1980), p. 559, 553, folder SA/FPA/C/B/6/7/1; John A. Murphy, "Sex Education Broadcasts: The Duty of Parents," *Times of London*, November 17, 1969; Jacinth Whittaker, "Now, Pornography for the Kids of 8," *Birmingham Free Press*, November 7, 1969, both in folder SA/FPA/A17/123, all in Family Planning Association Papers.

27. "School Sex Education Required in Three States and D.C., but Most States Allow Local Districts to Decide," *Family Planning Perspectives* 12, no. 6 (1980): 308; "That Schools Teach of Sex Is Still Controversial," *New York Times*, February 27, 1977, p. 150; "New York State and Sex Education," *SIECUS Report* 5, no. 3 (1977): 6; "School Sex Court Gets High Court OK," *Chicago Tribune*, December 8, 1970, p. B6; "Summary of Actions of the Supreme Court Announced Yesterday," *New York Times*, April 6,

1976, p. 25; "Protesters Proclaim, 'Right's on Our Side,'" *Christian Science Monitor*, February 14, 1970, p. 13; Commission on Professional Rights and Responsibilities, National Education Association, *Suggestions for Defense against Extremist Attack: Sex Education in the Public Schools* (Washington, DC: National Education Association, n.d. [1970]), p. 4, folder 10, box 999, Manuscript Collection 2266, National Education Association Records, Gelman Library, George Washington University, Washington, DC.

28. "Rappitup," "Stop All This Havering about Sex!" *Evening Times*, July 10, 1969, folder SA/FPA/A17/122, Family Planning Association Papers; "Concern Grows on BBC Lessons" (unidentified clipping, n.d. [1971]), box 80 [no folders], section 1, NVLA Papers; "Sex Courses Bring Picketing Threat by Parents," *Washington Post*, March 3, 1968, p. F6.

29. "'Spring Awakening' More Than a Curiosity Piece," *Chicago Tribune*, February 22, 1979, p. A3; Ronald Goldman and Juliette Goldman, "The Research Bases for Sex Education" (MS, November 10–11, 1984), pp. 4–5, volume 17, Foreign Correspondence, RFSU Papers; Mary Calderone to Ronald Goldman, January 21, 1981, folder 10, box 6, Collection 83-M184, Calderone Papers.

30. Thorsten Sjövall, "Why Sex Education?" in International Planned Parenthood Federation, Europe and Near East Region, *Regional Council Sex Education Seminar, Baden/Vienna, 6–8 October 1970* (London: IPPF Europe and Near East Region, 1970), 4; Bernard, "Most Swedes Want Sex in Curriculum," 8; "The Sexual Rights of Children and Youth," *SIECUS Report* 8, no. 2 (1979): 3; Lester A. Kirkendall to Mary Calderone, June 6, 1979; Lester A. Kirkendall and Ronald Moglia, "The Sexual Rights of Children and Youth" (MS 1979), both in folder 23, box 30, Collection 83-M184, Calderone Papers; WHO Regional Office for Europe, "Consultation on Sexuality, Summary Report" (MS, December 15, 1983), pp. 1–3, volume 17, Foreign Correspondence, RFSU Papers.

31. "Sex Education and Parental Rights in International Law," 3; Emrys Jones to Alastair Service, July 19, 1982, folder SA/FPA/C/B/2/15/1, Family Planning Association Papers; Brita Blomquist to Milanka Jaksic, June 15, 1973, volume 12, Foreign Correspondence, RFSU Papers; Lester A. Kirkendall, "Education for Sexuality in the Orient," *SIECUS Report* 1, no. 2 (1972): 5.

32. Bruce D. Carlson to John S. Nagel, November 27, 1974; Barry Schuman to Nagel, November 11, 1974, both in grant 07110570, reel 1200; Clay I. Onah to Robert Edwards, April 17, 1975, grant 07350359, reel 1158, all in Ford Foundation Archives, New York; "Health Education and Family Planning Program in Uganda. Monthly Report of George A. Saxton, Jr., M.D., M.P.H." (MS, April 1968), folder 3, box 2; AFSC International Service Division, "Hong Kong Family Planning Program. Program Developments during 1967" (MS, March 1968), folder 21, box 12; Corinne Johnson to Members of the Committee on Family Planning and

Population Education, January 26, 1972, folder 11, box 1; American Friends Service Committee, "Family Planning and Population Education in Latin America" (MS, October 1970), folder 1, box 2, all in Henry Joel Cadbury Papers, Special Collections, Bryn Mawr College, Bryn Mawr, Pennsylvania; Paula Pelaez, "Chile," in *Responsible Parenthood and Sex Education*, ed. Susan Burke (London: International Planned Parenthood Federation, 1970), 82; "Report on Ed Duckles [*sic*] trip to Central and South America. February 8 to March 14, 1969" (MS, 1969), p. 12, folder 1, box 2, Cadbury Papers.

33. Elisabeth Wettergren to Benigno S. Aquino, October 10, 1969, volume 8, Foreign Correspondence, RFSU Papers; Wettergren to H. S. Hoyman, September 28, 1971; K. Yamaguchi to "Miss Wemen," April 3, 1971; "Object of Study" (MS, 1971), enclosed with Takeo Asai to Truz von Ahlefeld, May 21, 1971, all in volume 10, Foreign Correspondence, RFSU Papers; *Final Report on the Third Seminar on Sex Education and Social Development* (Stockholm: Division for Population, Health and Nutrition of the Swedish International Development Authority, 1977), 3; *Second Seminar on Sex Education and Social Development in Sweden, Latin America and the Caribbean* (Stockholm: Swedish International Development Authority, 1974), 100.

34. "Urge Every School to Teach Sex Education," *Chicago Tribune*, April 13, 1967, folder 119, box 12, Institute for Sex Education Records; Eighth International Conference of the IPPF, "Daily Bulletin"; IPPF, *Regional Council Sex Education Seminar, Baden/Vienna, 6–8 October 1970*, 3; UNESCO, *Regional Meeting of Experts on Sex Education* (UNESCO Regional Office of Education for Latin America and the Caribbean, 1971), 4; Bo Lewin, "Family Planning and Sex Education for Young People," in *The Adolescent Dilemma: International Perspectives on the Family Planning Rights of Minors*, ed. Hyman Rodman and Jan Trost (Westport, CT: Praeger, 1986), 203.

35. Pierre Pradervand, "Excerpts from the Letters of Pierre Pradervand from West Africa, 1971–1973, Regarding Sex Education, Local Beliefs, Western Approaches" (MS, n.d. [1973]), p. 7, General Collection, Kinsey Institute Archives; "Mexican Government's Increased Program Support Leads to Doubling of Contraceptive Use in 2.5 Years," *International Family Planning Digest* 3, no. 4 (1977): 13; N. H. Rajaratnam, "Suggestions" (MS, August 16, 1965), p. 1, folder 3/1/35; "Petition to the National Liberation Council through Lt-General J. A. Ankrah, Chairman" (MS, 1966), enclosed with J.T.K. Aggrey to Principal Secretary, August 8, 1966, folder 3/1/121, both in Ghana Education Service Records, Record Group 3/1, Ghana National Archives, Accra, Ghana.

36. Planned Parenthood Association of Ghana, "Discussion Paper. Sex Education in Ghana" (MS, July 1971), p. 1, enclosed with E. K. Okoh to F. W. Beecham, September 6, 1971, folder 3/1/35, Ghana Education Service Records; *Planned Parenthood Association of Ghana* (n.p., October 1976),

26; Maung Sein to Anita Gradin, May 1, 1975, volume 13, Foreign Correspondence, RFSU Papers; Hermongenes Alvarez, "Uruguay," in Burke, *Responsible Parenthood and Sex Education*, 111; Barry Schuman to John S. Nagel, November 11, 1974, grant 07110570, reel 1200, Ford Foundation Archives.

37. Government of India, Ministry of Health, Family Planning, Works, Housing, and Urban Development, *Family Planning Programme Today: Some Questions and Answers* (n.p., December 1970), p. 13, folder 30, box 13, Alan Frank Guttmacher Papers, Center for the History of Medicine, Frances A. Countway Library of Medicine, Harvard University, Boston; J. Mayone Stycos, "Desexing Birth Control," *Family Planning Perspectives* 9, no. 6 (1977): 286–87; Burke, *Responsible Parenthood and Sex Education*, 15; Pierre Pradervand, "Report on the First National Seminar on Family Planning" (MS, December 11–16, 1972), p. 3, grant 07350359, reel 1158, Ford Foundation Archives; Co-Ordinated Action Programme for the Advancement of Population Education (CAPAPE), UNESCO, *Study of the Contribution of Population Education to Educational Renewal and Innovation in El Salvador, the Republic of Korea, Philippines, and Tunisia* (Paris: UNESCO, 1980), 25, 45; "Report of Edwin Duckles' Trip to Central and South America. January 30 to March 14, 1970" (MS, 1970), p. 11, folder 1, box 2, Cadbury Papers.

38. UNESCO, *Population Education: A Contemporary Concern* (Paris: UNESCO, 1978), 23–24; John W. Dykstra, "Imperative: Education for Reproductive Responsibility," *Phi Delta Kappan* 49 (May 1968): 503; Caroline S. Cochran, "Baltimore—Population and Family Planning Education" (MS, n.d. [1967]), "Correspondence Re: Meeting 5/1, 2/70" folder, box PC-102, Accession II, Population Council Papers; Art Hurow memorandum, August 5, 1971, School of Education of the University of North Carolina Papers, Collection 40043, University Archives, University of North Carolina, Chapel Hill.

39. Sloan Wayland, "Population Education as It Exists Today: A Global Perspective" (MS, 1971), p. 1, "Population Education as It Exists Today: A Global Perspective" folder, Sloan R. Wayland Papers, Pocket Knowledge (BETA) File View, Teachers College Archives; Matthew Connelly, *Fatal Misconception: The Struggle to Control World Population* (Cambridge, MA: Harvard University Press, 2008), 162–63; Inderjeet Parmar, *Foundations of the American Century: The Ford, Carnegie, and Rockefeller Foundations in the Rise of American Power* (New York: Columbia University Press, 2012), 2; John S. Nagel to Richard W. Dye, April 12, 1975; Barry Schuman to Nagel, November 11, 1974, both in grant 07110570, reel 1200, Ford Foundation Archives.

40. "Population-Related Activities at Teachers College, Columbia University" (MS, n.d. [1983?]), "Population Education" folder, Wayland Papers; David Kline to Stephen Viederman, April 20, 1970, "Correspondence re

Meetings, 5/1, 2/70" folder; Thomas Poffenberger and B. P. Lulla, "The Baroda-Michigan Population Education Program" (MS, 1970), "Project Proposals—International" folder, both in box PC-S102; Stephen Vieder-man, "Proposals for the Population Council's Program in Population Education" (MS, October 2, 1970), p. 8, "Population Education—A Report" folder, box PC-S101, all in Accession II, Population Council Papers; "Some Thoughts about a Population Education Network" (MS, 1973), p. 4, "Population Education and Studies (1973) 1" folder, box 12, Center for Studies in Education and Development Papers, Harvard University Archives, Cambridge, Massachusetts; B. L. Raina, *A Quest for a Small Family* (New Delhi: Commonwealth Publishers, 1991), 198.

41. UNESCO, *Population Education: A Contemporary Concern*, 25; Edward W. Pohlman and K. Seshagiri Rao, "Population Education *versus* Sex Education," in *Population Education: A Panel Discussion*, ed. B. Kuppuswamy et al. (Delhi: Institute for Social and Psychological Research, 1971), 7–8, 3–4, 5.

42. Irwin Slesnick, "Reaction to Basic Paper from Non-Participants," in Kuppuswamy et al., *Population Education*, 101–2; Raina, *A Quest for a Small Family*, 191–92; "Population, Sex Teaching Found Not Widespread," *International Family Planning Digest* 2, no. 1 (1976): 560; V. K. Rao, *Population Education* (New Delhi: APH Publishing, 2001), 16; T. Sjövall, "The Relative Priority for IPPF Policy of Maternal and Child Health, etc. and Population Control" (MS, September 1970), volume 10, Foreign Correspondence, RFSU Papers.

43. Pohlman and Rao, "Population Education *versus* Sex Education," 10; Stephen Viederman to John H. Tanton, August 27, 1970, "Teachers Requests—Misc." folder, box PC-S101, Accession II, Population Council Papers; Stephen Viederman, "Population Education in the Schools: Status and Needs," in *Readings on Population Information and Education. Background Papers for a Ford Foundation Meeting on Population. Elsinore, Denmark, June, 1972* (New York: Ford Foundation, 1973), 328; David Kline, "Why, What, and How Population Education in the Schools?" (MS, November 30, 1972), p. 6, "Population Education and Studies (1973) 2" folder; David Kline, John Middleton, and Lewis J. Perelman, "PACER: Population Abatement through Communication, Education, and Reinforcement" (MS, May 1, 1972), p. 37, both in box 12, Center for Studies in Education and Development Papers; Rosario P. Alberto and Mara Jesusa A. Ledesma, *Population Education in Asia: A Synthesis* (Honolulu: East-West Center, March 1977), 5–6.

44. Felicitas Arellano-Reyes and Carmelita L. Villaneuva, *Introducing Human Sexuality into the Population Education Curriculum* (Makatia, Rizal, Philippines: Population Center Foundation, 1976), 16; "Sex Education in Mexico," *SIECUS Report* 5, no. 3 (1977): 7; Elisabeth E. Mueller to Stephen

Viederman, June 10, 1970, folder 70, PC-FC box 54, Accession II, Population Council Papers; N. V. Vaswani and Indira Kapoor, "School Teachers' Attitude towards Population Education, Views on Age of Marriage and Family Size," in *Why Sex Education? Report of the Seminar*, ed. Indian Council for Child Welfare (New Delhi: March 29–30, 1976), 31–32.

45. "School Use of Sex Pamphlet Stirs Angry Debate in French Town," *New York Times*, December 26, 1972, p. 35; "Sex Education Planned in French Schools," *New York Times*, January 5, 1973, p. 3; William Farr, "France: Cautious Start to Sex Instruction," *Times Educational Supplement*, February 22, 1974, p. 15; Mark Webster, "Unwilling to School," *Times Educational Supplement*, December 31, 1976, p. 6.

46. Robert M. Bjork, "An International Perspective on Various Issues in Sex Education as an Aspect of Health Education," *Journal of School Health* 39 (October 1969): 526; "Teacher in Pill Talk Gets the Sack," *Daily Sketch* (UK), March 18, 1969; untitled clipping, *Nottingham Evening Post*, March 28, 1969, both in folder SA/FPA/A17/122, Family Planning Association Papers; "Teacher Defends Showing of Explicit Sex Filmstrip," *New York Times*, April 6, 1974, p. 35; "Merola Drops Inquiry of a Teacher Showing Students Sex Film, Saying Law Was Not Violated," *New York Times*, May 23, 1974, p. 21; "Sex Education Softened," *Los Angeles Times*, May 25, 1975, p. SE1; Helen Smyth, *Rocking the Cradle: Contraception, Sex, and Politics in New Zealand* (Wellington: Steele Roberts, 2000), 168–69; Albert G. Chanter, *Sex Education in the Primary School* (London: Macmillan, 1966), 4–5.

47. Wolf Bleek, *Sexual Relationships and Birth Control in Ghana: A Case Study of a Rural Town* (Amsterdam: Universiteit van Amsterdam, 1976), 53–54; Anthony A. D'Souza, *Sex Education and Personality Development* (New Delhi: USHA Publications, 1979), 25; Concerned Parents Association (Geelong, Australia), *Alert*, no. 3 (April 1981): 5, "Australian Festival of Light" folder, box 131, section 1, NVLA Papers; Ann Leslie, "Sex out of School Hours," *Sunday Mirror*, February 11, 1968; Josephine Type, "Sex Education Is Still a Delicate Issue," *South Wales Weekly Argus*, May 9, 1968, both in folder SA/FPA/A17/121, Family Planning Association Papers; "Women Victim of Sexual Taboos, Psychiatrist Says," *Los Angeles Times*, May 22, 1970, p. E8.

48. "Gay Rights: Is a Backlash Forming?" *Los Angeles Times*, July 29, 1977, p. F1; "The Homosexual in the Classroom," *New York Times*, October 24, 1977, p. 28; "San Francisco Schools to Teach Tolerance of Homosexuals," *Washington Post*, June 7 1977, p. A2; *House of Lords Official Report* Vol. 406 No. 98 (March 14, 1980), p. 1375, folder SA/FPA/C/B/6/7/1, Family Planning Association Papers; Bernard Moran, "Our Teenagers and Sex Education," *Challenge Weekly* (New Zealand) 41, no. 9 (March 18, 1983), p. 11, "MW 1978" visit folder, box 129, section 1, NVLA Papers.

49. Moran, "Our Teenagers and Sex Education," 10; Kozakiewicz and Rea, *A Survey on the Status of Sex Education in European Member Countries*, 22; Lewin, "Family Planning and Sex Education for Young People," 207; "Population, Sex Teaching Found Not Widespread," 7.

50. "That Schools Teach of Sex Is Still Controversial"; Howard M. Bahr, "Changes in Family Life in Middletown, 1924–1977," *Public Opinion Quarterly* 44, no. 1 (1980): 42; Gerard Lucas, "Sex Education Today," *World Health* [no vol. number] (July–August 1969): 37.

## CHAPTER FOUR: A RIGHT TO KNOWLEDGE?

1. *Report of the International Conference on Population and Development. Cairo, 5–13 September 1994* (New York: United Nations, 1995), 49; Stanley Johnson, *The Politics of Population: The International Conference on Population and Development* (London: Earthscan, 1995), 153–54; Jocelyn DeJong memorandum, March 23, 1994, reel 7009; Aziz Ahmed Khattab, "Sex Education in Egypt. [Thirty Years' Personal Experience]" (MS, n.d. [1995]), reel 6855, both in grant 09451109, Ford Foundation Archives, New York.

2. Swedish Association for Sexuality Education, *Breaking Through: A Guide to Sexual and Reproductive Health and Rights* (Stockholm: RFSU, 2004), 15–17; *Report of the International Conference on Population and Development*, 146; "The Poor Lose Out in Battle between Church and State," *Guardian*, October 31, 1994, p. 9; Michelle Goldberg, *The Means of Reproduction: Sex, Power, and the Future of the World* (New York: Penguin, 2009), 104; "Pakistani Leader Attends Conference Despite Islamists," *Christian Science Monitor*, September 6, 1994, p. 7.

3. Johnson, *The Politics of Population*, 157; Goldberg, *Means of Reproduction*, 112; Fatima Amer, "The Problems of Sex Education within the Context of Islamic Teachings—Towards a Clearer Vision of the British Case," *Muslim Education Quarterly* 14, no. 2 (1997): 16, 24, 26.

4. Swedish Association for Sexuality Education, *Passion for Rights: Ten Years of Fighting for Sexual and Reproductive Health* (Stockholm: RFSU, 2004), 69.

5. "AIDS lecture October 6, 1987" (MS, 1989), pp. 1–2, folder 3, box 148, C. Everett Koop Papers, National Library of Medicine, Bethesda, Maryland.

6. Yoshiro Hatano and Tsuguo Shimazaki, "Japan," in *The Continuum Complete International Encyclopedia of Sexuality*, ed. Robert T. Francoeur and Raymond J. Noonan (Bloomington, IN: Kinsey Institute, 2004), online edition; James L. Shortridge, "Siecus Is Pioneering a Worldwide Sexuality Education Effort," *SIECUS Report* 24, no. 3 (1996): 2.

7. "Family Feuds," *New York Times*, August 5, 1990, p. EDUC26; Debra W. Haffner, "1992 Report Card on the States: Sexual Rights in America," *SIECUS Report* 20, no. 3 (1992); "Abstinence Is Focus of U.S. Sex Education," *New York Times*, December 15, 1999, p. A18; "U.S. Shows Respect," *Daily Journal* (Kankakee, IL), February 10, 1987, enclosed with Coleen Kelly Mast to C. Everett Koop, February 19, 1987, folder 7, box 84, Koop Papers; "Sex and Schools," *Time*, November 24, 1986, "AIDS. Education—Newspaper Clippings" folder, box 101, AIDS History Project Collection, One: National Gay and Lesbian Archives, Los Angeles; "Dr. Koop Defends His Crusade on AIDS," *New York Times*, April 6, 1987, p. B8.

8. "Sex Lesson Rules Mean Pupils May Miss Aids Advice," *Guardian*, March 7, 1987, p. 2; "Condoms Pose Sex Lesson Problem in Catholic Schools," *Guardian*, April 16, 1987, p. 4; "Children 'Need Lessons on Aids,'" *Guardian*, July 15, 1987, p. 4; Paul Meredith, "Children's Rights and Education," in *Legal Concepts of Childhood*, ed. Julia Fonda (Portland, OR: Hart Publishing, 2001), 211–12.

9. Hugo Roling, "The Problem of Sex Education in the Netherlands in the 20th Century," in *Cultures of Child Health in Britain and the Netherlands in the 20th Century*, ed. Marijke Gijswijt-Hofstra and Hilary Marland (Amsterdam: Rodopi, 2003), 255; Jay Friedman, "Cross-Cultural Perspectives on Sexuality Education," *SIECUS Report* 20, no. 6 (1992): 9; Osmo Kontula, *Reproductive Health Behaviour of Young Europeans*, vol. 2 (Strasbourg: Council of Europe, 2004), 48; Kristin Luker, *When Sex Goes to School* (New York: Norton, 2006), 209; Thomas Phelim Kelly, "Ireland," in Francoeur and Noonan, *Continuum Complete International Encyclopedia of Sexuality*; Anna Titkow, "Poland," in *From Abortion to Contraception: A Resource to Public Policies and Reproductive Behavior in Central and Eastern Europe from 1917 to the Present*, ed. Henry David (Westport, CT: Greenwood, 1999), 187; Corinne Nativel, "Teen Pregnancy and Reproductive Policies in France," in *When Children Become Parents: Welfare State Responses to Teenage Pregnancy*, ed. Anne Dagueree and Corinne Nativel (Bristol, UK: Policy Press, 2006), 127; United Nations Family Planning Association, *Thematic Evaluation of Adolescent Reproductive Health Programmes* (New York: UNFPA, 1997), 24.

10. Melanie Gallant and Eleanor Maticka-Tyndale, "School-Based HIV Prevention Programmes for African Youth," *Social Science and Medicine* 58 (April 2004): 1337–38; Monica Dynowski Smith, *Profile of Youth in Botswana* (Gabarone: Intersectoral Committee on Family Life Education, 1989), 5; *Final Report of the UNESCO Regional Seminar on HIV/AIDS and Education within the School System for English-Speaking Countries in Eastern and Southern Africa* (Paris: UNESCO, 1995), 12–13, 72; Colleen McLaughlin et al., *Old Enough to Know: Consulting Children about Sex and AIDS Education in Africa* (Cape Town: HSRC Press, 2012), 41.

11. Christopher Mensah Chrismek, *Sex Education and Social Harmony*, vol. 1 (Accra, Ghana: Chrismek Rights' Foundation, 2004), 15, 27–28, 36–39; Michael Aketewah, *Current Social Studies for West African Senior Schools* (Kumasi, Ghana: 4th Born Printing Press, 2007 [2004]), 114; Gifty Gyamera, *Religious and Moral Education for Senior Secondary Schools* (Accra, Ghana: Gogan Publishing, 2007), 94; Luke Gyesi-Appiah, *HIV/AIDS—Condom or Abstinence* (Cape Coast, Ghana: L. Nyakod Printing Works, 2007), 12.

12. Margaret E. Greene et al., *In This Generation: Sexual and Reproductive Health Policies for a Youthful World* (Washington, DC: Population Action International, 2002), 28–29; James T. Sears, "In(ter)ventions of Male Sexualities and HIV Education: Case Studies in the Philippines," in *A Dangerous Knowing: Sexuality, Pedagogy, and Popular Culture*, ed. Debbie Epstein and James T. Sears (London and New York: Cassell, 1999), 106; S. P. Ruhela and Ahrar Husain, *Sex Education in India in the 21st Century* (Delhi: Indian Publishers Distributors, 2002), ix; Nancy E. Riley and Edith Bowles, "Premarital Sexual Behavior in the People's Republic of China: A Review of Critical Problems and Issues," p. 13, in "Conference on Adolescent Sexuality in Asia" (MS, September 24–28, 1990), Research Information Services, East-West Center, Honolulu, Hawai'i; Joanna McMillan, *Sex, Science, and Morality in China* (London: Routledge, 2006), 57.

13. Margaret Gecaga, "Sex Education in the Context of Changing Family Roles," in *Responsible Leadership in Marriage and Family*, ed. Mary N. Getui (2005; Nairobi, Kenya: Acton Publishers, 2008), 55; Shishir Bhate, "Should a Child Be Told about 'The Birds and the Bees?'" in Ruhela and Husain, *Sex Education in India in the 21st Century*, 4–5; "Progress or Pornography?" *News China*, December 1, 2011, p. 18; Alessandra Aresu, "Sex Education in Modern and Contemporary China: Interrupted Debates across the Last Century," *International Journal of Educational Development* 29, no. 5 (2009): 539; Azzah Shararah Baydoun, "Sex Education in Lebanon: Between Secular and Religious Discourses," in *Deconstructing Sexuality in the Middle East*, ed. Pinar Ilkkaracan (Hampshire, UK: Ashgate, 2008), 91.

14. Office of the Secretary memorandum, October 18, 1985, folder 4, box 1323; Inter-Agency Working Group, "Core Curriculum Guide for Strengthening Health and Family Life Education in Teacher Training Colleges in the Eastern Caribbean" (MS, 1993), p. 73, folder 5, box 1321; "Workshop for Primary School Teachers in Health and Family Life Education, 12–14 November 1986" (MS, 1986), pp. 2–3, folder 8, box 1322, all in Carnegie Corporation of New York Papers, Rare Books and Manuscripts Library, Columbia University.

15. Ruth Landau, "Trip Report" (n.d., 1987), enclosed with Landau to Kerstin Strid, January 27, 1987, volume 22, IPPF Correspondence; "Ottar Fund," *People* 13, no. 2 (1986), enclosed with Maj Fant and Kerstin Strid to "World List of Family Planning Addresses," June 6, 1986, volume 18,

Foreign Correspondence, both in Papers of Riksförbundet för Sexuell Upplysning [RFSU], Labour Movement Archives and Library, Stockholm, Sweden; Le Thi Nham Tuyet and Vuong Xuan Tinh, eds., *Reproductive Culture in Vietnam* (Hanoi: Gioi Publishers, 1999), foreword [n.p.]; Anna Runeborg, *Sexuality—A Super Force: Young People, Sexuality, and Rights in the Era of HIV/AIDS* (Stockholm: Swedish International Development Cooperation Agency, 2002), 27, 34–35.

16. *Summary of Proceedings of the First African Youth Conference on Sexual Health* (Accra, Ghana: GUNSA National Secretariat, 1996), 28; Ford Foundation, *Sexuality and Social Change: Making the Connection; Strategies for Action and Investment* (New York: Ford Foundation, 1995), 32–33; Debra Haffner, "Should We Do It the Swedish Way?" *SIECUS Report* 18, no. 5 (1990): 10.

17. Carmen Barroso, "From Reproductive to Sexual Rights," in *Routledge Handbook of Sexuality, Health and Rights*, ed. Peter Aggleton and Richard Parker (London: Routledge, 2010), 386; "International Guidelines on Sex Education Reignite Debate," *Singapore News*, September 4, 2009; "Unesco Assailed over Sex Education Guidelines," *International Herald Tribune*, September 3, 2009, p. 8.

18. "Swedes Instill a Sense of Responsibility," *New York Times*, November 8, 1987, p. EDUC19; Maureen A. Kelly and Michael McGee, "Report from a Study Tour: Teen Sexuality Education in Netherlands, France, and Germany," *SIECUS Report* 27, no. 2 (December 1998/January 1999): 11–12.

19. Nativel, "Teen Pregnancy and Reproductive Policies in France," 125; Syed Ali Ashraf, "Sex Education and the Decadence of European Civilization," *Muslim Education Quarterly* 11, no. 4 (1994): 1; J. Mark Halstead, "Values and Sex Education in a Multicultural Society," in *Sex Education and Religion*, ed. Michael J. Reiss and Shaikh Abdul Mabud (Cambridge: Islamic Academy, 1998), 238; Syed Ali Ashraf, "The Islamic Concept of Sex as the Basis of Sex Education," *Muslim Education Quarterly* 13, no. 2 (1996): 2; Shaikh Abdul Mabud, "An Islamic View of Sex Education," in *Sex Education and Religion*, 114; "'Cameron Did Not Want a Yes Man': Sayeeda Warsi, David Cameron's New Shadow Minister for Community Cohesion, Is the First Muslim to Sit in Either a Cabinet or Shadow Cabinet," *Guardian*, July 11, 2007, p. 10.

20. Isabel Kaprielian-Churchill, "Refugees in Education in Canadian Schools," *International Review of Education* 42, no. 4 (1996): 361; Shahnaz Khan, "Muslim Women: Negotiations in the Third Space," *Signs* 23, no. 2 (1998): 480; Fida Sanjakdar, "'Teacher Talk': The Problems, Perspectives, and Possibilities for Developing a Comprehensive Sexual Health Education Curriculum for Australian Muslim Students," *Sex Education* 9, no. 3 (2009): 265–66; "Liberal Sexual Mores Present a 'Threat' to Swedish Muslims," *Jakarta Post*, June 24, 2001, p. 1; Tiffany Bartz, "Sex Education in

Multicultural Norway," *Sex Education* 7, no. 1 (2007): 18–20, 24; Roling, "The Problem of Sex Education in the Netherlands," 255; Jan Steutel and Ben Spiecker, "Sex Education, State Policy, and the Principle of Mutual Consent," *Sex Education* 4, no. 1 (2004): 52; Rachel Parker et al., "Sexuality Education in Europe: An Overview of Current Policies," *Sex Education* 9, no. 3 (2008): 237.

21. "Church Turns the Clock Back on Poland's Sexual Taboos," *Observer* (UK), May 2, 1993, p. 18; "Behind the Priests' Back," *Guardian*, October 3, 1995, p. B5; Kontula, *Reproductive Health Behaviour of Young Europeans*, 56; Igor S. Kon, "Russia," in Francoeur and Noonan, *Continuum Complete International Encyclopedia of Sexuality*; Igor S. Kon, "Sexual Culture and Politics in Contemporary Russia," in *Sexuality and Gender in Postcommunist Eastern Europe and Russia*, ed. Aleksandar Stulhofer and Theo Sandfort (New York: Haworth Press, 2005), 119.

22. Jennifer S. Butler, *Born Again: The Christian Right Globalized* (London: Pluto Press, 2006), 103, 130; Goldberg, *Means of Reproduction*, 156–57; Shelley Jones and Bonny Norton, "Uganda's ABC Program on HIV/AIDS Prevention: A Discursive Site of Struggle," in *Language and HIV/AIDS*, ed. Christina Higgins and Bonny Norton (Bristol, UK: Multilingual Matters, 2010), 160–61.

23. Goldberg, *Means of Reproduction*, 104; "Women's Meeting Agrees on Right to Say No to Sex," *New York Times*, September 11, 1995, p. A1; United Nations Family Planning Association, *Thematic Evaluation of Adolescent Reproductive Health Programmes* (New York: UNFPA, 1997), 25; "Deadly Serious," *Guardian*, June 30, 1999, p. B2; "Islamic States and US Right Fight to Turn Back Clock," *Guardian*, September 22, 1999, p. 6.

24. Gordon Urquhart, "That's Not Faith, That's Provocation: Catholics and Muslims Are Uniting in a Pernicious New Alliance," *Guardian*, November 12, 1999, p. 22; Butler, *Born Again*, 52; Goldberg, *Means of Reproduction*, 157.

25. Doug Ireland, "U.S and Evil Axis—Allies for Abstinence," *Nation*, May 16, 2002; Susan Rose, "Going Too Far? Sex, Sin, and Social Policy," *Social Forces* 84, no. 2 (2005): 1211–12; A. K. Ghosh, "Lifestyle Education: Need for Wholesome, Responsible Attitude to Sex," *Statesman* (New Delhi), May 30, 2005, p. 1; Avadesh Kumar Singh, "Against," in "Debate Contest: Sex Education Should Be Made Compulsory in Schools," *Pratiyogita Darpan*, July 2008, p. 171.

26. *Communication and Advocacy Strategies: Adolescent Reproductive and Sexual Health. Booklet 1. Demographic Profile* (Bangkok: UNESCO PROAP Regional Clearing House, 1999), 12; Mary Hunag Soo Lee, *Communication and Advocacy Strategies: Adolescent Reproductive and Sexual Health. Case Study: Malaysia* (Bangkok: UNESCO PROAP Regional Clearing House, 1999), 16; Gyamera, *Religious and Moral Education for Senior Secondary Schools*, 93;

Pornruedee Nitrat, "Thai Adolescents' Sexual Behaviors and School-Based Sex Education: Perspectives of Stakeholders in Chanthaburi Province, Thailand" (PhD diss., University of North Carolina–Chapel Hill, 2007), 88.

27. "Moral Responsibility," *Statesman* (New Delhi), August 22, 2007, p. 1; K. D. Whitehead, "Sex Education: Vatican Guidelines," *Crisis* 14, no. 5 (1996); R. Wanjohi, "Views of the Catholic Church: Youth and Family Life Education," in *Adolescent Fertility. Proceedings of a Workshop Held at Kwale, Coast Province, Kenya, August 1986*, ed. K. O. Rogo (Nairobi: Kenya Medical Association, 1987), 96; "Safe Textuality," *Outlook* (India), April 8–14, 2008, p. 20.

28. "Sex Classes Urged after Scandal at School," *South China Morning Post*, September 24, 2001, p. 12; Gallant and Maticka-Tyndale, "School-Based HIV Prevention Programmes for African Youth," 1349; Mbukeni Herbert Mnguni, *Education as a Social Institution and Ideological Process: From the Negritude Education in Senegal to Bantu Education in South Africa* (Münster, Germany: Waxmann Verlag, 1998), 75; "Women's Organization Opposes Decision to Introduce Sex Education in Schools," *Hindu* (Chennai), March 8, 2007, p. 1; Kabita Chakraboty, "Unmarried Muslim Youth and Sex Education: The *bustees* of Kolkata," in *Health, Culture, and Religion in South Asia: Critical Perspectives*, ed. Assa Doron and Alex Broom (New York: Routledge, 2011), 77; "Teacher Arrested for Sodomy," *Jakarta Post*, April 8, 2004, p. 5.

29. Peter Lewis Allen, *The Wages of Sin: Sex and Disease, Past and Present* (Chicago: University of Chicago Press, 2000), 147; "Books Stir Sex Education Debate in Britain," *Chicago Tribune*, December 22, 1986, p. 36; "Bigotry Fear If Gay Sex Teaching Is Banned," *Guardian*, December 9, 1987, p. 3; "Section 28 'No Bar to Gay Issues,'" *Guardian*, July 26, 1988, p. 4; Wanjira Kiama, "Men Who Have Sex with Men in Kenya," in *AIDS and Men: Taking Risks or Taking Responsibility?* ed. Martin Foreman (London: Panos/Zed Books, 1999), 115; *The Voices and Identities of Botswana's School Children: Gender, Sexuality, HIV/AIDS, and Life Skills in Education* (Nairobi: United Nations Children's Fund, 2005), 109.

30. Baydoun, "Sex Education in Lebanon," 94; Harriet Evans, *Women and Sexuality in China: Female Sexuality and Gender since 1949* (New York: Continuum, 1997), 38; "Sex Education Termed a Crime against Youth," *Hindu* (Chennai), April 21, 2007, p. 1; Mabud, "An Islamic View of Sex Education," 109, 112.

31. Gert Hekma, "A Dutch Concert: Sex Education in Multicultural Schools," *Thamyris* 7, nos. 1 and 2 (Amsterdam: Najade Press, 2000), 252, 255–56.

32. Hera Cook, "Getting 'Foolishly Hot and Bothered'? Parents and Teachers and Sex Education in the 1940s," *Sex Education* 12, no. 5 (2012): 560; Pierre Pradervand, "Report of the First International Seminar on Sex

Education for Countries of Francophone Subsaharan Africa" (MS, April 16–25, 1973), p. 2, grant 07350359, reel 1158, Ford Foundation Archives; Runeborg, *Sexuality—A Super Force*, 15; Saskia Belleman, "Let's Talk about Sex," *Guardian*, November 19, 1993, p. A16; Figen Cok, "Reflections on an Adolescent Sexuality Education Program in Turkey," *SIECUS Report* 28, no. 4 (2000): 17.

33. Cok, "Reflections on an Adolescent Sexuality Education Program," 17; Swedish Association for Sexuality Education, *Breaking Through: A Guide to Sexual and Reproductive Health and Rights* (Stockholm: RFSU, 2004), 43; Stine H. Bang Svendsen, "Elusive Acts: Pleasure and Politics in Norwegian Sex Education," *Sex Education* 12, no. 4 (2012): 400; Mary M. Krueger, "The Omnipresent Need: Professional Training for Sexuality Education Teachers," *SIECUS Report* 19, no. 4 (1994): 3; McLaughlin et al., *Old Enough to Know*, 62; Paula Maycock et al., *Relationships and Sexuality Education (RSE) in the Context of Social, Personal, and Health Education (SPHE)* (Dublin: Crisis Pregnancy Center, 2007), 172.

34. Iffat Farah et al., *Where Are the Gaps? HIV and Gender Pre-Service Teacher Training Curriculum and Practices in East Africa* (London: Commonwealth Secretariat, 2009), 81–82; McLaughlin et al., *Old Enough to Know*, 55, 42, 77; Market and Research Development Center, *Report. Evaluation of the National AIDS Program. January 1996–June 2001 in Vietnam* (Hanoi: n.p., May 2002), 59, Vietnam Development Information Center, Hanoi.

35. "Teachers Unwilling to Give Sex Lessons," *South China Morning Post*, July 18, 1996, p. 5; Igor S. Kon, "Russia," in Francoeur and Noonan, *Complete International Encyclopedia of Sexuality*; Alan Guttmacher Institute, *Risk and Responsibility: Teaching Sex Education in America's Schools* (New York: Guttmacher Institute, 1989), p. 12, folder 10, box 1916, Collection 2281, National Education Association Records, Gelman Library, George Washington University; "Flash Points," *New York Times*, August 5, 1990, p. EDUC23; Lana D. Muraskin to Gloria Primm Brown, August 21, 1987, folder 4, box 1192, Carnegie Corporation of New York Papers; "Classroom Conundrums," in *Sex Exposed: Sexuality and the Pornography Debate*, ed. Lynne Segal and Mary McIntosh (New Brunswick, NJ: Rutgers University Press, 1993), 203.

36. Mathabo Khau, "Sexuality Education in Rural Lesotho Schools: Challenges and Possibilities," *Sex Education* 12, no. 4 (2012): 413; Sabina Faiz Rashid, "Communicating with Rural Adolescents about Sex Education: Experiences from BRAC, Bangladesh," in *Towards Adulthood: Exploring the Sexual and Reproductive Health of Adolescents in South Asia*, ed. Sarah Bott et al. (Geneva: World Health Organization, 2003), 171; McLaughlin et al., *Old Enough to Know*, 72; Uwem Edimo Eslet, "Nigeria," in Francoeur and Noonan, *Complete International Encyclopedia of Sexuality*; Nitrat, "Thai

Adolescents' Sexual Behaviors and School-Based Sex Education," 29, 204; "Unwanted Lessons in Sex Education for Thai Teachers," *South China Morning Post*, April 9, 2005, p. 2; "Implementation of Project to Strengthen the Role of the School in Health Development and School Health and Family Life Education. Dominica 1986" (MS, 1986), p. 8, folder 8, box 1322, Carnegie Corporation of New York Papers; *Voices and Identities of Botswana's School Children*, 68–69.

37. "No Sex Please, We're in School," *South China Morning Post*, February 10, 2001, p. 7; Maureen Freely, "They Never Tell Us the Things We Really Want to Know," *Independent*, November 1, 1999, p. 8; Nitrat, "Thai Adolescents' Sexual Behaviors and School-Based Sex Education," 203.

38. Pempelani Mufane, "Stakeholder Perceptions and Attitudes towards Sexual and Reproductive Health Education in Namibia," *Sex Education* 8, no. 2 (2008): 152–53; McLaughlin et al., *Old Enough to Know*, 62; Andrea Irvin, *Taking Steps of Courage: Teaching Adolescents about Sexuality and Gender in Nigeria and Cameroun* (New York: International Women's Health Coalition, 2000), 4; Isak Niehaus, "Towards a Dubious Liberation: Masculinity, Sexuality, and Power in South African Lowveld Schools, 1953–1999," *Journal of Southern African Studies* 26, no. 3 (2000): 405; Anoop Khanna, *Adolescent Sexual Behaviour and Quality of Life* (Jaipur, India: Shruti Publications, 2009), 135; Shreejana Pokharel, "School-Based Sex Education in Western Nepal: Uncomfortable for Both Teachers and Students," *Reproductive Health Matters* 14, no. 28 (2006): 158; "Is Sex Education Appropriate for Middle School Students?" *Beijing Review* 50, no. 4 (2007): 46.

39. Tsuguo Shimazaki, "A Closer Look at Sexuality Education and Japanese Youth," *SIECUS Report* 22, no. 2 (December 1993/January 1994): 13; Maycock et al., *Relationships and Sexuality Education*, 163, 131; *Eastern Caribbean Intercountry Meeting on School Health and Family Life Education, Sponsored by the Carnegie Corporation of New York and Pan American Health Organization (as Executing Agency), St. Christopher–Nevis, June 3–5, 1991* (n.p., 1991), p. 9, folder 1, box 1323, Carnegie Corporation of New York Papers.

40. "Teenage Girls Demand Better Sex Education," *Observer* (London), February 26, 2006, p. 10; Donald Langille et al., "So Many Bricks in the Wall: Young Women in Nova Scotia Speak about Barriers to School-Based Sexual Health Education," *Sex Education* 1, no. 3 (2001): 253; Social Sector Policy Unit, Policy Analysis Division, Ministry of Finance and Economic Planning, *In-Depth Assessment of the Ghana National Family Planning Programme: 1970–1990* (Accra: Social Sector Policy Unit, 1992), 260; Pokharel, "School-Based Sex Education in Western Nepal," 158–59; "Rural Sex Education Frustrated by Ignorance," *Guardian*, September 3, 1994, p. 10.

41. Pokharel, "School-Based Sex Education in Western Nepal," 158; Michael J. Kelly, SJ, *Education: For an Africa without AIDS* (Nairobi: Paulines Publications Africa, 2008), 155; *Handbook for Educating on Adolescent*

*Reproductive and Sexual Health*, book 2 (Bangkok: UNESCO, 1998), 2; "AIDS Survey Sparks Call for Classes," *South China Morning Post*, February 10, 1996, p. 5; Center for Reproductive Law and Policy, *State of Denial: Adolescent Reproductive Rights in Zimbabwe* (New York: Center for Reproductive Law and Policy, 2002), 57; AnnDenise Brown et al., *Sexual Relations among Young People in Developing Countries: Evidence from WHO Case Studies* (Geneva: Department of Reproductive Health and Research, World Health Organization, 2001), 31; Lakshmi Goparaju, "Ignorance and Inequality: Youth Sexuality in India and Its Implications to HIV Spread" (PhD diss., Syracuse University, 1998), 206; "Concern over Ignorance of HIV among Taiwanese Youth," *BBC Monitoring Asia Pacific*, July 22, 2004, p. 1; Doris Essah, "School Children Learning about Sex and Love," in *Sex and Gender in an Era of Aids: Ghana at the Turn of the Millennium*, ed. Christine Oppong et al. (Accra: Sub-Saharan Publishers, 2006), 200–201; Wanda Nowicka, "Roman Catholic Fundamentalism against Women's Reproductive Rights in Poland," *Reproductive Health Matters* 4, no. 8 (1996): 26; *Reality Counts: Focusing on Sexuality and Rights in the Fight against HIV/AIDS* (Stockholm: RFSU, 2004), 64.

42. "Recommendation for Grant/FAP Action" (MS, March 13, 1997), grant 09300818, reel 7347, frames 147–48, Ford Foundation Archives; Virginia Guzman et al., "Democracy in the Country but Not in the Home? Religion, Politics, and Women's Rights in Chile," *Third World Quarterly* 31, no. 6 (2010): 977–79.

# CONCLUSION

1. Rex Stanton Rogers to T. J. Proom, January 11, 1976, box 80 [no folders], section 5, Papers of the National Viewers' and Listeners' Association, Albert Sloman Library, University of Essex, Colchester, United Kingdom; Rex S. Rogers, *Sex Education: Rationale and Reaction* (Cambridge: Cambridge University Press, 1974).

2. Proom to Rogers, March 4, 1976, box 80, section 5, NVLA Papers.

3. See, e.g., John Boli, Francisco O. Ramirez, and John W. Meyer, "Explaining the Origins and Expansion of Mass Education," *Comparative Education Review* 29, no. 2 (1985): 148; John W. Meyer, "World Models, National Curricula, and the Centrality of the Individual," in *School Knowledge in Comparative and Historical Perspective*, ed. Aaron Benavot and Cecilia Braslavsky (Hong Kong: Spring, 2007), 268–70.

4. K. H. Kavanagh, *Sex Education: Its Uses and Abuses* (London: Responsible Society, n.d. [1972]), "Sex Education" folder, box 14, section 2, NVLA Papers.

5. Paul Cole Beach and James Likoudis, "Sex Education: The New Man-icheanism. Part II. A New Ideology," *Child and Family* 10, no. (1971): 316; Lisa Arai, *Teenage Pregnancy: The Making and Unmaking of a Problem* (Bristol, UK: Policy Press, 2009), 95.

6. Rogers to Proom, January 11, 1976, box 80, section 5, NVLA Papers; Marta Suplicy, "Sexuality Education in Brazil," *SIECUS Report* 22, no. 2 (December 1993/January 1994): 3.

7. Kenneth Cmiel, "The Recent History of Human Rights," in *The Human Rights Revolution: An International History*, ed. Akira Iriye, Petra Goedde, and William I. Hitchcock (New York: Oxford University Press, 2012), 36; Michael Ignatieff et al., *Human Rights as Politics and Idolatry* (Princeton, NJ: Princeton University Press, 2001), 53; Sally Gibson, "The Language of the Right: Sex Education Debates in South Australia," *Sex Education* 7, no. 3 (2007): 240.

8. Clark W. Hetherington, "Play Leadership in Sex Education," *Social Hygiene* 1, no. 1 (1914): 37; Lucien Viborel, "Venus Remains Unsatiated: Youth Should Preserve Its Cool-Headedness!" International Union against the Venereal Diseases and the Treponematoses, *Bulletin of Information for the Regional Office for Europe* (Rotterdam: IUAVD, July 1959), 25; Makoto Yamaguchi, "Sex Problems and Sex Education in Japan," in *Responsible Parenthood and Family Life Education. Proceedings of the Seminar of the Western Pacific Region of the International Planned Parenthood Federation* (Hong Kong: IPPF, 1972), 28; "Progress or Pornography?" *News China*, December 1, 2011, p. 18; "Let's Talk about Sex," *Sunday Star-Times* (Wellington, New Zealand), May 21, 2006, p. C1.

9. "Schools Flunk Sex Education Test," *Los Angeles Times*, May 14, 1981, p. 111; "Study of Sex Education Programs," *School and Society* 97 (Summer 1969): 271; Carl Gustaf Boethius, "Comparisons: A Discussion of Some Topics from Country Reports," in *The Other Curriculum: European Strategies for School Sex Education*, ed. Philip Meredith (London: IPPF, 1989), 346.

10. James A. Michener, "Sex Education: A Success in Our Social-Studies Classes," *Clearing House* 12, no. 8 (1938): 464; Catherine Gasquoine Hartley, *Sex Education and National Health* (London: Leonard Parsons, 1920), 47.

11. "Should Public Schools Teach the 'Facts of Life'?" *Forum and Century* 102 (October 1939): 172; letter by Mrs. O. R. Martin, *St. Louis Argus*, November 6, 1970, folder 10, box 9, Helen Manley Papers, Missouri Historical Society, Saint Louis; L. Townsend, "Teaching Sex in Primary Schools" (MS, n.d. [1970]), box 80, section 5, NVLA Papers.

12. Matthew Gutmann, *Fixing Men: Sex, Birth Control, and AIDS in Mexico* (Berkeley: University of California Press, 2007), 125; Joseph Ribal, *Learning Sex Roles: American and Scandinavian Contrasts* (San Francisco: Canfield Press, 1973), 255.

# MANUSCRIPT COLLECTIONS

AIDS History Project Collection. One: National Gay and Lesbian Archives. Los Angeles.

American Social Health Association. Papers. Social Welfare History Archives. University of Minnesota, Minneapolis.

Balliet, Thomas M. Papers. New York University Archives.

Blackburn, Eunice R. Papers. Presbyterian Historical Society. Philadelphia.

Bureau of Social Hygiene. Papers. Rockefeller Archive Center. Tarrytown, New York.

Cadbury, Henry Joel. Papers. Bryn Mawr College, Special Collections. Bryn Mawr, Pennsylvania.

Calderone, Mary S. Papers. Arthur and Elizabeth Schlesinger Library, Radcliffe College. Cambridge, Massachusetts.

Carnegie Corporation of New York. Papers. Columbia University Rare Books and Manuscript Library. New York City.

Center for Studies in Education and Development. Papers. Harvard University Archives. Cambridge, Massachusetts.

Department of Education Records. California State Archives. Sacramento.

Family Planning Association. Papers. Wellcome Library. London.

Gebhard Era Correspondence Collection. Kinsey Institute Archives. Bloomington, Indiana.

Ghana Education Service Records. Ghana National Archives. Accra, Ghana.

Guttmacher, Alan Frank. Papers. Francis A. Countway Library of Medicine, Harvard University. Boston.

HCA/Albany Trust Collection. Hall-Carpenter Archives, London School of Economics.

Institute for Sex Education Records. Richard J. Daley Library, Special Collections, University of Illinois at Chicago.

Koop, C. Everett. Papers. National Library of Medicine. Bethesda, Maryland.

Malinowski, Bronisław. Papers. Hall-Carpenter Archives, London School of Economics.

Manley, Helen. Papers. Missouri History Museum Archives. Saint Louis.

Medical Women's Federation. Papers. Wellcome Library. London.

Microfilmed Grant Collection. Ford Foundation Archives. New York.

Moore, Veranus A. Papers. Division of Rare and Manuscript Collections, Cornell University Library. Ithaca, New York.

National Education Association Records. Gelman Library, George Washington University. Washington, DC.

National Union of Women Teachers Collection. Institute of Education Archives, University of London.

National Viewers' and Listeners' Association. Papers. Albert Sloman Library, University of Essex. Colchester, United Kingdom.

National Vigilance Association. Papers. Women's Library. London.

Planned Parenthood Federation of America II Collection. Sophia Smith Collection, Smith College. Northampton, Massachusetts.

Population Council. Papers. Rockefeller Archive Center. Tarrytown, New York.

Presbyterian Board of Christian Education Records. Presbyterian Historical Society. Philadelphia.

Records of International Conferences, Commissions, and Expositions. National Archives II. College Park, Maryland.

Records of the Public Health Service. National Archives II. College Park, Maryland.

Records of the Supreme Commander for the Allied Powers. National Archives II. College Park, Maryland.

Records of the White House Conference on Child Health and Protection. Hoover Institution Archives. Stanford, California.

Riksförbundet för Sexuell Upplysning (Swedish Association for Sexuality Education). Papers. Labour Movement Archives and Library. Stockholm, Sweden.

Rockefeller Family Archives. Rockefeller Archive Center. Tarrytown, New York.

Rugen, Mabel. Papers. Bentley Historical Library, University of Michigan. Ann Arbor.

School of Education of the University of North Carolina. Papers. University Archives, University of North Carolina. Chapel Hill.

Sears, James T. Papers. Duke University Rare Book, Manuscript and Special Collections Library. Durham, North Carolina.

Society of Medical Officers. Papers. Wellcome Library. London.

Stone, Abraham. Papers. Francis A. Countway Library of Medicine, Harvard University. Boston.

United Federation of Teachers Records. Robert F. Wagner Archives, Tamiment Library, New York University.

Vertical Files Collection. Kinsey Institute Archives. Bloomington, Indiana.

Wayland, Sloan R. Papers. Teachers College Archives, Teachers College Columbia University. New York.

# INDEX